5-6-73

Fannie Farmer's Book of Good Dinners

FANNIE MERRITT FARMER
1857–1915

"The seat of courage is the stomach."

Director
Boston Cooking School, 1891–1902

Author
Boston Cooking School Cook Book
First edition, 1896

A Book of Good Dinners For My Friend, Or,
What to Have for Dinner
First edition, 1905

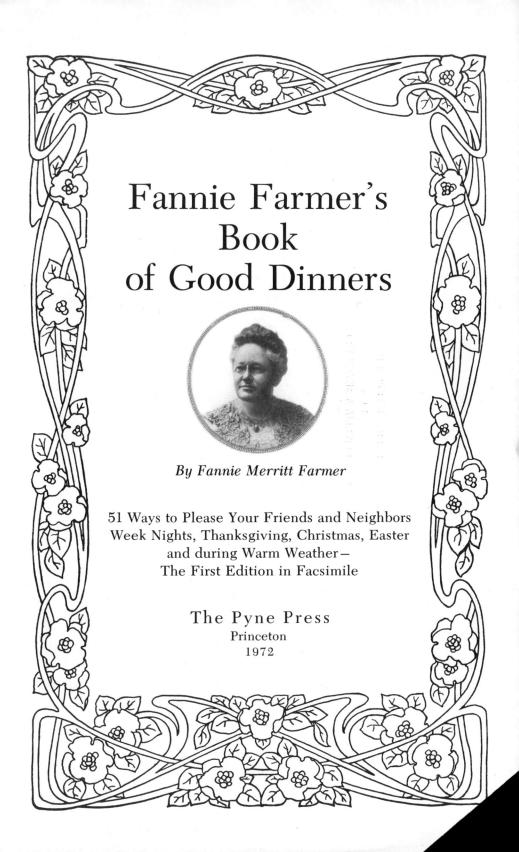

Fannie Farmer's Book of Good Dinners

By Fannie Merritt Farmer

51 Ways to Please Your Friends and Neighbors
Week Nights, Thanksgiving, Christmas, Easter
and during Warm Weather—
The First Edition in Facsimile

The Pyne Press
Princeton
1972

Contents

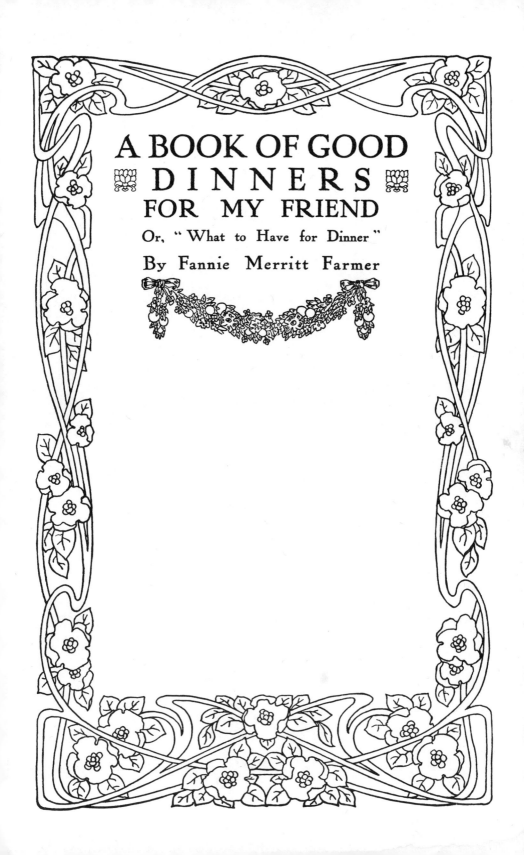

A BOOK OF GOOD
DINNERS
FOR MY FRIEND

Or, " What to Have for Dinner "

By Fannie Merritt Farmer

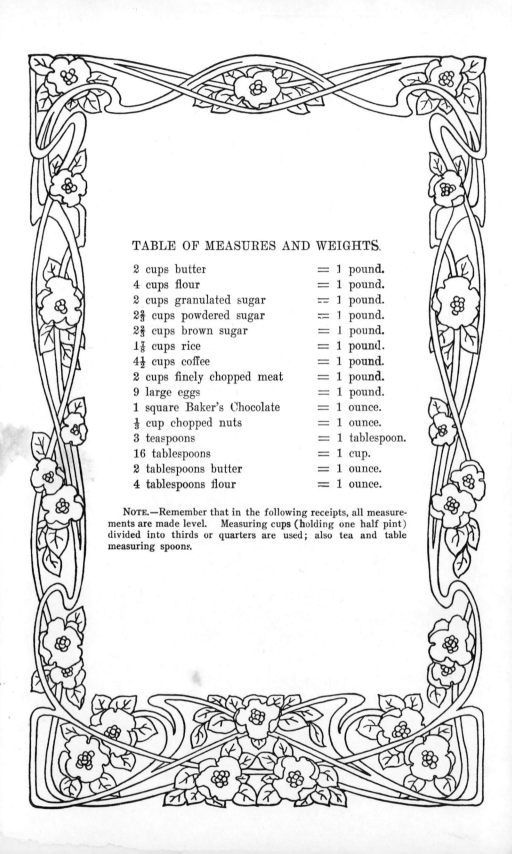

TABLE OF MEASURES AND WEIGHTS.

2 cups butter	= 1 pound.
4 cups flour	= 1 pound.
2 cups granulated sugar	= 1 pound.
2⅔ cups powdered sugar	= 1 pound.
2⅔ cups brown sugar	= 1 pound.
1⅞ cups rice	= 1 pound.
4½ cups coffee	= 1 pound.
2 cups finely chopped meat	= 1 pound.
9 large eggs	= 1 pound.
1 square Baker's Chocolate	= 1 ounce.
⅓ cup chopped nuts	= 1 ounce.
3 teaspoons	= 1 tablespoon.
16 tablespoons	= 1 cup.
2 tablespoons butter	= 1 ounce.
4 tablespoons flour	= 1 ounce.

NOTE.—Remember that in the following receipts, all measurements are made level. Measuring cups (holding one half pint) divided into thirds or quarters are used; also tea and table measuring spoons.

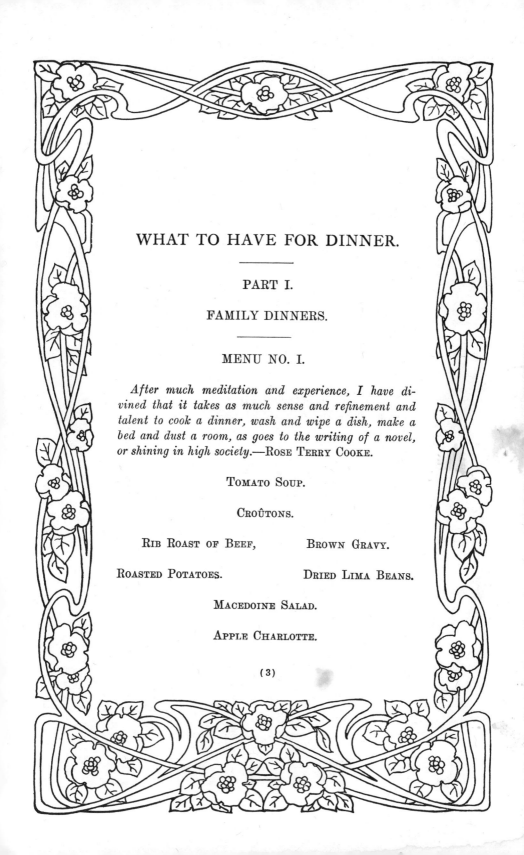

WHAT TO HAVE FOR DINNER.

PART I.

FAMILY DINNERS.

MENU NO. I.

After much meditation and experience, I have divined that it takes as much sense and refinement and talent to cook a dinner, wash and wipe a dish, make a bed and dust a room, as goes to the writing of a novel, or shining in high society.—ROSE TERRY COOKE.

TOMATO SOUP.

CROÛTONS.

RIB ROAST OF BEEF,   BROWN GRAVY.

ROASTED POTATOES.   DRIED LIMA BEANS.

MACEDOINE SALAD.

APPLE CHARLOTTE.

(3)

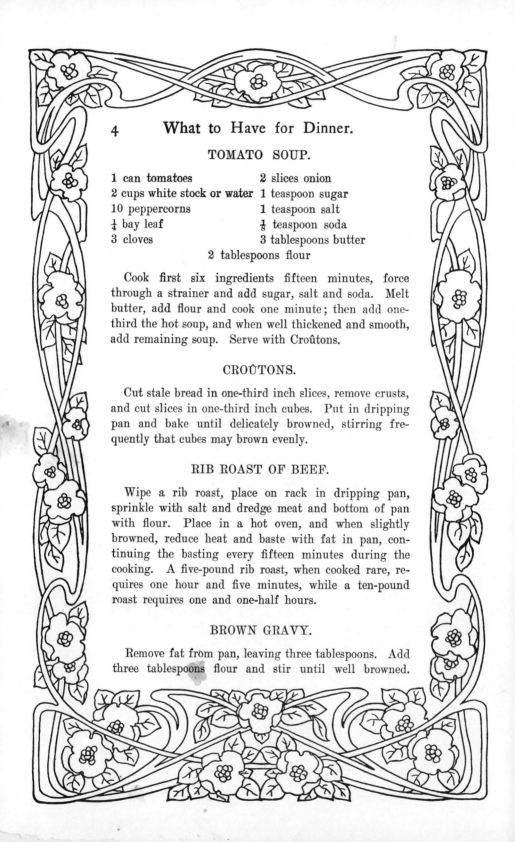

What to Have for Dinner.

TOMATO SOUP.

1 can tomatoes	2 slices onion
2 cups white stock or water	1 teaspoon sugar
10 peppercorns	1 teaspoon salt
$\frac{1}{4}$ bay leaf	$\frac{1}{8}$ teaspoon soda
3 cloves	3 tablespoons butter
	2 tablespoons flour

Cook first six ingredients fifteen minutes, force through a strainer and add sugar, salt and soda. Melt butter, add flour and cook one minute; then add one-third the hot soup, and when well thickened and smooth, add remaining soup. Serve with Croûtons.

CROÛTONS.

Cut stale bread in one-third inch slices, remove crusts, and cut slices in one-third inch cubes. Put in dripping pan and bake until delicately browned, stirring frequently that cubes may brown evenly.

RIB ROAST OF BEEF.

Wipe a rib roast, place on rack in dripping pan, sprinkle with salt and dredge meat and bottom of pan with flour. Place in a hot oven, and when slightly browned, reduce heat and baste with fat in pan, continuing the basting every fifteen minutes during the cooking. A five-pound rib roast, when cooked rare, requires one hour and five minutes, while a ten-pound roast requires one and one-half hours.

BROWN GRAVY.

Remove fat from pan, leaving three tablespoons. Add three tablespoons flour and stir until well browned.

Pour on, gradually, while stirring constantly, one and
one-half cups boiling water. Bring to boiling point,
season with salt and pepper, then strain.

ROAST POTATOES.

Wash and pare potatoes, and parboil twelve minutes in
boiling, salted water. Drain and place on rack in pan,
where meat is roasting, and bake until soft. Baste with
fat in pan, when basting meat.

DRIED LIMA BEANS.

1½ cups dried Lima beans 1 tablespoon butter
¾ cup cream   Salt
     Pepper

Soak beans over-night, in cold water. Drain, add cold
water to cover and bring slowly to boiling point. Let
simmer until tender, drain, add cream, butter, salt and
pepper.

MACEDOINE SALAD.

1 cup, each, cold cooked carrots and turnips, cut in
  strips
1 cup cold cooked potatoes, cut in balls
1 cup cold cooked string beans
2 tablespoons parsley, finely chopped

Marinate the vegetables separately with French Dressing. Arrange in sections on a dish, having the base of
shredded lettuce, garnish with lettuce and sprinkle
chopped parsley over all.

To Shred Lettuce.

Remove leaves from stalk, wash, drain, and cut in
narrow strips, using scissors.

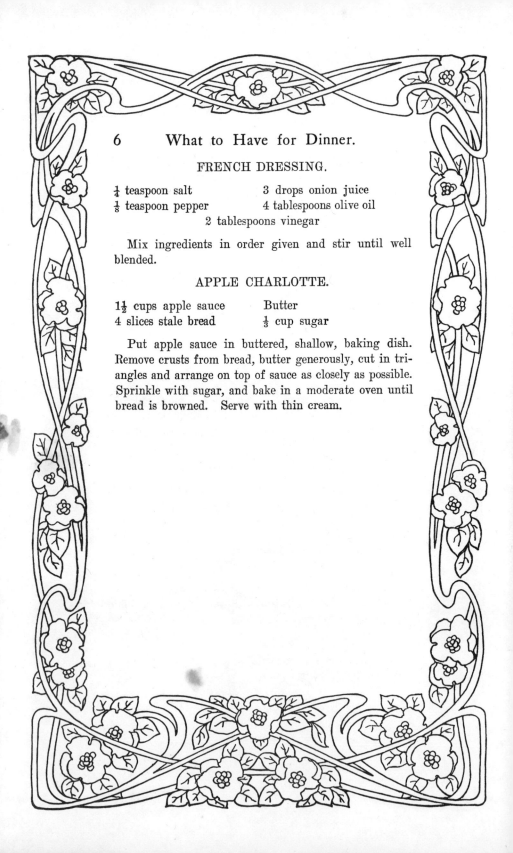

FRENCH DRESSING.

¼ teaspoon salt   3 drops onion juice
⅛ teaspoon pepper   4 tablespoons olive oil
         2 tablespoons vinegar

Mix ingredients in order given and stir until well blended.

APPLE CHARLOTTE.

1½ cups apple sauce   Butter
4 slices stale bread   ⅓ cup sugar

Put apple sauce in buttered, shallow, baking dish. Remove crusts from bread, butter generously, cut in triangles and arrange on top of sauce as closely as possible. Sprinkle with sugar, and bake in a moderate oven until bread is browned. Serve with thin cream.

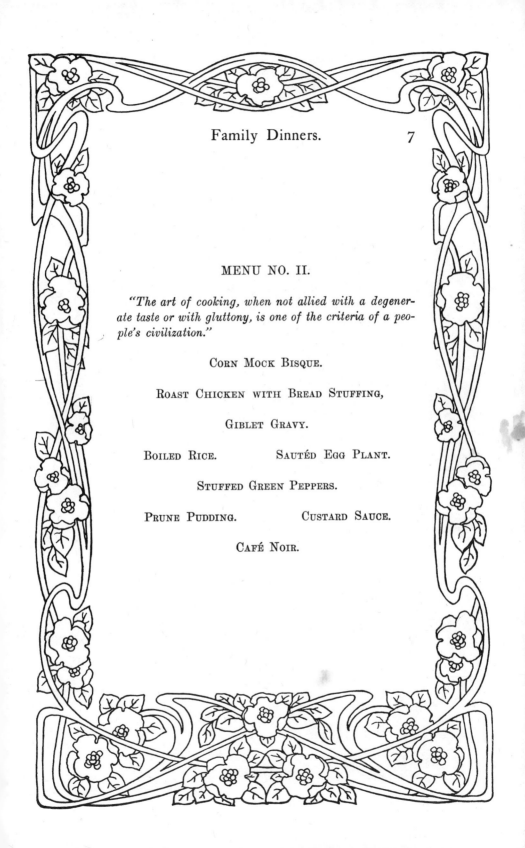

MENU NO. II.

"The art of cooking, when not allied with a degenerate taste or with gluttony, is one of the criteria of a people's civilization."

CORN MOCK BISQUE.

ROAST CHICKEN WITH BREAD STUFFING,

GIBLET GRAVY.

BOILED RICE.   SAUTÉD EGG PLANT.

STUFFED GREEN PEPPERS.

PRUNE PUDDING.   CUSTARD SAUCE.

CAFÉ NOIR.

CORN MOCK BISQUE SOUP.

1 can corn	$\frac{1}{2}$ can tomatoes
1 quart milk	$\frac{1}{4}$ teaspoon soda
1 slice onion	$\frac{1}{3}$ cup butter
3 tablespoons flour	2 teaspoons salt
$\frac{1}{4}$ cup cold water	$\frac{1}{8}$ teaspoon pepper

$\frac{1}{8}$ teaspoon paprika

Scald milk with corn and onion. Mix flour with cold water to form a smooth paste, and add to scalded milk; then cook twenty minutes, stirring constantly at first, and rub through a sieve. Cook tomatoes ten minutes, add soda, and rub through a sieve. Combine mixtures and strain into tureen in which is butter in small pieces, and seasonings.

ROAST CHICKEN.

Dress, clean, stuff and truss a four-pound chicken. Rub entire surface with salt and spread breast and legs with soft butter, using four tablespoons. Place on back on rack in dripping pan and dredge bird and bottom of pan generously with flour.

Place in a hot oven and when flour is well browned, reduce heat and baste. Turn, having breast side down, and baste every ten minutes during the remainder of the cooking, using one-fourth cup butter, melted in three-fourths cup boiling water, adding more water, if necessary, to prevent burning. A four-pound chicken requires from one and one-half to one and three-fourths hours. If a chicken is roasted breast down, the breast meat is more juicy and of finer flavor than it otherwise would be.

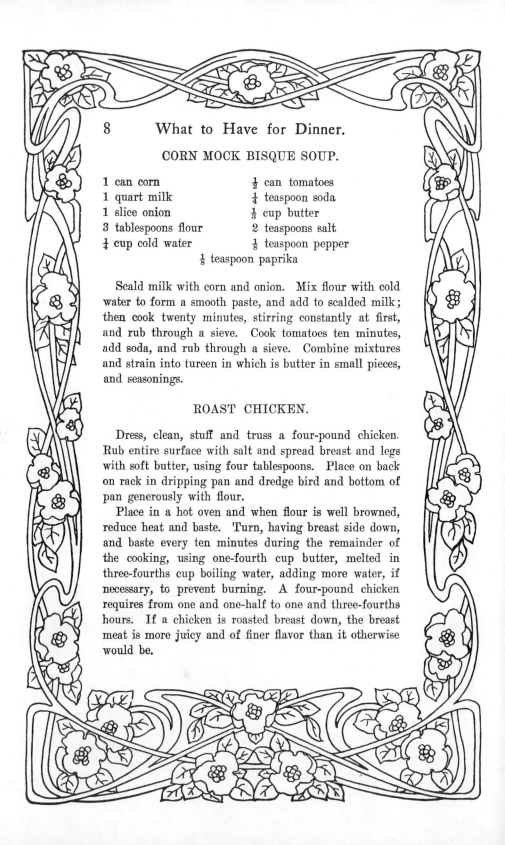

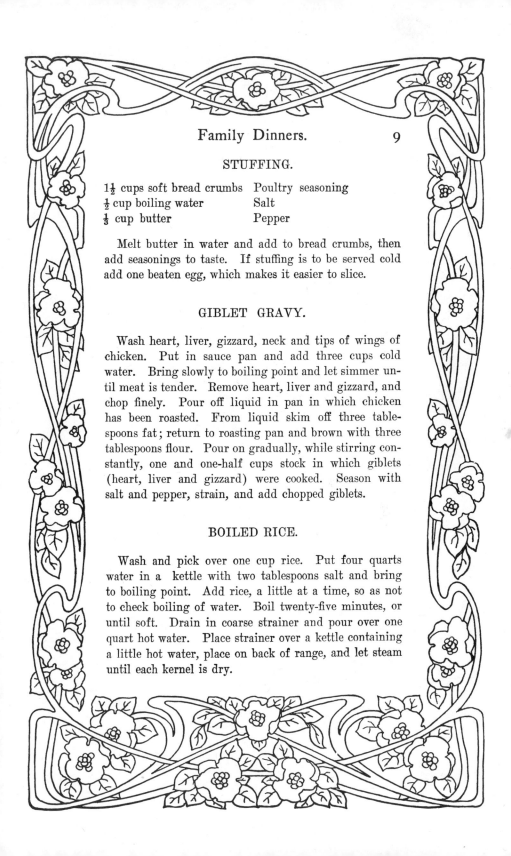

STUFFING.

1½ cups soft bread crumbs   Poultry seasoning
½ cup boiling water   Salt
⅓ cup butter   Pepper

Melt butter in water and add to bread crumbs, then add seasonings to taste. If stuffing is to be served cold add one beaten egg, which makes it easier to slice.

GIBLET GRAVY.

Wash heart, liver, gizzard, neck and tips of wings of chicken. Put in sauce pan and add three cups cold water. Bring slowly to boiling point and let simmer until meat is tender. Remove heart, liver and gizzard, and chop finely. Pour off liquid in pan in which chicken has been roasted. From liquid skim off three tablespoons fat; return to roasting pan and brown with three tablespoons flour. Pour on gradually, while stirring constantly, one and one-half cups stock in which giblets (heart, liver and gizzard) were cooked. Season with salt and pepper, strain, and add chopped giblets.

BOILED RICE.

Wash and pick over one cup rice. Put four quarts water in a kettle with two tablespoons salt and bring to boiling point. Add rice, a little at a time, so as not to check boiling of water. Boil twenty-five minutes, or until soft. Drain in coarse strainer and pour over one quart hot water. Place strainer over a kettle containing a little hot water, place on back of range, and let steam until each kernel is dry.

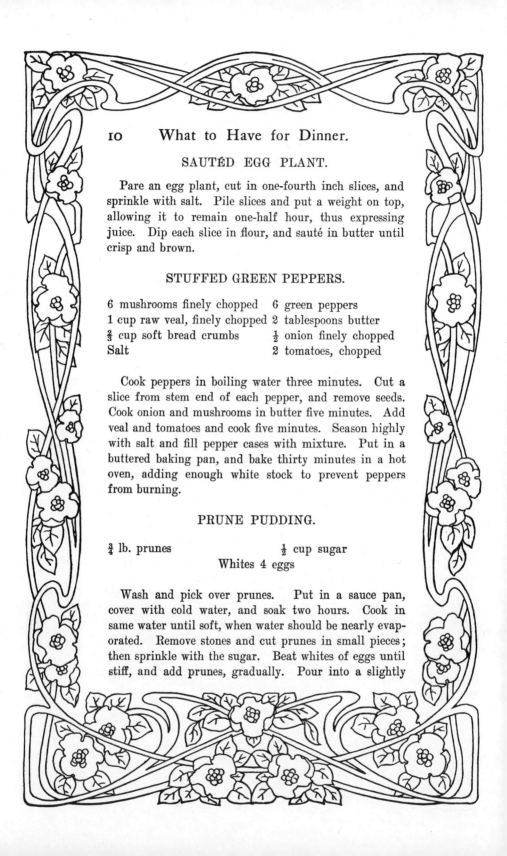

SAUTÉD EGG PLANT.

Pare an egg plant, cut in one-fourth inch slices, and sprinkle with salt. Pile slices and put a weight on top, allowing it to remain one-half hour, thus expressing juice. Dip each slice in flour, and sauté in butter until crisp and brown.

STUFFED GREEN PEPPERS.

6 mushrooms finely chopped	6 green peppers
1 cup raw veal, finely chopped	2 tablespoons butter
⅔ cup soft bread crumbs	½ onion finely chopped
Salt	2 tomatoes, chopped

Cook peppers in boiling water three minutes. Cut a slice from stem end of each pepper, and remove seeds. Cook onion and mushrooms in butter five minutes. Add veal and tomatoes and cook five minutes. Season highly with salt and fill pepper cases with mixture. Put in a buttered baking pan, and bake thirty minutes in a hot oven, adding enough white stock to prevent peppers from burning.

PRUNE PUDDING.

¾ lb. prunes	½ cup sugar
	Whites 4 eggs

Wash and pick over prunes. Put in a sauce pan, cover with cold water, and soak two hours. Cook in same water until soft, when water should be nearly evaporated. Remove stones and cut prunes in small pieces; then sprinkle with the sugar. Beat whites of eggs until stiff, and add prunes, gradually. Pour into a slightly buttered pudding dish, and bake in a moderate oven twenty-five minutes. Chill and serve with Custard Sauce or whipped cream, sweetened and flavored.

CUSTARD SAUCE.

1½ cups scalded milk	3 tablespoons sugar
Yolks 3 eggs	Few grains salt
	½ teaspoon vanilla

Beat egg yolks slightly, add sugar and salt; then add hot milk, gradually, while stirring constantly. Cook in double boiler until mixture thickens, stirring constantly at first and afterwards occasionally. Strain, chill and flavor.

CAFÉ NOIR (BOILED).

1 cup ground coffee	½ egg
½ cup cold water	3 cups boiling water

Wash an egg and break shell and all into a cup and beat slightly. Mix coffee with one-half the egg and one-half the cold water. Turn into a granite ware coffee pot, (which has been previously scalded with boiling water,) add boiling water, stuff spout of coffee pot with soft paper, place pot on front of range, and let boil three minutes. Add remaining cold water and let stand on back of range, where coffee will not boil, for ten minutes. Serve in after-dinner coffee cups with cut sugar.

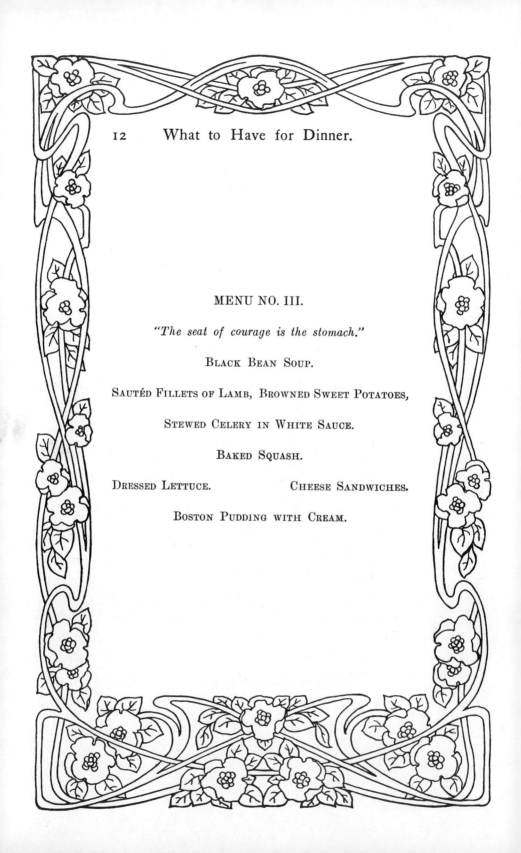

MENU NO. III.

"The seat of courage is the stomach."

BLACK BEAN SOUP.

SAUTÉD FILLETS OF LAMB, BROWNED SWEET POTATOES,

STEWED CELERY IN WHITE SAUCE.

BAKED SQUASH.

DRESSED LETTUCE.   CHEESE SANDWICHES.

BOSTON PUDDING WITH CREAM.

BLACK BEAN SOUP.

2 cups black beans	Bit of bay leaf
3 quarts cold water	Sprig of parsley
3 cloves	1½ tablespoons butter
4 peppercorns	1½ tablespoons flour
3 stalks celery	½ tablespoon salt
1 onion, sliced	Few grains cayenne
1 slice carrot	1 lemon, cut in thin
1 slice turnip	slices

1 hard boiled egg, cut in thin slices

Soak beans, over-night, in cold water to cover. Drain, add cold water, bring to boiling point and let simmer until soft; then force through a purée strainer. Cook seasoning in butter five minutes, add flour and cook one minute, then add to soup with salt and cayenne. Put sliced lemon and egg in tureen and strain over the hot soup.

SAUTÉD FILLETS OF LAMB.

Order two pounds lamb cut from fore quarter. Remove bones, and cut meat in strips one inch in thickness; then flatten with a cleaver to three-fourths inch in thickness. Arrange on a platter and pour over a marinade made by mixing three tablespoons olive oil, three tablespoons vinegar, two-thirds teaspoon salt, one-half onion finely chopped, and one tablespoon parsley finely chopped. Cover and let stand, over-night, or for several hours. Remove pieces of vegetables from fillets and sauté in a hot frying pan, using as little butter as possible.

BROWNED SWEET POTATOES.

Cut boiled sweet potatoes into slices one-fourth inch thick, arrange in a shallow baking pan, spread with

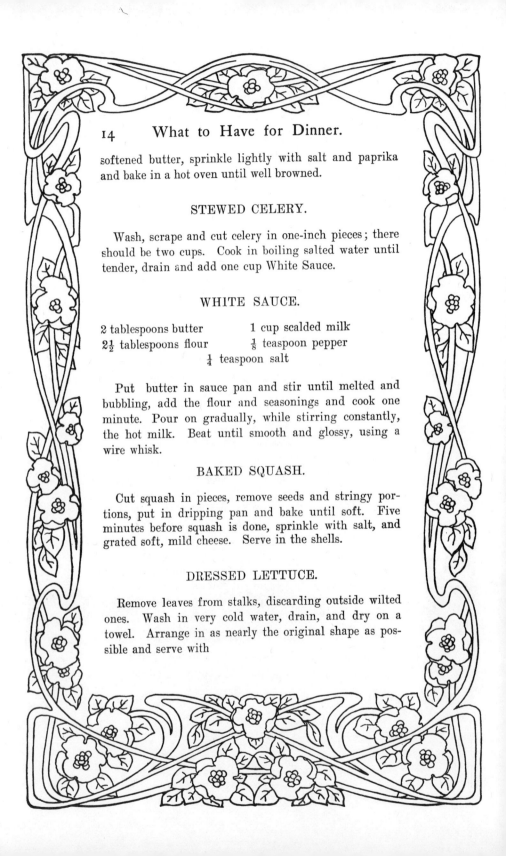

softened butter, sprinkle lightly with salt and paprika and bake in a hot oven until well browned.

STEWED CELERY.

Wash, scrape and cut celery in one-inch pieces; there should be two cups. Cook in boiling salted water until tender, drain and add one cup White Sauce.

WHITE SAUCE.

2 tablespoons butter	1 cup scalded milk
$2\frac{1}{2}$ tablespoons flour	$\frac{1}{8}$ teaspoon pepper
	$\frac{1}{4}$ teaspoon salt

Put butter in sauce pan and stir until melted and bubbling, add the flour and seasonings and cook one minute. Pour on gradually, while stirring constantly, the hot milk. Beat until smooth and glossy, using a wire whisk.

BAKED SQUASH.

Cut squash in pieces, remove seeds and stringy portions, put in dripping pan and bake until soft. Five minutes before squash is done, sprinkle with salt, and grated soft, mild cheese. Serve in the shells.

DRESSED LETTUCE.

Remove leaves from stalks, discarding outside wilted ones. Wash in very cold water, drain, and dry on a towel. Arrange in as nearly the original shape as possible and serve with

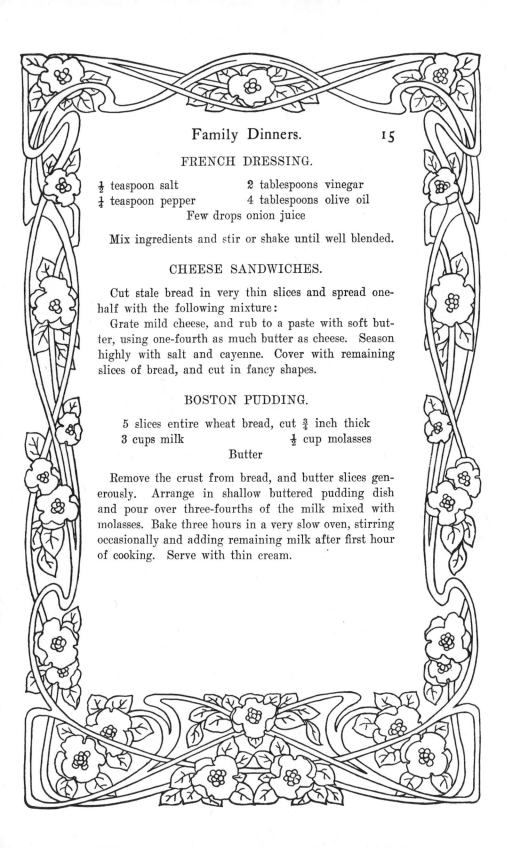

FRENCH DRESSING.

½ teaspoon salt   2 tablespoons vinegar
¼ teaspoon pepper   4 tablespoons olive oil
Few drops onion juice

Mix ingredients and stir or shake until well blended.

CHEESE SANDWICHES.

Cut stale bread in very thin slices and spread one-half with the following mixture:
Grate mild cheese, and rub to a paste with soft butter, using one-fourth as much butter as cheese. Season highly with salt and cayenne. Cover with remaining slices of bread, and cut in fancy shapes.

BOSTON PUDDING.

5 slices entire wheat bread, cut ¾ inch thick
3 cups milk   ½ cup molasses
Butter

Remove the crust from bread, and butter slices generously. Arrange in shallow buttered pudding dish and pour over three-fourths of the milk mixed with molasses. Bake three hours in a very slow oven, stirring occasionally and adding remaining milk after first hour of cooking. Serve with thin cream.

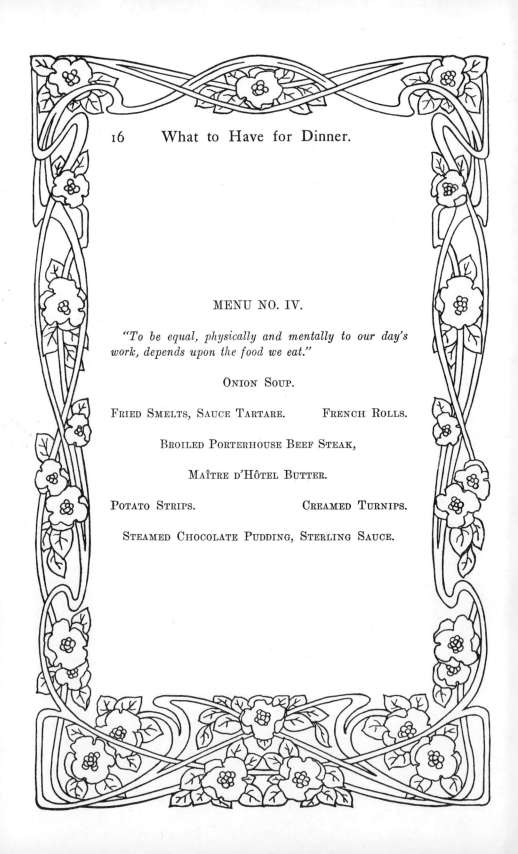

MENU NO. IV.

"To be equal, physically and mentally to our day's work, depends upon the food we eat."

ONION SOUP.

FRIED SMELTS, SAUCE TARTARE.   FRENCH ROLLS.

BROILED PORTERHOUSE BEEF STEAK,

MAÎTRE D'HÔTEL BUTTER.

POTATO STRIPS.   CREAMED TURNIPS.

STEAMED CHOCOLATE PUDDING, STERLING SAUCE.

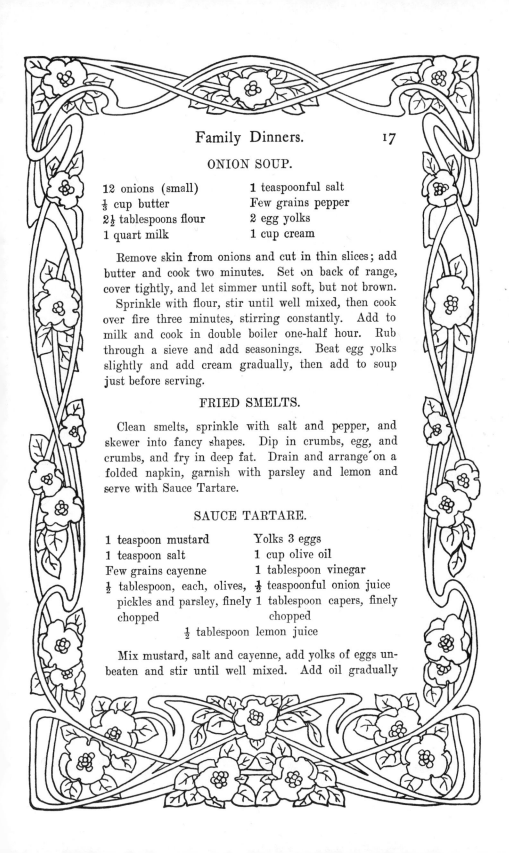

ONION SOUP.

12 onions (small)
⅓ cup butter
2½ tablespoons flour
1 quart milk

1 teaspoonful salt
Few grains pepper
2 egg yolks
1 cup cream

Remove skin from onions and cut in thin slices; add butter and cook two minutes. Set on back of range, cover tightly, and let simmer until soft, but not brown. Sprinkle with flour, stir until well mixed, then cook over fire three minutes, stirring constantly. Add to milk and cook in double boiler one-half hour. Rub through a sieve and add seasonings. Beat egg yolks slightly and add cream gradually, then add to soup just before serving.

FRIED SMELTS.

Clean smelts, sprinkle with salt and pepper, and skewer into fancy shapes. Dip in crumbs, egg, and crumbs, and fry in deep fat. Drain and arrange on a folded napkin, garnish with parsley and lemon and serve with Sauce Tartare.

SAUCE TARTARE.

1 teaspoon mustard
1 teaspoon salt
Few grains cayenne
½ tablespoon, each, olives, pickles and parsley, finely chopped

Yolks 3 eggs
1 cup olive oil
1 tablespoon vinegar
½ teaspoonful onion juice
1 tablespoon capers, finely chopped

½ tablespoon lemon juice

Mix mustard, salt and cayenne, add yolks of eggs unbeaten and stir until well mixed. Add oil gradually

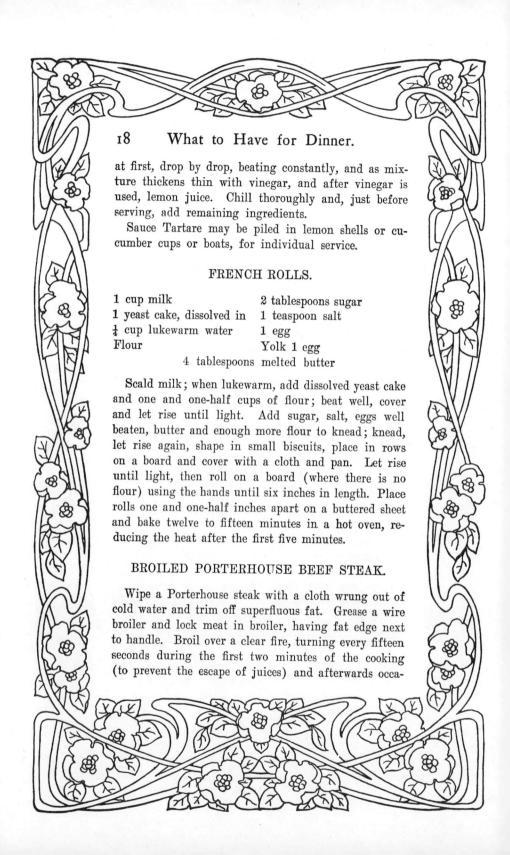

at first, drop by drop, beating constantly, and as mixture thickens thin with vinegar, and after vinegar is used, lemon juice. Chill thoroughly and, just before serving, add remaining ingredients.

Sauce Tartare may be piled in lemon shells or cucumber cups or boats, for individual service.

FRENCH ROLLS.

1 cup milk	2 tablespoons sugar
1 yeast cake, dissolved in	1 teaspoon salt
¼ cup lukewarm water	1 egg
Flour	Yolk 1 egg

4 tablespoons melted butter

Scald milk; when lukewarm, add dissolved yeast cake and one and one-half cups of flour; beat well, cover and let rise until light. Add sugar, salt, eggs well beaten, butter and enough more flour to knead; knead, let rise again, shape in small biscuits, place in rows on a board and cover with a cloth and pan. Let rise until light, then roll on a board (where there is no flour) using the hands until six inches in length. Place rolls one and one-half inches apart on a buttered sheet and bake twelve to fifteen minutes in a hot oven, reducing the heat after the first five minutes.

BROILED PORTERHOUSE BEEF STEAK.

Wipe a Porterhouse steak with a cloth wrung out of cold water and trim off superfluous fat. Grease a wire broiler and lock meat in broiler, having fat edge next to handle. Broil over a clear fire, turning every fifteen seconds during the first two minutes of the cooking (to prevent the escape of juices) and afterwards occa-

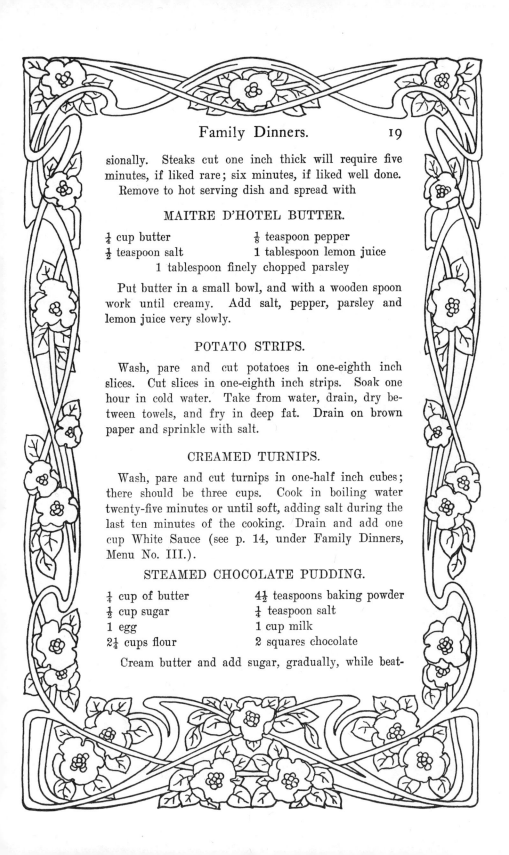

sionally. Steaks cut one inch thick will require five minutes, if liked rare; six minutes, if liked well done. Remove to hot serving dish and spread with

MAITRE D'HOTEL BUTTER.

¼ cup butter⠀⠀⠀⠀⠀⅛ teaspoon pepper
½ teaspoon salt⠀⠀⠀⠀1 tablespoon lemon juice
⠀⠀⠀1 tablespoon finely chopped parsley

Put butter in a small bowl, and with a wooden spoon work until creamy. Add salt, pepper, parsley and lemon juice very slowly.

POTATO STRIPS.

Wash, pare and cut potatoes in one-eighth inch slices. Cut slices in one-eighth inch strips. Soak one hour in cold water. Take from water, drain, dry between towels, and fry in deep fat. Drain on brown paper and sprinkle with salt.

CREAMED TURNIPS.

Wash, pare and cut turnips in one-half inch cubes; there should be three cups. Cook in boiling water twenty-five minutes or until soft, adding salt during the last ten minutes of the cooking. Drain and add one cup White Sauce (see p. 14, under Family Dinners, Menu No. III.).

STEAMED CHOCOLATE PUDDING.

¼ cup of butter⠀⠀⠀⠀4½ teaspoons baking powder
½ cup sugar⠀⠀⠀⠀⠀⠀¼ teaspoon salt
1 egg⠀⠀⠀⠀⠀⠀⠀⠀⠀⠀1 cup milk
2¼ cups flour⠀⠀⠀⠀⠀⠀2 squares chocolate

Cream butter and add sugar, gradually, while beat-

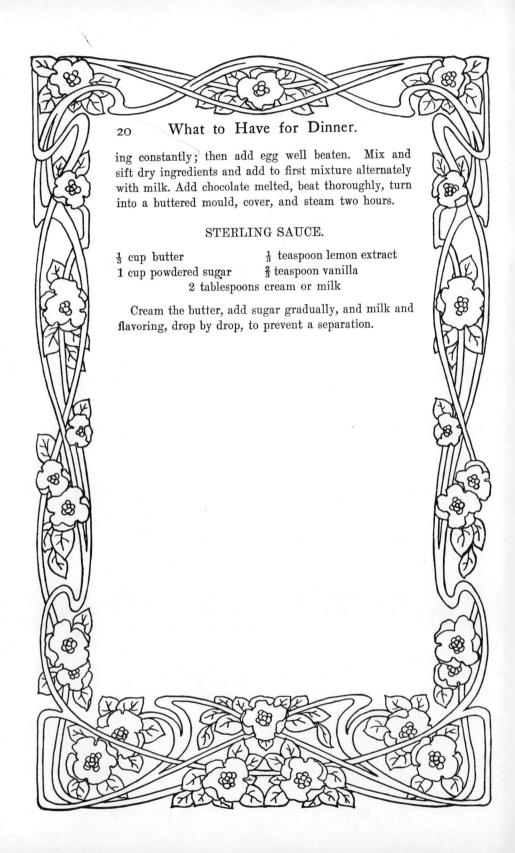

ing constantly; then add egg well beaten. Mix and sift dry ingredients and add to first mixture alternately with milk. Add chocolate melted, beat thoroughly, turn into a buttered mould, cover, and steam two hours.

STERLING SAUCE.

⅓ cup butter   ⅓ teaspoon lemon extract
1 cup powdered sugar   ⅔ teaspoon vanilla
         2 tablespoons cream or milk

Cream the butter, add sugar gradually, and milk and flavoring, drop by drop, to prevent a separation.

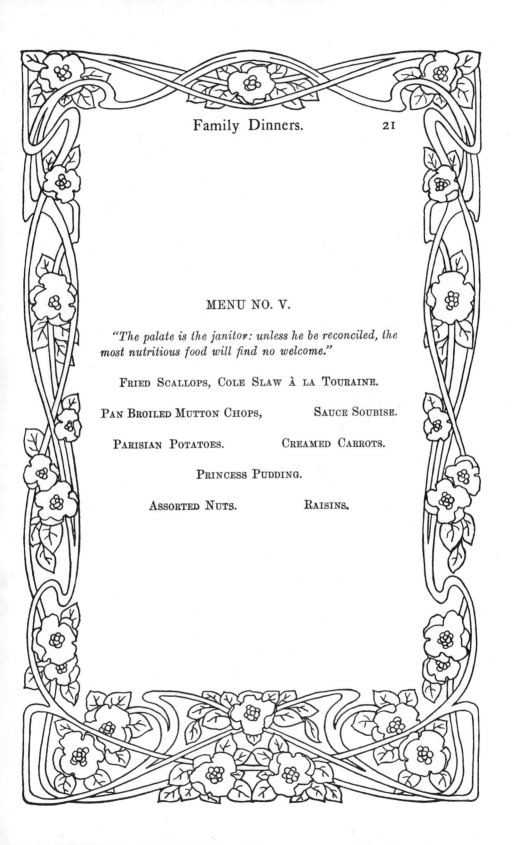

MENU NO. V.

"The palate is the janitor: unless he be reconciled, the most nutritious food will find no welcome."

FRIED SCALLOPS, COLE SLAW À LA TOURAINE.

PAN BROILED MUTTON CHOPS,   SAUCE SOUBISE.

PARISIAN POTATOES.   CREAMED CARROTS.

PRINCESS PUDDING.

ASSORTED NUTS.   RAISINS.

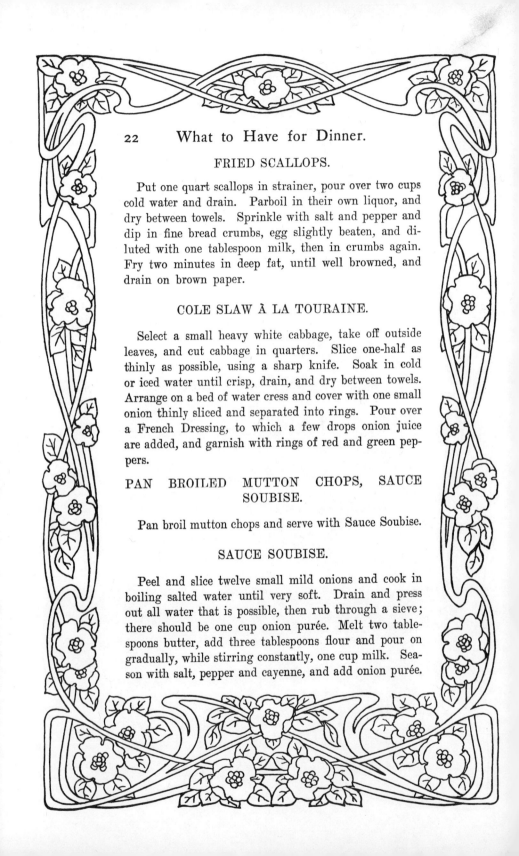

FRIED SCALLOPS.

Put one quart scallops in strainer, pour over two cups cold water and drain. Parboil in their own liquor, and dry between towels. Sprinkle with salt and pepper and dip in fine bread crumbs, egg slightly beaten, and diluted with one tablespoon milk, then in crumbs again. Fry two minutes in deep fat, until well browned, and drain on brown paper.

COLE SLAW À LA TOURAINE.

Select a small heavy white cabbage, take off outside leaves, and cut cabbage in quarters. Slice one-half as thinly as possible, using a sharp knife. Soak in cold or iced water until crisp, drain, and dry between towels. Arrange on a bed of water cress and cover with one small onion thinly sliced and separated into rings. Pour over a French Dressing, to which a few drops onion juice are added, and garnish with rings of red and green peppers.

PAN BROILED MUTTON CHOPS, SAUCE SOUBISE.

Pan broil mutton chops and serve with Sauce Soubise.

SAUCE SOUBISE.

Peel and slice twelve small mild onions and cook in boiling salted water until very soft. Drain and press out all water that is possible, then rub through a sieve; there should be one cup onion purée. Melt two tablespoons butter, add three tablespoons flour and pour on gradually, while stirring constantly, one cup milk. Season with salt, pepper and cayenne, and add onion purée.

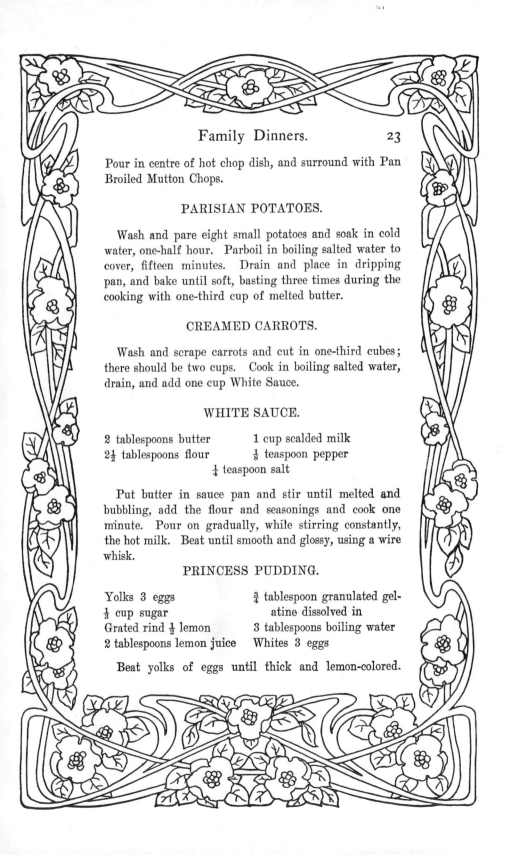

Pour in centre of hot chop dish, and surround with Pan Broiled Mutton Chops.

PARISIAN POTATOES.

Wash and pare eight small potatoes and soak in cold water, one-half hour. Parboil in boiling salted water to cover, fifteen minutes. Drain and place in dripping pan, and bake until soft, basting three times during the cooking with one-third cup of melted butter.

CREAMED CARROTS.

Wash and scrape carrots and cut in one-third cubes; there should be two cups. Cook in boiling salted water, drain, and add one cup White Sauce.

WHITE SAUCE.

2 tablespoons butter   1 cup scalded milk
2½ tablespoons flour   ⅛ teaspoon pepper
     ¼ teaspoon salt

Put butter in sauce pan and stir until melted and bubbling, add the flour and seasonings and cook one minute. Pour on gradually, while stirring constantly, the hot milk. Beat until smooth and glossy, using a wire whisk.

PRINCESS PUDDING.

Yolks 3 eggs   ¾ tablespoon granulated gel-
⅓ cup sugar   atine dissolved in
Grated rind ½ lemon   3 tablespoons boiling water
2 tablespoons lemon juice   Whites 3 eggs

Beat yolks of eggs until thick and lemon-colored.

and add sugar gradually, while beating constantly; then add grated rind of lemon, lemon juice and dissolved gelatine. As soon as mixture begins to thicken, cut and fold in whites of eggs beaten until stiff. Mould, chill and serve with whipped cream.

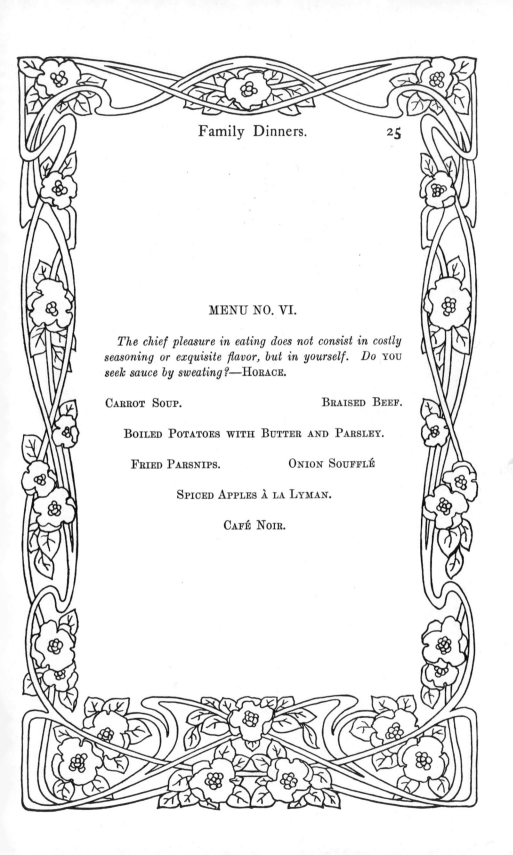

MENU NO. VI.

The chief pleasure in eating does not consist in costly seasoning or exquisite flavor, but in yourself. Do YOU *seek sauce by sweating?*—HORACE.

CARROT SOUP.   BRAISED BEEF.

BOILED POTATOES WITH BUTTER AND PARSLEY.

FRIED PARSNIPS.   ONION SOUFFLÉ

SPICED APPLES À LA LYMAN.

CAFÉ NOIR.

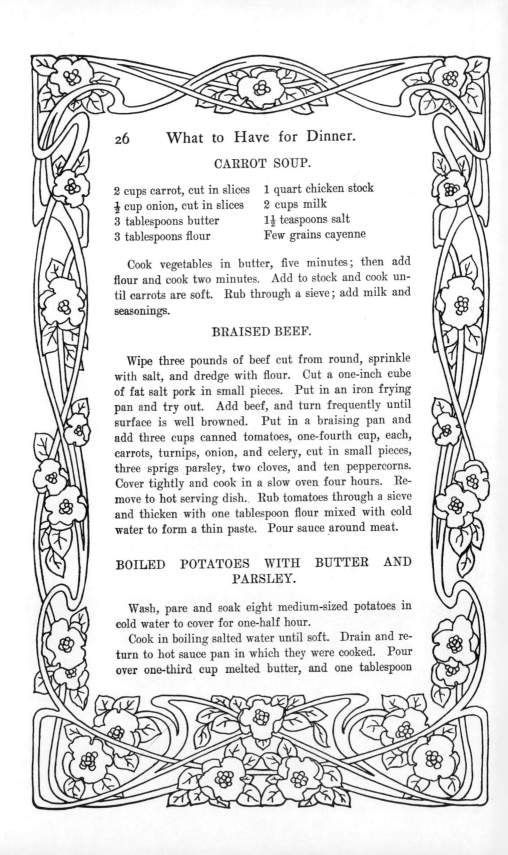

CARROT SOUP.

2 cups carrot, cut in slices	1 quart chicken stock
½ cup onion, cut in slices	2 cups milk
3 tablespoons butter	1½ teaspoons salt
3 tablespoons flour	Few grains cayenne

Cook vegetables in butter, five minutes; then add flour and cook two minutes. Add to stock and cook until carrots are soft. Rub through a sieve; add milk and seasonings.

BRAISED BEEF.

Wipe three pounds of beef cut from round, sprinkle with salt, and dredge with flour. Cut a one-inch cube of fat salt pork in small pieces. Put in an iron frying pan and try out. Add beef, and turn frequently until surface is well browned. Put in a braising pan and add three cups canned tomatoes, one-fourth cup, each, carrots, turnips, onion, and celery, cut in small pieces, three sprigs parsley, two cloves, and ten peppercorns. Cover tightly and cook in a slow oven four hours. Remove to hot serving dish. Rub tomatoes through a sieve and thicken with one tablespoon flour mixed with cold water to form a thin paste. Pour sauce around meat.

BOILED POTATOES WITH BUTTER AND PARSLEY.

Wash, pare and soak eight medium-sized potatoes in cold water to cover for one-half hour.

Cook in boiling salted water until soft. Drain and return to hot sauce pan in which they were cooked. Pour over one-third cup melted butter, and one tablespoon finely chopped parsley. Let stand on back of range until serving time.

FRIED PARSNIPS.

Wash parsnips, using a small brush to remove all particles of dirt. Cook in boiling salted water, one hour or until soft; drain, cover with cold water, again drain, and rub off skins. Cut lengthwise in slices one-fourth inch thick. Sprinkle with salt, dredge with flour, and sauté in butter until brown.

ONION SOUFFLÉ.

Cook onions in boiling salted water until soft, drain, and force through a sieve; there should be one and one-fourth cups onion pulp. Melt four tablespoons butter, add four tablespoons flour, and pour on gradually one-third cup water in which onions have been cooked, and one-third cup cream; then add onion pulp. Season with salt and pepper. Beat yolks of three eggs until thick and lemon colored, and add to first mixture. Cut and fold in whites of egg beaten until stiff and dry. Turn into a buttered baking dish, and bake twenty-five minutes in a moderate oven. Serve at once.

SPICED APPLE À LA LYMAN.

6 large apples	1 teaspoon cinnamon
¾ cup sugar	¼ teaspoon salt
	¼ cup water

Wipe, core and pare apples and arrange in baking dish. Mix sugar, cinnamon and salt, and fill cavities. Add water and bake until apples are soft, basting often with syrup in dish. Remove from oven, cool slightly and

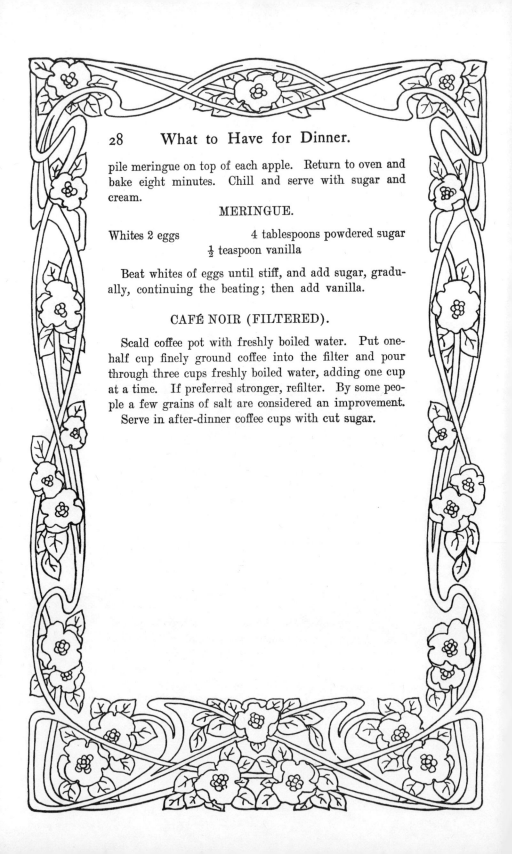

pile meringue on top of each apple. Return to oven and bake eight minutes. Chill and serve with sugar and cream.

MERINGUE.

Whites 2 eggs   4 tablespoons powdered sugar
½ teaspoon vanilla

Beat whites of eggs until stiff, and add sugar, gradually, continuing the beating; then add vanilla.

CAFÉ NOIR (FILTERED).

Scald coffee pot with freshly boiled water. Put one-half cup finely ground coffee into the filter and pour through three cups freshly boiled water, adding one cup at a time. If preferred stronger, refilter. By some people a few grains of salt are considered an improvement. Serve in after-dinner coffee cups with cut sugar.

MENU NO. VII.

*"We grow like what we eat. Bad food depresses;
good food exalts us like an inspiration."*

JULIENNE SOUP.

BOILED FOWL,   CELERY SAUCE.

RICED POTATOES À LA COLBURG.

SPINACH, SWEDISH STYLE.   TOMATO JELLY SALAD.

HEALTH FOOD BREAD SANDWICHES.

CHOCOLATE ICE CREAM WITH ZWIEBACK.

JULIENNE SOUP.

1½ quarts brown soup stock   ¼ cup string beans
⅓ cup, each, carrot and tur- 2 tablespoons canned green
    nip   peas

Cut carrot, turnip and string beans into very thin
strips, one inch long, and cook in boiling salted water
until soft.   Add to brown stock with peas.

BROWN SOUP STOCK.

5 lbs. shin of beef   4 cloves
2½ quarts cold water   ½ bay leaf
⅓ cup, each, carrot, turnip, 1 sprig thyme
    celery and onion, cut in 1 sprig marjoram
    small pieces   2 sprigs parsley
10 peppercorns   1 tablespoon salt

Wipe beef and cut in one-half inch cubes.   Brown one-
fourth of meat in a hot frying pan in marrow from marrow bone.   Add cold water to remaining meat and bone
and let stand one-half hour, then add browned meat.
Bring slowly to boiling point, cover, and let simmer
seven hours.   Add vegetables and seasonings, and let
simmer one hour.   Strain and cool.   Remove fat and
clear before serving.

BOILED FOWL.

Dress, clean and truss a four-pound fowl.   Place on a
trivet in kettle, half surround with boiling water and add
one sliced onion, three slices carrot, two stalks celery,
one sprig parsley, and one-half teaspoon peppercorns.
Bring quickly to boiling point, then let simmer until

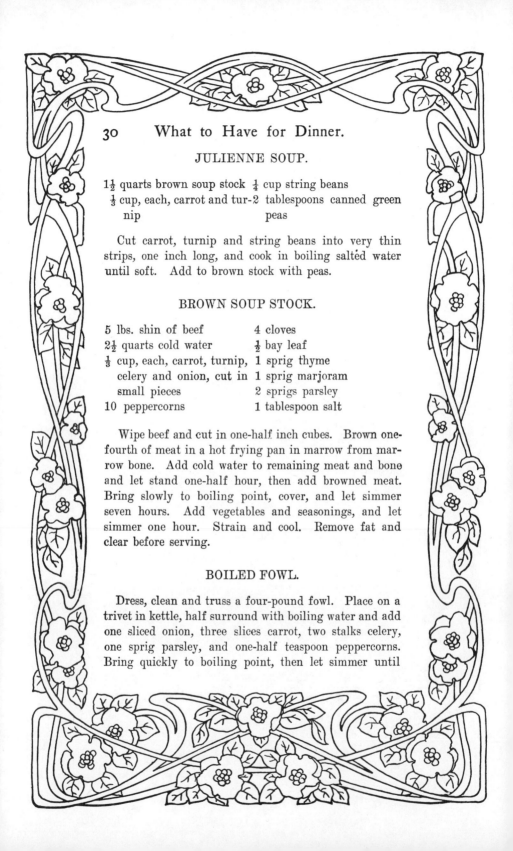

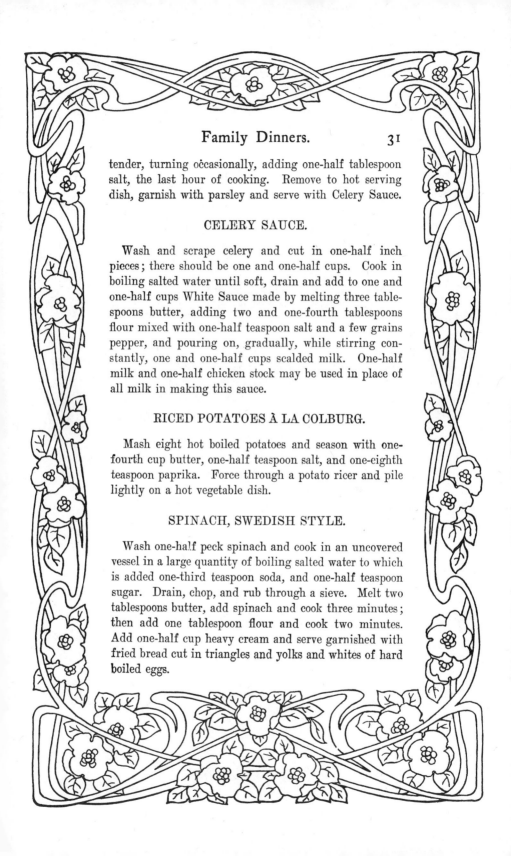

tender, turning occasionally, adding one-half tablespoon salt, the last hour of cooking. Remove to hot serving dish, garnish with parsley and serve with Celery Sauce.

CELERY SAUCE.

Wash and scrape celery and cut in one-half inch pieces; there should be one and one-half cups. Cook in boiling salted water until soft, drain and add to one and one-half cups White Sauce made by melting three tablespoons butter, adding two and one-fourth tablespoons flour mixed with one-half teaspoon salt and a few grains pepper, and pouring on, gradually, while stirring constantly, one and one-half cups scalded milk. One-half milk and one-half chicken stock may be used in place of all milk in making this sauce.

RICED POTATOES À LA COLBURG.

Mash eight hot boiled potatoes and season with one-fourth cup butter, one-half teaspoon salt, and one-eighth teaspoon paprika. Force through a potato ricer and pile lightly on a hot vegetable dish.

SPINACH, SWEDISH STYLE.

Wash one-half peck spinach and cook in an uncovered vessel in a large quantity of boiling salted water to which is added one-third teaspoon soda, and one-half teaspoon sugar. Drain, chop, and rub through a sieve. Melt two tablespoons butter, add spinach and cook three minutes; then add one tablespoon flour and cook two minutes. Add one-half cup heavy cream and serve garnished with fried bread cut in triangles and yolks and whites of hard boiled eggs.

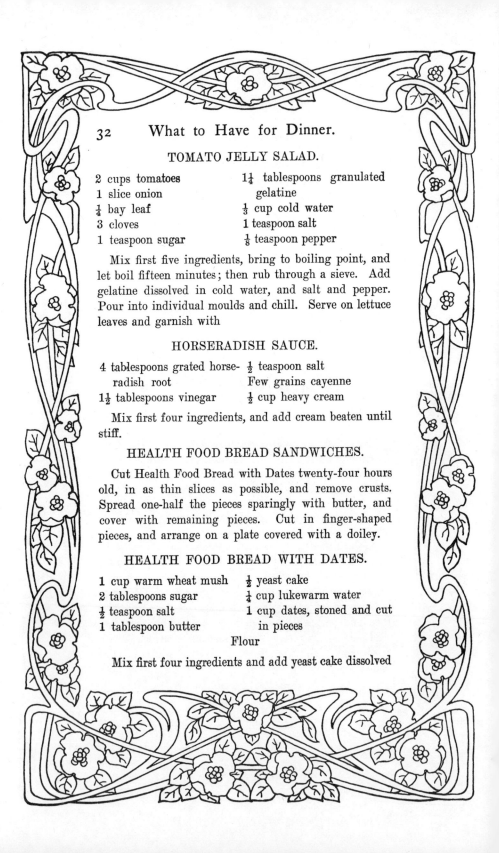

TOMATO JELLY SALAD.

2 cups tomatoes
1 slice onion
¼ bay leaf
3 cloves
1 teaspoon sugar

1¼ tablespoons granulated gelatine
⅓ cup cold water
1 teaspoon salt
⅛ teaspoon pepper

Mix first five ingredients, bring to boiling point, and let boil fifteen minutes; then rub through a sieve. Add gelatine dissolved in cold water, and salt and pepper. Pour into individual moulds and chill. Serve on lettuce leaves and garnish with

HORSERADISH SAUCE.

4 tablespoons grated horse-radish root
1½ tablespoons vinegar

½ teaspoon salt
Few grains cayenne
½ cup heavy cream

Mix first four ingredients, and add cream beaten until stiff.

HEALTH FOOD BREAD SANDWICHES.

Cut Health Food Bread with Dates twenty-four hours old, in as thin slices as possible, and remove crusts. Spread one-half the pieces sparingly with butter, and cover with remaining pieces. Cut in finger-shaped pieces, and arrange on a plate covered with a doiley.

HEALTH FOOD BREAD WITH DATES.

1 cup warm wheat mush
2 tablespoons sugar
½ teaspoon salt
1 tablespoon butter

½ yeast cake
¼ cup lukewarm water
1 cup dates, stoned and cut in pieces

Flour

Mix first four ingredients and add yeast cake dissolved

in lukewarm water and flour to knead. Cover and let rise until mixture has doubled its bulk. Cut down, add dates, and shape in a loaf. Put in buttered bread pan, let rise, and bake fifty minutes in a moderate oven.

CHOCOLATE ICE CREAM WITH ZWIEBACK.

2 cups scalded milk	2 squares chocolate
1¼ cups sugar	1 tablespoon vanilla
1 tablespoon flour	1 cup heavy cream
2 eggs	3 cups Zwieback, dried and
¼ teaspoon salt	broken in small pieces

3 cups thin cream

Mix sugar, flour and salt, add eggs slightly beaten and milk gradually; cook over hot water until a coating is formed on the spoon, stirring constantly at first, afterwards occasionally. Melt chocolate, dilute with hot mixture, then add to remaining mixture. Cool, add thin cream and vanilla; strain and freeze. Just before serving, add heavy cream beaten until stiff, and Zwieback.

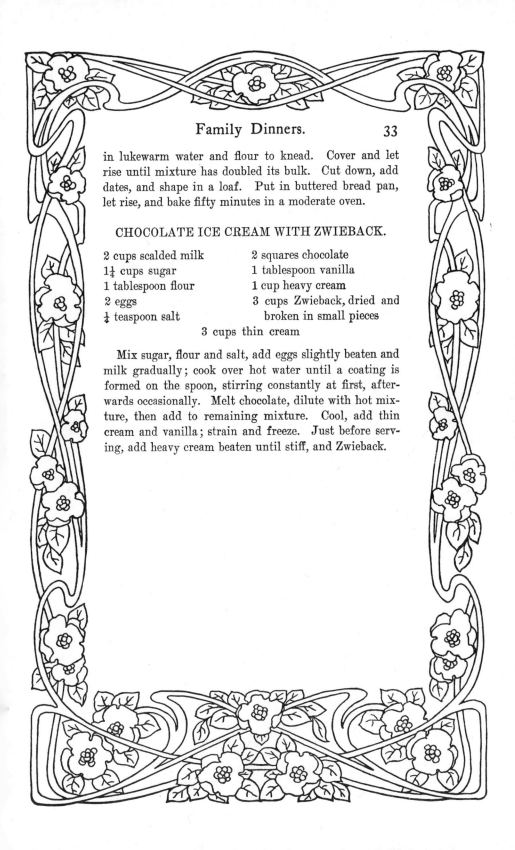

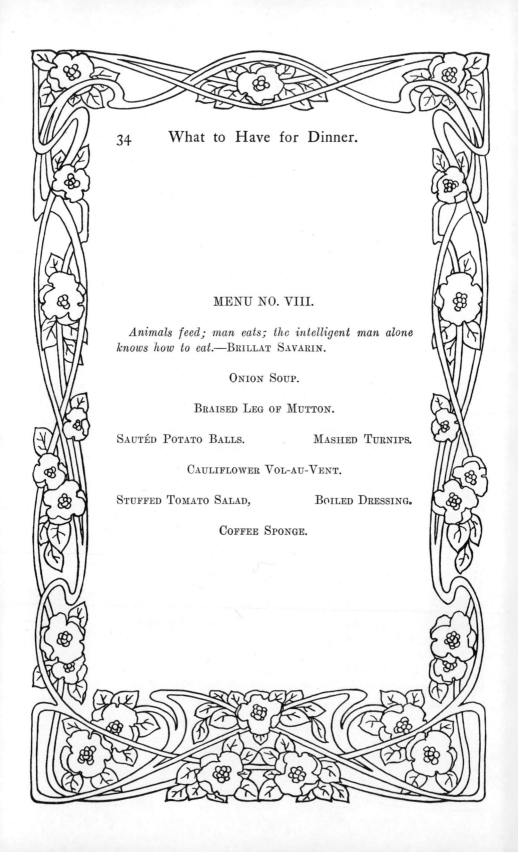

MENU NO. VIII.

Animals feed; man eats; the intelligent man alone knows how to eat.—BRILLAT SAVARIN.

ONION SOUP.

BRAISED LEG OF MUTTON.

SAUTÉD POTATO BALLS.   MASHED TURNIPS.

CAULIFLOWER VOL-AU-VENT.

STUFFED TOMATO SALAD,   BOILED DRESSING.

COFFEE SPONGE.

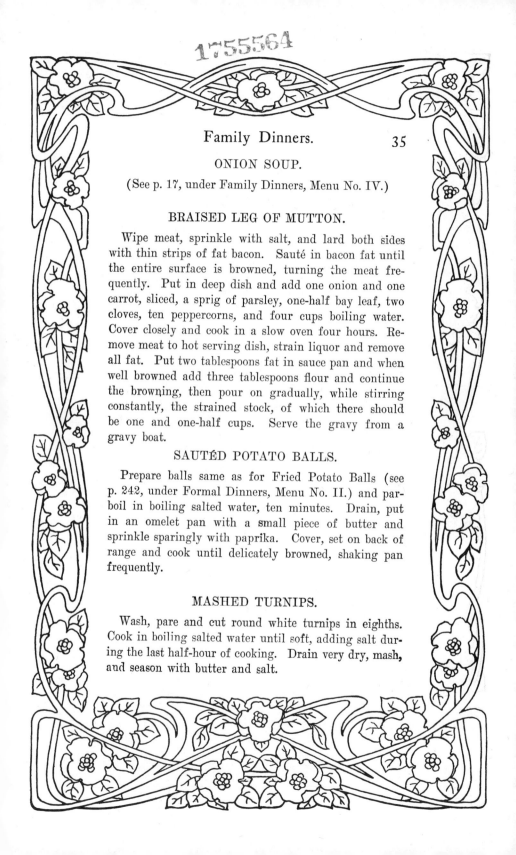

ONION SOUP.

(See p. 17, under Family Dinners, Menu No. IV.)

BRAISED LEG OF MUTTON.

Wipe meat, sprinkle with salt, and lard both sides with thin strips of fat bacon. Sauté in bacon fat until the entire surface is browned, turning the meat frequently. Put in deep dish and add one onion and one carrot, sliced, a sprig of parsley, one-half bay leaf, two cloves, ten peppercorns, and four cups boiling water. Cover closely and cook in a slow oven four hours. Remove meat to hot serving dish, strain liquor and remove all fat. Put two tablespoons fat in sauce pan and when well browned add three tablespoons flour and continue the browning, then pour on gradually, while stirring constantly, the strained stock, of which there should be one and one-half cups. Serve the gravy from a gravy boat.

SAUTÉD POTATO BALLS.

Prepare balls same as for Fried Potato Balls (see p. 242, under Formal Dinners, Menu No. II.) and parboil in boiling salted water, ten minutes. Drain, put in an omelet pan with a small piece of butter and sprinkle sparingly with paprika. Cover, set on back of range and cook until delicately browned, shaking pan frequently.

MASHED TURNIPS.

Wash, pare and cut round white turnips in eighths. Cook in boiling salted water until soft, adding salt during the last half-hour of cooking. Drain very dry, mash, and season with butter and salt.

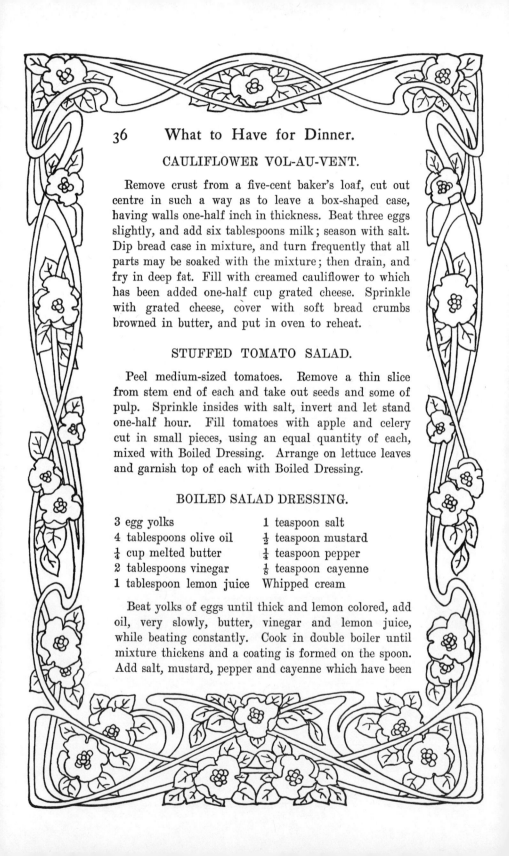

CAULIFLOWER VOL-AU-VENT.

Remove crust from a five-cent baker's loaf, cut out centre in such a way as to leave a box-shaped case, having walls one-half inch in thickness. Beat three eggs slightly, and add six tablespoons milk; season with salt. Dip bread case in mixture, and turn frequently that all parts may be soaked with the mixture; then drain, and fry in deep fat. Fill with creamed cauliflower to which has been added one-half cup grated cheese. Sprinkle with grated cheese, cover with soft bread crumbs browned in butter, and put in oven to reheat.

STUFFED TOMATO SALAD.

Peel medium-sized tomatoes. Remove a thin slice from stem end of each and take out seeds and some of pulp. Sprinkle insides with salt, invert and let stand one-half hour. Fill tomatoes with apple and celery cut in small pieces, using an equal quantity of each, mixed with Boiled Dressing. Arrange on lettuce leaves and garnish top of each with Boiled Dressing.

BOILED SALAD DRESSING.

3 egg yolks	1 teaspoon salt
4 tablespoons olive oil	$\frac{1}{2}$ teaspoon mustard
$\frac{1}{4}$ cup melted butter	$\frac{1}{4}$ teaspoon pepper
2 tablespoons vinegar	$\frac{1}{8}$ teaspoon cayenne
1 tablespoon lemon juice	Whipped cream

Beat yolks of eggs until thick and lemon colored, add oil, very slowly, butter, vinegar and lemon juice, while beating constantly. Cook in double boiler until mixture thickens and a coating is formed on the spoon. Add salt, mustard, pepper and cayenne which have been

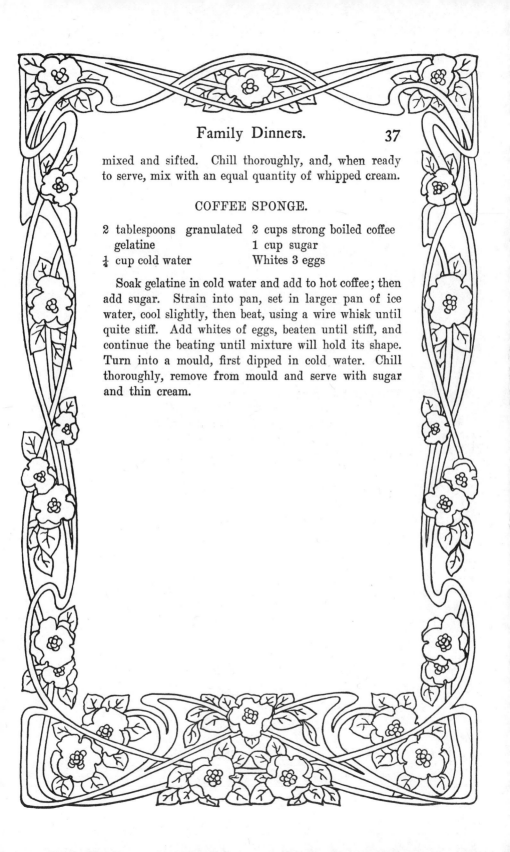

mixed and sifted. Chill thoroughly, and, when ready to serve, mix with an equal quantity of whipped cream.

COFFEE SPONGE.

2 tablespoons granulated gelatine
¼ cup cold water

2 cups strong boiled coffee
1 cup sugar
Whites 3 eggs

Soak gelatine in cold water and add to hot coffee; then add sugar. Strain into pan, set in larger pan of ice water, cool slightly, then beat, using a wire whisk until quite stiff. Add whites of eggs, beaten until stiff, and continue the beating until mixture will hold its shape. Turn into a mould, first dipped in cold water. Chill thoroughly, remove from mould and serve with sugar and thin cream.

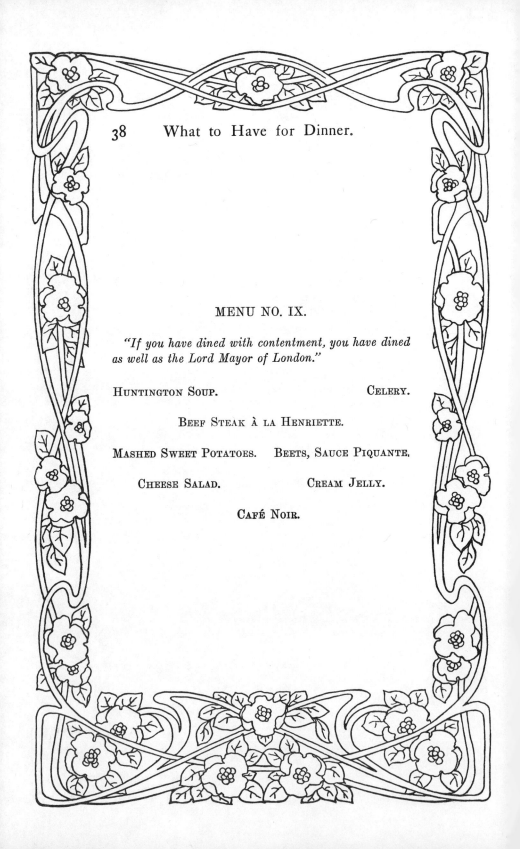

MENU NO. IX.

"If you have dined with contentment, you have dined as well as the Lord Mayor of London."

HUNTINGTON SOUP.   CELERY.

BEEF STEAK À LA HENRIETTE.

MASHED SWEET POTATOES.   BEETS, SAUCE PIQUANTE.

CHEESE SALAD.   CREAM JELLY.

CAFÉ NOIR.

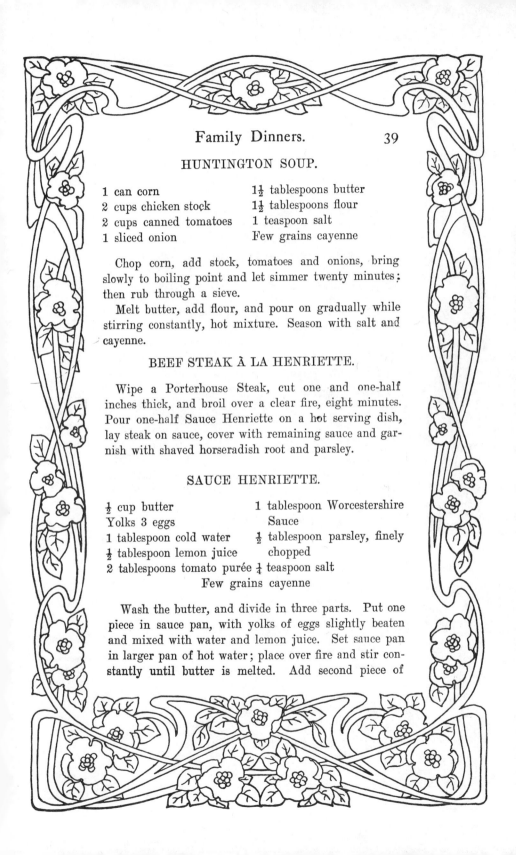

HUNTINGTON SOUP.

1 can corn	1½ tablespoons butter
2 cups chicken stock	1½ tablespoons flour
2 cups canned tomatoes	1 teaspoon salt
1 sliced onion	Few grains cayenne

Chop corn, add stock, tomatoes and onions, bring slowly to boiling point and let simmer twenty minutes; then rub through a sieve.

Melt butter, add flour, and pour on gradually while stirring constantly, hot mixture. Season with salt and cayenne.

BEEF STEAK À LA HENRIETTE.

Wipe a Porterhouse Steak, cut one and one-half inches thick, and broil over a clear fire, eight minutes. Pour one-half Sauce Henriette on a hot serving dish, lay steak on sauce, cover with remaining sauce and garnish with shaved horseradish root and parsley.

SAUCE HENRIETTE.

½ cup butter	1 tablespoon Worcestershire
Yolks 3 eggs	Sauce
1 tablespoon cold water	½ tablespoon parsley, finely
¼ tablespoon lemon juice	chopped
2 tablespoons tomato purée	¼ teaspoon salt
Few grains cayenne	

Wash the butter, and divide in three parts. Put one piece in sauce pan, with yolks of eggs slightly beaten and mixed with water and lemon juice. Set sauce pan in larger pan of hot water; place over fire and stir constantly until butter is melted. Add second piece of

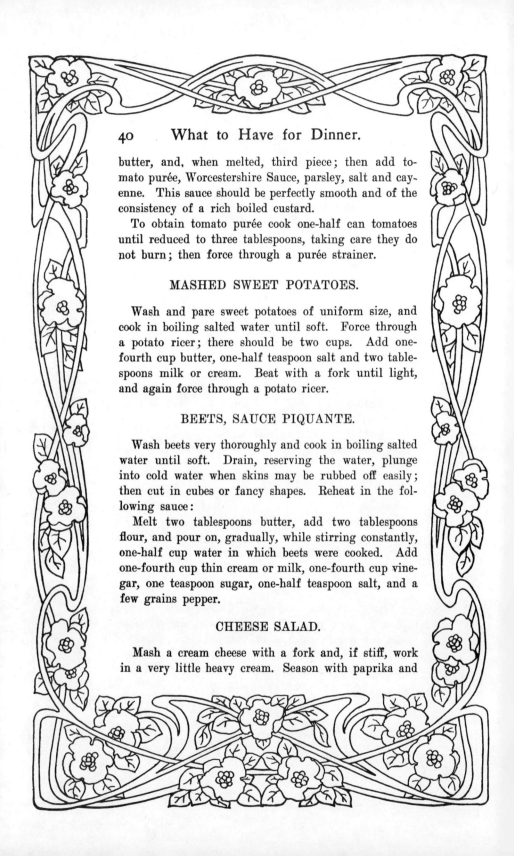

butter, and, when melted, third piece; then add tomato purée, Worcestershire Sauce, parsley, salt and cayenne. This sauce should be perfectly smooth and of the
consistency of a rich boiled custard.

To obtain tomato purée cook one-half can tomatoes
until reduced to three tablespoons, taking care they do
not burn; then force through a purée strainer.

MASHED SWEET POTATOES.

Wash and pare sweet potatoes of uniform size, and
cook in boiling salted water until soft. Force through
a potato ricer; there should be two cups. Add one-
fourth cup butter, one-half teaspoon salt and two tablespoons milk or cream. Beat with a fork until light,
and again force through a potato ricer.

BEETS, SAUCE PIQUANTE.

Wash beets very thoroughly and cook in boiling salted
water until soft. Drain, reserving the water, plunge
into cold water when skins may be rubbed off easily;
then cut in cubes or fancy shapes. Reheat in the following sauce:

Melt two tablespoons butter, add two tablespoons
flour, and pour on, gradually, while stirring constantly,
one-half cup water in which beets were cooked. Add
one-fourth cup thin cream or milk, one-fourth cup vinegar, one teaspoon sugar, one-half teaspoon salt, and a
few grains pepper.

CHEESE SALAD.

Mash a cream cheese with a fork and, if stiff, work
in a very little heavy cream. Season with paprika and

make in the form of balls. Arrange lettuce in form of nests by putting two leaves with stem ends together. Put three cheese balls in each nest. Pour over a French Dressing, (p. 6, Family Dinners, Menu No. I.), and sprinkle one-half the nests with finely chopped parsley and the other half with paprika, having alternate nests of green and red.

CREAM JELLY.

1 tablespoon granulated gelatine
2 tablespoons cold water
$\frac{1}{4}$ cup scalded cream

$\frac{1}{4}$ cup sugar
Whip from 3 cups thin cream
1 teaspoon vanilla **or**

2 teaspoons maraschino

Soak gelatine in cold water and dissolve in hot cream. Add sugar and flavoring and strain. Beat until mixture begins to thicken, then cut and fold in whip from cream. Turn into a mould first dipped in cold water, and chill.

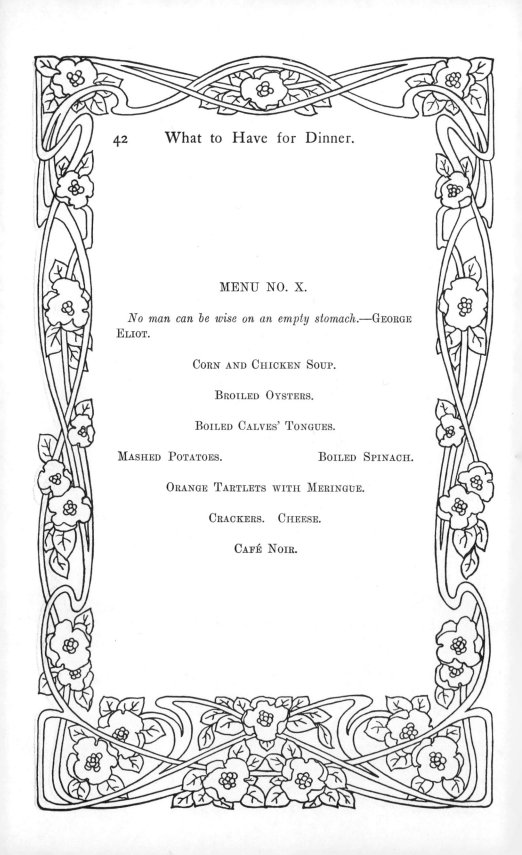

MENU NO. X.

No man can be wise on an empty stomach.—GEORGE ELIOT.

CORN AND CHICKEN SOUP.

BROILED OYSTERS.

BOILED CALVES' TONGUES.

MASHED POTATOES.   BOILED SPINACH.

ORANGE TARTLETS WITH MERINGUE.

CRACKERS.   CHEESE.

CAFÉ NOIR.

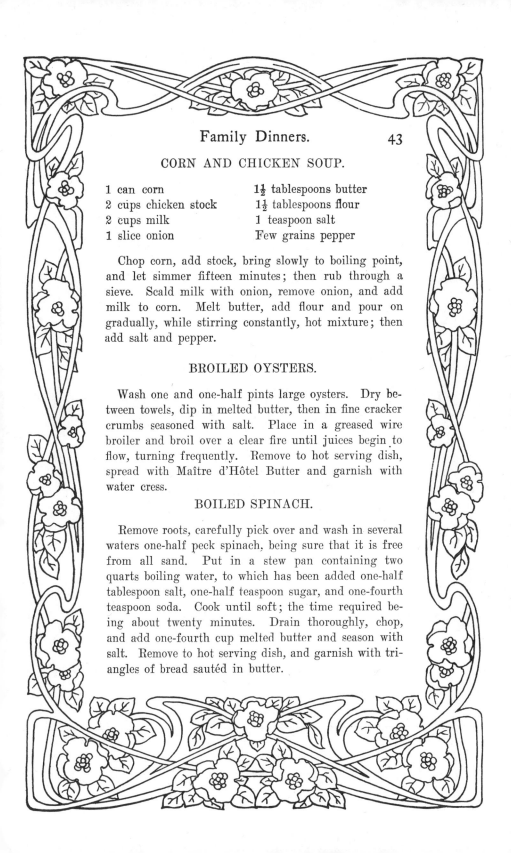

CORN AND CHICKEN SOUP.

1 can corn	1½ tablespoons butter
2 cups chicken stock	1½ tablespoons flour
2 cups milk	1 teaspoon salt
1 slice onion	Few grains pepper

Chop corn, add stock, bring slowly to boiling point, and let simmer fifteen minutes; then rub through a sieve. Scald milk with onion, remove onion, and add milk to corn. Melt butter, add flour and pour on gradually, while stirring constantly, hot mixture; then add salt and pepper.

BROILED OYSTERS.

Wash one and one-half pints large oysters. Dry between towels, dip in melted butter, then in fine cracker crumbs seasoned with salt. Place in a greased wire broiler and broil over a clear fire until juices begin to flow, turning frequently. Remove to hot serving dish, spread with Maître d'Hôtel Butter and garnish with water cress.

BOILED SPINACH.

Remove roots, carefully pick over and wash in several waters one-half peck spinach, being sure that it is free from all sand. Put in a stew pan containing two quarts boiling water, to which has been added one-half tablespoon salt, one-half teaspoon sugar, and one-fourth teaspoon soda. Cook until soft; the time required being about twenty minutes. Drain thoroughly, chop, and add one-fourth cup melted butter and season with salt. Remove to hot serving dish, and garnish with triangles of bread sautéd in butter.

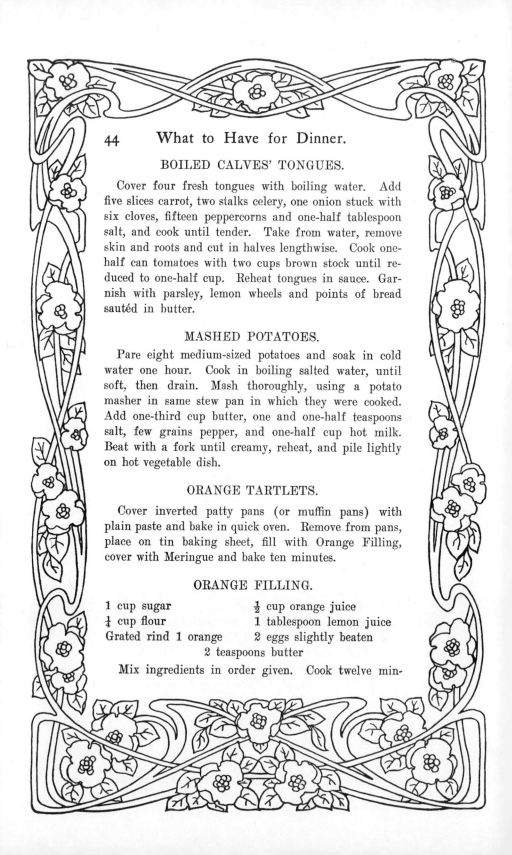

BOILED CALVES' TONGUES.

Cover four fresh tongues with boiling water. Add five slices carrot, two stalks celery, one onion stuck with six cloves, fifteen peppercorns and one-half tablespoon salt, and cook until tender. Take from water, remove skin and roots and cut in halves lengthwise. Cook one-half can tomatoes with two cups brown stock until reduced to one-half cup. Reheat tongues in sauce. Garnish with parsley, lemon wheels and points of bread sautéd in butter.

MASHED POTATOES.

Pare eight medium-sized potatoes and soak in cold water one hour. Cook in boiling salted water, until soft, then drain. Mash thoroughly, using a potato masher in same stew pan in which they were cooked. Add one-third cup butter, one and one-half teaspoons salt, few grains pepper, and one-half cup hot milk. Beat with a fork until creamy, reheat, and pile lightly on hot vegetable dish.

ORANGE TARTLETS.

Cover inverted patty pans (or muffin pans) with plain paste and bake in quick oven. Remove from pans, place on tin baking sheet, fill with Orange Filling, cover with Meringue and bake ten minutes.

ORANGE FILLING.

1 cup sugar	½ cup orange juice
¼ cup flour	1 tablespoon lemon juice
Grated rind 1 orange	2 eggs slightly beaten
	2 teaspoons butter

Mix ingredients in order given. Cook twelve min-

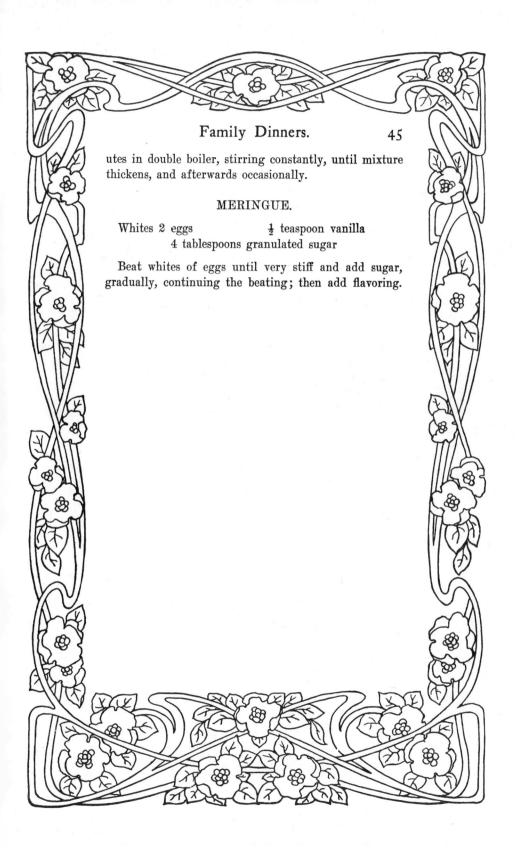

utes in double boiler, stirring constantly, until mixture thickens, and afterwards occasionally.

MERINGUE.

Whites 2 eggs $\frac{1}{2}$ teaspoon vanilla
4 tablespoons granulated sugar

Beat whites of eggs until very stiff and add sugar, gradually, continuing the beating; then add flavoring.

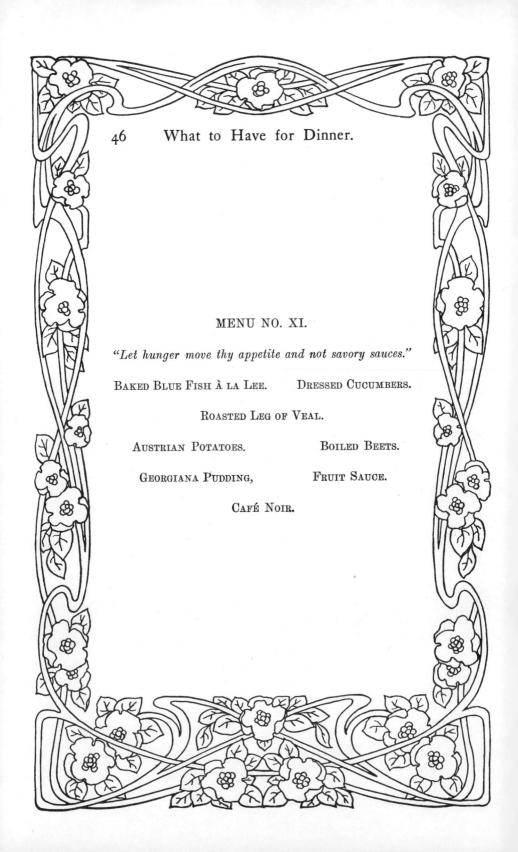

MENU NO. XI.

"Let hunger move thy appetite and not savory sauces."

BAKED BLUE FISH À LA LEE.   DRESSED CUCUMBERS.

ROASTED LEG OF VEAL.

AUSTRIAN POTATOES.   BOILED BEETS.

GEORGIANA PUDDING,   FRUIT SAUCE.

CAFÉ NOIR.

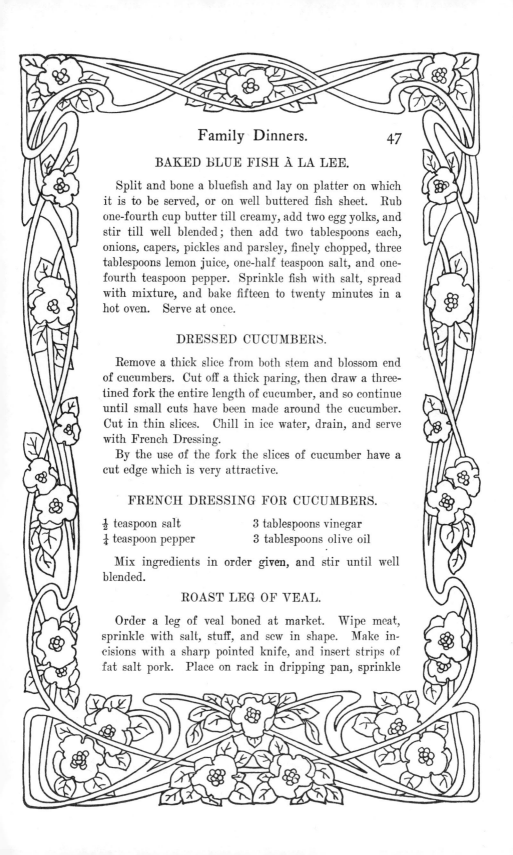

BAKED BLUE FISH À LA LEE.

Split and bone a bluefish and lay on platter on which it is to be served, or on well buttered fish sheet. Rub one-fourth cup butter till creamy, add two egg yolks, and stir till well blended; then add two tablespoons each, onions, capers, pickles and parsley, finely chopped, three tablespoons lemon juice, one-half teaspoon salt, and one-fourth teaspoon pepper. Sprinkle fish with salt, spread with mixture, and bake fifteen to twenty minutes in a hot oven. Serve at once.

DRESSED CUCUMBERS.

Remove a thick slice from both stem and blossom end of cucumbers. Cut off a thick paring, then draw a three-tined fork the entire length of cucumber, and so continue until small cuts have been made around the cucumber. Cut in thin slices. Chill in ice water, drain, and serve with French Dressing.

By the use of the fork the slices of cucumber have a cut edge which is very attractive.

FRENCH DRESSING FOR CUCUMBERS.

½ teaspoon salt	3 tablespoons vinegar
¼ teaspoon pepper	3 tablespoons olive oil

Mix ingredients in order given, and stir until well blended.

ROAST LEG OF VEAL.

Order a leg of veal boned at market. Wipe meat, sprinkle with salt, stuff, and sew in shape. Make incisions with a sharp pointed knife, and insert strips of fat salt pork. Place on rack in dripping pan, sprinkle

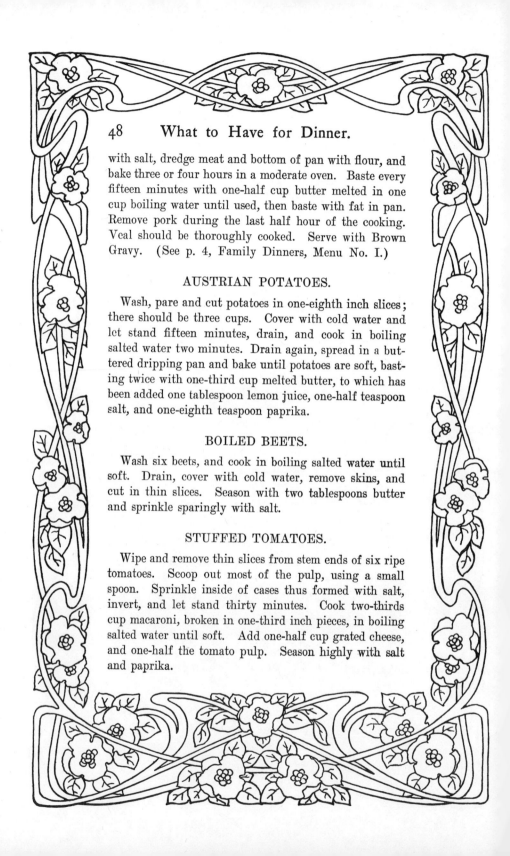

with salt, dredge meat and bottom of pan with flour, and bake three or four hours in a moderate oven. Baste every fifteen minutes with one-half cup butter melted in one cup boiling water until used, then baste with fat in pan. Remove pork during the last half hour of the cooking. Veal should be thoroughly cooked. Serve with Brown Gravy. (See p. 4, Family Dinners, Menu No. I.)

AUSTRIAN POTATOES.

Wash, pare and cut potatoes in one-eighth inch slices; there should be three cups. Cover with cold water and let stand fifteen minutes, drain, and cook in boiling salted water two minutes. Drain again, spread in a buttered dripping pan and bake until potatoes are soft, basting twice with one-third cup melted butter, to which has been added one tablespoon lemon juice, one-half teaspoon salt, and one-eighth teaspoon paprika.

BOILED BEETS.

Wash six beets, and cook in boiling salted water until soft. Drain, cover with cold water, remove skins, and cut in thin slices. Season with two tablespoons butter and sprinkle sparingly with salt.

STUFFED TOMATOES.

Wipe and remove thin slices from stem ends of six ripe tomatoes. Scoop out most of the pulp, using a small spoon. Sprinkle inside of cases thus formed with salt, invert, and let stand thirty minutes. Cook two-thirds cup macaroni, broken in one-third inch pieces, in boiling salted water until soft. Add one-half cup grated cheese, and one-half the tomato pulp. Season highly with salt and paprika.

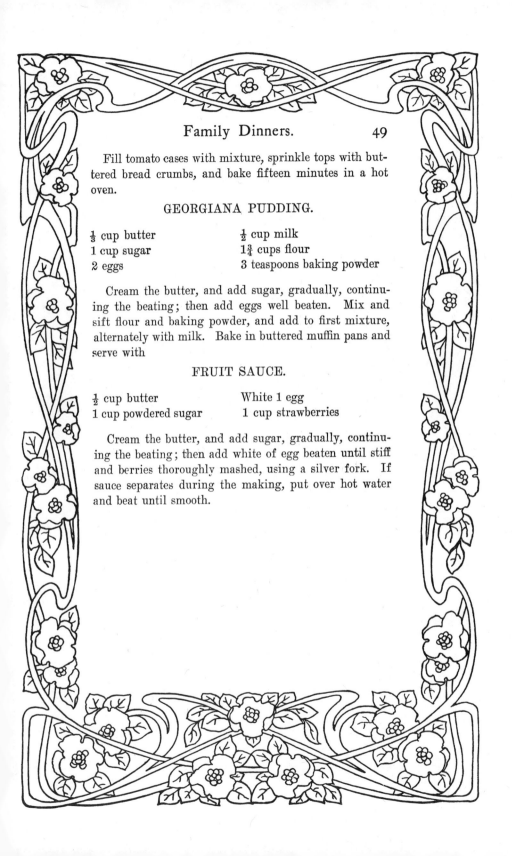

Fill tomato cases with mixture, sprinkle tops with buttered bread crumbs, and bake fifteen minutes in a hot oven.

GEORGIANA PUDDING.

⅓ cup butter	½ cup milk
1 cup sugar	1¾ cups flour
2 eggs	3 teaspoons baking powder

Cream the butter, and add sugar, gradually, continuing the beating; then add eggs well beaten. Mix and sift flour and baking powder, and add to first mixture, alternately with milk. Bake in buttered muffin pans and serve with

FRUIT SAUCE.

½ cup butter	White 1 egg
1 cup powdered sugar	1 cup strawberries

Cream the butter, and add sugar, gradually, continuing the beating; then add white of egg beaten until stiff and berries thoroughly mashed, using a silver fork. If sauce separates during the making, put over hot water and beat until smooth.

MENU NO. XII.

A dinner lubricates business.—LORD STOWELL.

CREAM OF CELERY SOUP.   BROWNED CRACKERS.

BRAISED FOWL,   CHESTNUT STUFFING.

MASHED POTATOES.   BRUSSELS SPROUTS WITH CELERY.

FARINA CUPS WITH CURRANT JELLY.

LEMON CREAM SHERBET.   BRANDY SNAPS.

STUFFED RAISINS.

CAFÉ NOIR.

CREAM OF CELERY SOUP.

5 stalks celery	3 tablespoons flour
4 cups milk	Salt
2 slices onion	Pepper
3 tablespoons butter	½ cup cream

Chop celery and pound in a mortar. Cook in double boiler with onion and milk thirty minutes. Melt the butter, add flour and cook one minute, then pour on gradually the hot milk, stirring constantly. Season with salt and pepper, add cream, strain into tureen and serve at once.

BROWNED CRACKERS.

Split common crackers, arrange in dripping pan and let stand in a slow oven until crisp and delicately browned.

BRAISED FOWL.

Dress, clean, stuff and truss a fowl. Try out a one and one-half inch cube of fat salt pork, and remove scraps. Sauté fowl in pork fat, until entire surface is well browned, turning frequently. Remove to a trivet in a deep pan and pour over fat remaining in pan cooked, three minutes, with one small sliced onion, four slices carrot, two sprigs parsley and one-half bay leaf. Add two cups boiling water, cover, and bake in a slow oven until tender, basting every twenty minutes. Serve with a sauce made by straining the stock remaining in pan, removing fat, and thickening with two tablespoons flour diluted with cold water to form a thin, smooth paste.

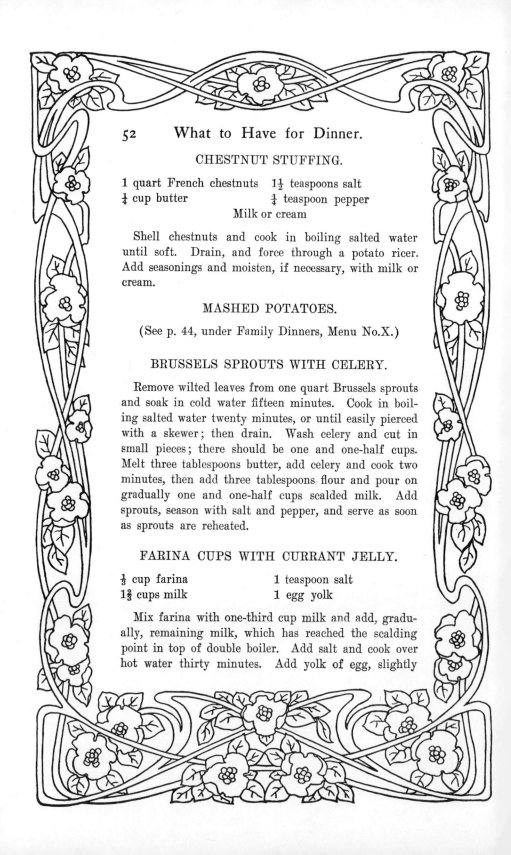

CHESTNUT STUFFING.

1 quart French chestnuts
¼ cup butter

1½ teaspoons salt
¼ teaspoon pepper

Milk or cream

Shell chestnuts and cook in boiling salted water until soft. Drain, and force through a potato ricer. Add seasonings and moisten, if necessary, with milk or cream.

MASHED POTATOES.

(See p. 44, under Family Dinners, Menu No.X.)

BRUSSELS SPROUTS WITH CELERY.

Remove wilted leaves from one quart Brussels sprouts and soak in cold water fifteen minutes. Cook in boiling salted water twenty minutes, or until easily pierced with a skewer; then drain. Wash celery and cut in small pieces; there should be one and one-half cups. Melt three tablespoons butter, add celery and cook two minutes, then add three tablespoons flour and pour on gradually one and one-half cups scalded milk. Add sprouts, season with salt and pepper, and serve as soon as sprouts are reheated.

FARINA CUPS WITH CURRANT JELLY.

⅓ cup farina
1⅔ cups milk

1 teaspoon salt
1 egg yolk

Mix farina with one-third cup milk and add, gradually, remaining milk, which has reached the scalding point in top of double boiler. Add salt and cook over hot water thirty minutes. Add yolk of egg, slightly

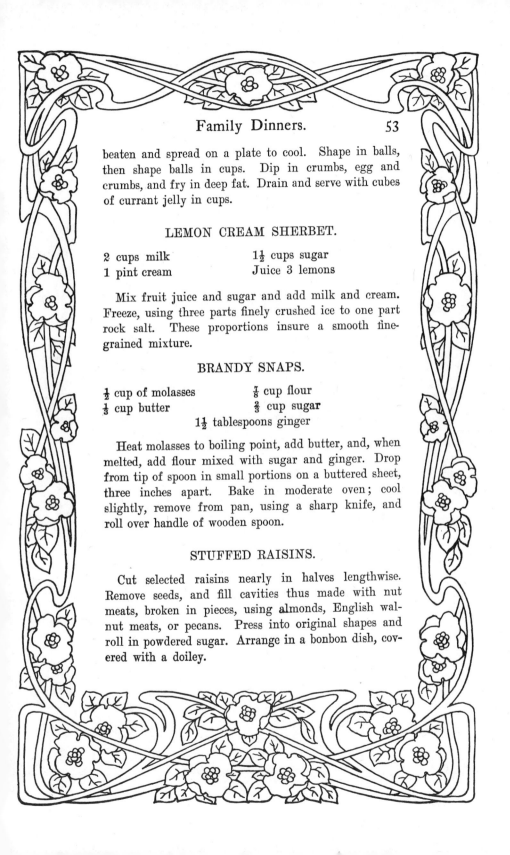

beaten and spread on a plate to cool. Shape in balls,
then shape balls in cups. Dip in crumbs, egg and
crumbs, and fry in deep fat. Drain and serve with cubes
of currant jelly in cups.

LEMON CREAM SHERBET.

2 cups milk   1½ cups sugar
1 pint cream   Juice 3 lemons

Mix fruit juice and sugar and add milk and cream.
Freeze, using three parts finely crushed ice to one part
rock salt. These proportions insure a smooth fine-
grained mixture.

BRANDY SNAPS.

½ cup of molasses   ⅞ cup flour
⅓ cup butter   ⅔ cup sugar
          1½ tablespoons ginger

Heat molasses to boiling point, add butter, and, when
melted, add flour mixed with sugar and ginger. Drop
from tip of spoon in small portions on a buttered sheet,
three inches apart. Bake in moderate oven; cool
slightly, remove from pan, using a sharp knife, and
roll over handle of wooden spoon.

STUFFED RAISINS.

Cut selected raisins nearly in halves lengthwise.
Remove seeds, and fill cavities thus made with nut
meats, broken in pieces, using almonds, English walnut meats, or pecans. Press into original shapes and
roll in powdered sugar. Arrange in a bonbon dish, covered with a doiley.

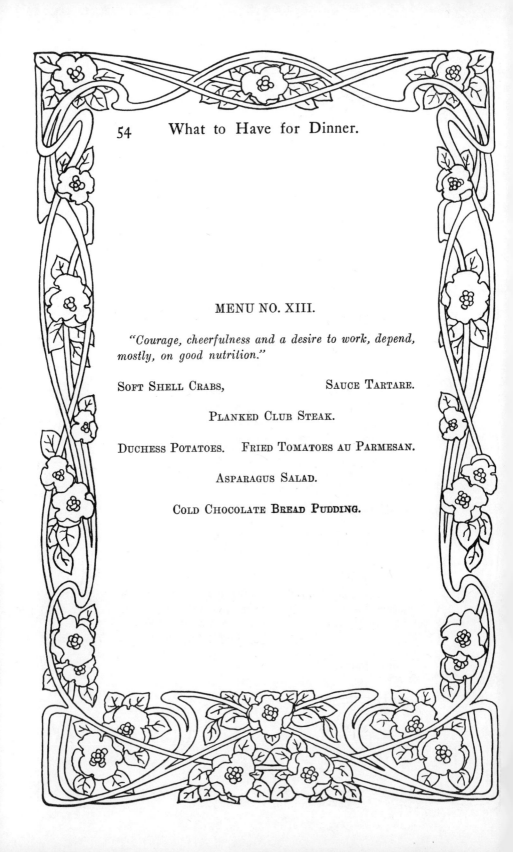

MENU NO. XIII.

"Courage, cheerfulness and a desire to work, depend, mostly, on good nutrition."

SOFT SHELL CRABS,   SAUCE TARTARE.

PLANKED CLUB STEAK.

DUCHESS POTATOES.   FRIED TOMATOES AU PARMESAN.

ASPARAGUS SALAD.

COLD CHOCOLATE BREAD PUDDING.

SOFT SHELL CRABS.

Clean crabs, sprinkle with salt, dip in egg and crumbs and fry in deep fat, turning often while frying. Serve with Sauce Tartare. (See p. 17, under Family Dinners, Menu No. IV.)

PLANKED CLUB STEAK.

Wash one-half cup butter, and add one-half tablespoon, each, red pepper, green pepper and parsley, finely chopped, one-fourth tablespoon onion, finely chopped, one clove of garlic finely chopped and one-half tablespoon lemon juice. Spread one-third of the mixture on the centre of a plank and arrange a border of Duchess Potatoes close to edge of plank, using a pastry bag and tube. Pan broil a Porterhouse Steak, cut one and one-half inches thick, four minutes, and remove to plank. Spread with remaining butter, and put in a hot oven to finish the cooking. Garnish with three large mushroom caps sautéd in butter.

DUCHESS POTATOES.

To three cups hot riced potatoes, add three tablespoons butter, one teaspoon salt, and the yolks of three eggs slightly beaten.

FRIED TOMATOES AU PARMESAN.

Select medium-sized tomatoes and cut in slices crosswise, sprinkle with salt and pepper, dredge with flour and sauté in butter. Arrange each slice on a round of toasted bread, sprinkle with grated cheese, and pile whipped cream on top.

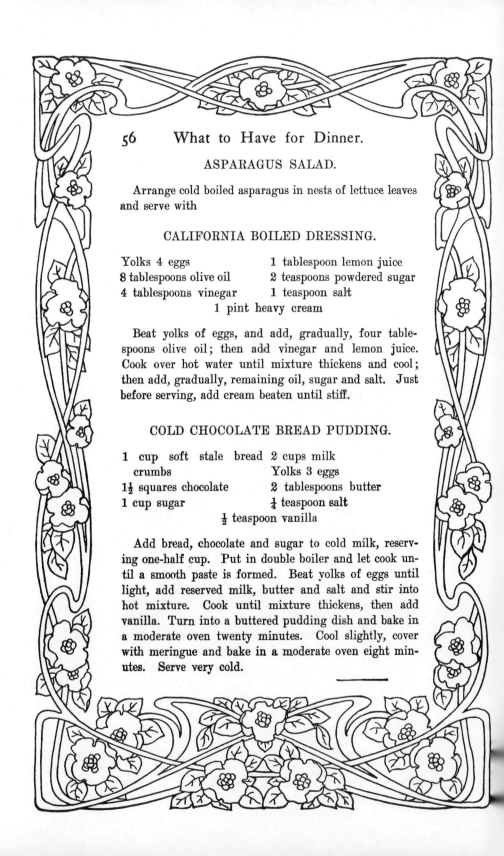

ASPARAGUS SALAD.

Arrange cold boiled asparagus in nests of lettuce leaves and serve with

CALIFORNIA BOILED DRESSING.

Yolks 4 eggs
8 tablespoons olive oil
4 tablespoons vinegar
1 tablespoon lemon juice
2 teaspoons powdered sugar
1 teaspoon salt
1 pint heavy cream

Beat yolks of eggs, and add, gradually, four table-spoons olive oil; then add vinegar and lemon juice. Cook over hot water until mixture thickens and cool; then add, gradually, remaining oil, sugar and salt. Just before serving, add cream beaten until stiff.

COLD CHOCOLATE BREAD PUDDING.

1 cup soft stale bread crumbs
1½ squares chocolate
1 cup sugar
2 cups milk
Yolks 3 eggs
2 tablespoons butter
¼ teaspoon salt
½ teaspoon vanilla

Add bread, chocolate and sugar to cold milk, reserving one-half cup. Put in double boiler and let cook until a smooth paste is formed. Beat yolks of eggs until light, add reserved milk, butter and salt and stir into hot mixture. Cook until mixture thickens, then add vanilla. Turn into a buttered pudding dish and bake in a moderate oven twenty minutes. Cool slightly, cover with meringue and bake in a moderate oven eight minutes. Serve very cold.

MERINGUE.

Beat the whites of three eggs until stiff and add, gradually, one-fourth cup powdered sugar, continuing the beating; then cut and fold in one-fourth cup powdered sugar and add one-half teaspoon vanilla.

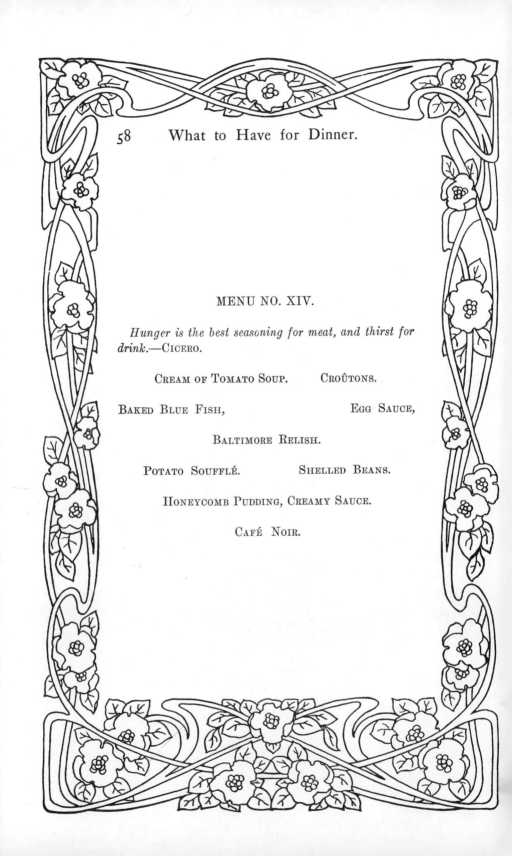

MENU NO. XIV.

Hunger is the best seasoning for meat, and thirst for drink.—CICERO.

CREAM OF TOMATO SOUP.   CROÛTONS.

BAKED BLUE FISH,   EGG SAUCE,

BALTIMORE RELISH.

POTATO SOUFFLÉ.   SHELLED BEANS.

HONEYCOMB PUDDING, CREAMY SAUCE.

CAFÉ NOIR.

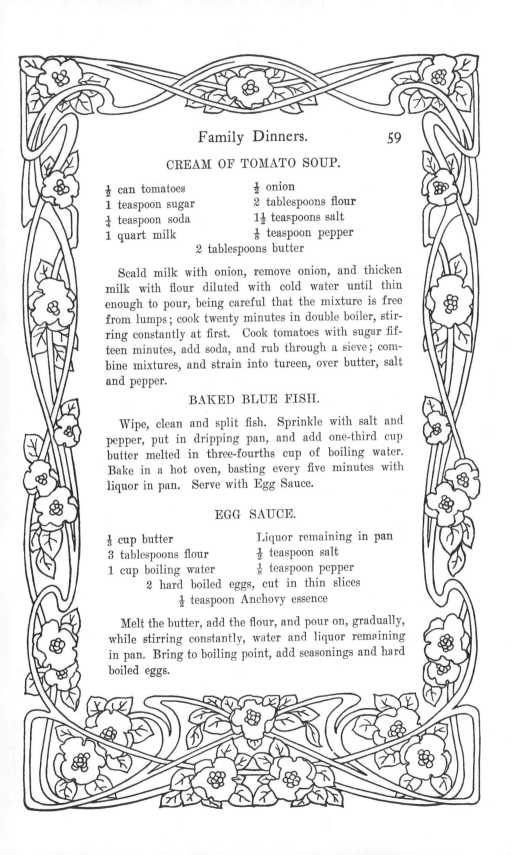

CREAM OF TOMATO SOUP.

½ can tomatoes   ½ onion
1 teaspoon sugar   2 tablespoons flour
¼ teaspoon soda   1½ teaspoons salt
1 quart milk   ⅛ teaspoon pepper
2 tablespoons butter

Scald milk with onion, remove onion, and thicken milk with flour diluted with cold water until thin enough to pour, being careful that the mixture is free from lumps; cook twenty minutes in double boiler, stirring constantly at first. Cook tomatoes with sugar fifteen minutes, add soda, and rub through a sieve; combine mixtures, and strain into tureen, over butter, salt and pepper.

BAKED BLUE FISH.

Wipe, clean and split fish. Sprinkle with salt and pepper, put in dripping pan, and add one-third cup butter melted in three-fourths cup of boiling water. Bake in a hot oven, basting every five minutes with liquor in pan. Serve with Egg Sauce.

EGG SAUCE.

⅓ cup butter   Liquor remaining in pan
3 tablespoons flour   ½ teaspoon salt
1 cup boiling water   ⅛ teaspoon pepper
2 hard boiled eggs, cut in thin slices
½ teaspoon Anchovy essence

Melt the butter, add the flour, and pour on, gradually, while stirring constantly, water and liquor remaining in pan. Bring to boiling point, add seasonings and hard boiled eggs.

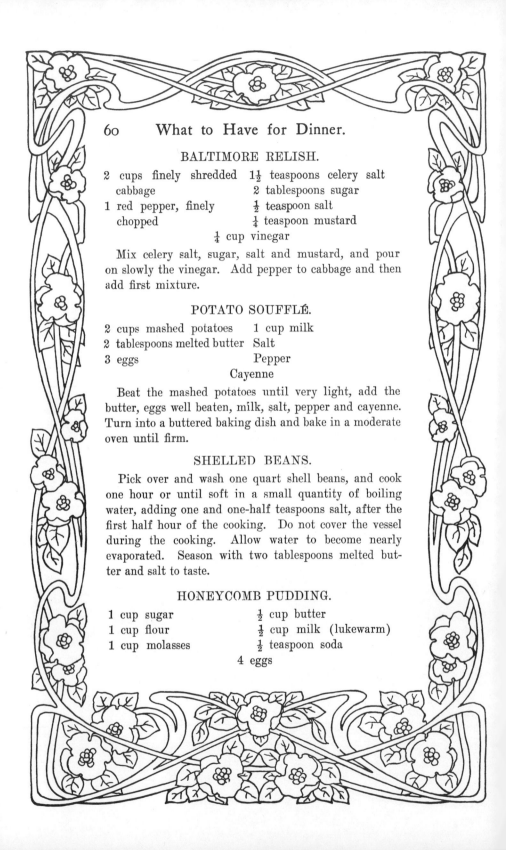

BALTIMORE RELISH.

2 cups finely shredded cabbage

1 red pepper, finely chopped

1½ teaspoons celery salt

2 tablespoons sugar

½ teaspoon salt

¼ teaspoon mustard

¼ cup vinegar

Mix celery salt, sugar, salt and mustard, and pour on slowly the vinegar. Add pepper to cabbage and then add first mixture.

POTATO SOUFFLÉ.

2 cups mashed potatoes

2 tablespoons melted butter

3 eggs

1 cup milk

Salt

Pepper

Cayenne

Beat the mashed potatoes until very light, add the butter, eggs well beaten, milk, salt, pepper and cayenne. Turn into a buttered baking dish and bake in a moderate oven until firm.

SHELLED BEANS.

Pick over and wash one quart shell beans, and cook one hour or until soft in a small quantity of boiling water, adding one and one-half teaspoons salt, after the first half hour of the cooking. Do not cover the vessel during the cooking. Allow water to become nearly evaporated. Season with two tablespoons melted butter and salt to taste.

HONEYCOMB PUDDING.

1 cup sugar

1 cup flour

1 cup molasses

½ cup butter

½ cup milk (lukewarm)

½ teaspoon soda

4 eggs

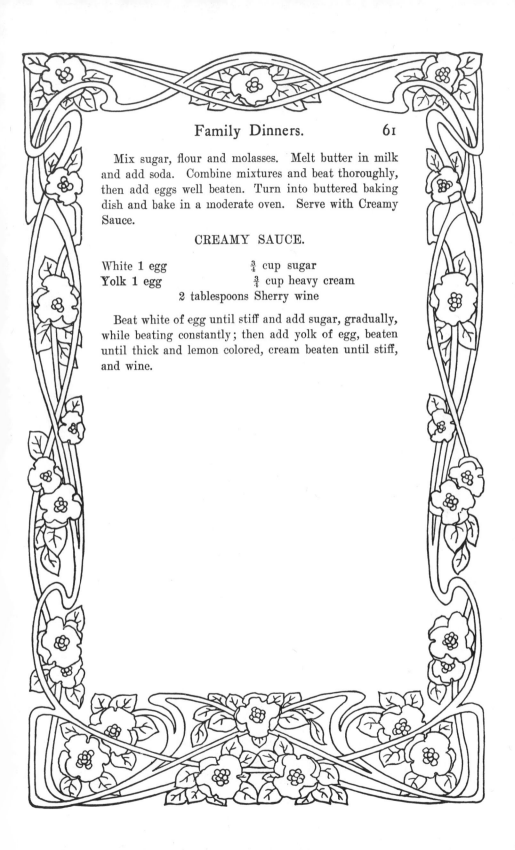

Mix sugar, flour and molasses. Melt butter in milk and add soda. Combine mixtures and beat thoroughly, then add eggs well beaten. Turn into buttered baking dish and bake in a moderate oven. Serve with Creamy Sauce.

CREAMY SAUCE.

White 1 egg $\frac{3}{4}$ cup sugar
Yolk 1 egg $\frac{3}{4}$ cup heavy cream
             2 tablespoons Sherry wine

Beat white of egg until stiff and add sugar, gradually, while beating constantly; then add yolk of egg, beaten until thick and lemon colored, cream beaten until stiff, and wine.

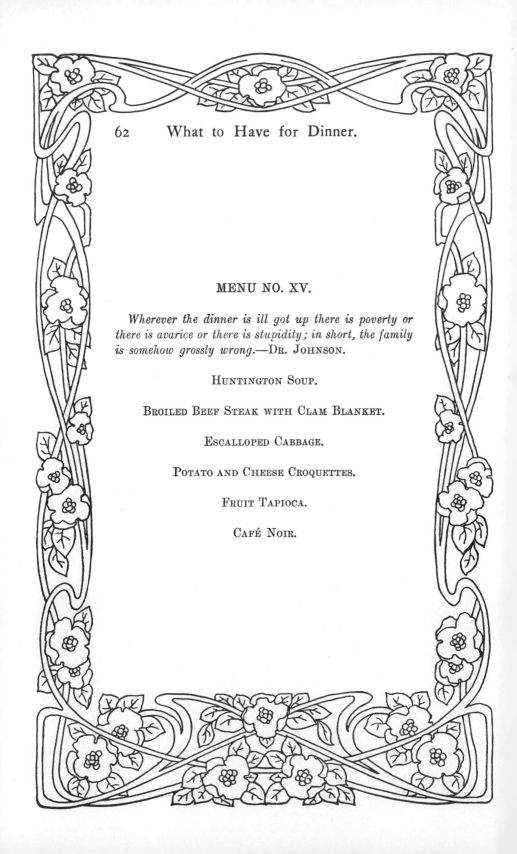

MENU NO. XV.

Wherever the dinner is ill got up there is poverty or there is avarice or there is stupidity; in short, the family is somehow grossly wrong.—Dr. Johnson.

Huntington Soup.

Broiled Beef Steak with Clam Blanket.

Escalloped Cabbage.

Potato and Cheese Croquettes.

Fruit Tapioca.

Café Noir.

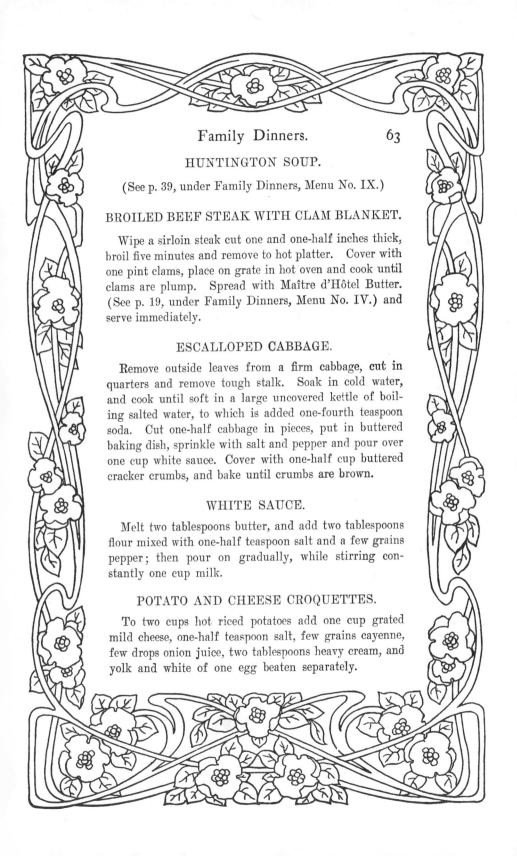

HUNTINGTON SOUP.

(See p. 39, under Family Dinners, Menu No. IX.)

BROILED BEEF STEAK WITH CLAM BLANKET.

Wipe a sirloin steak cut one and one-half inches thick, broil five minutes and remove to hot platter. Cover with one pint clams, place on grate in hot oven and cook until clams are plump. Spread with Maître d'Hôtel Butter. (See p. 19, under Family Dinners, Menu No. IV.) and serve immediately.

ESCALLOPED CABBAGE.

Remove outside leaves from a firm cabbage, cut in quarters and remove tough stalk. Soak in cold water, and cook until soft in a large uncovered kettle of boiling salted water, to which is added one-fourth teaspoon soda. Cut one-half cabbage in pieces, put in buttered baking dish, sprinkle with salt and pepper and pour over one cup white sauce. Cover with one-half cup buttered cracker crumbs, and bake until crumbs are brown.

WHITE SAUCE.

Melt two tablespoons butter, and add two tablespoons flour mixed with one-half teaspoon salt and a few grains pepper; then pour on gradually, while stirring constantly one cup milk.

POTATO AND CHEESE CROQUETTES.

To two cups hot riced potatoes add one cup grated mild cheese, one-half teaspoon salt, few grains cayenne, few drops onion juice, two tablespoons heavy cream, and yolk and white of one egg beaten separately.

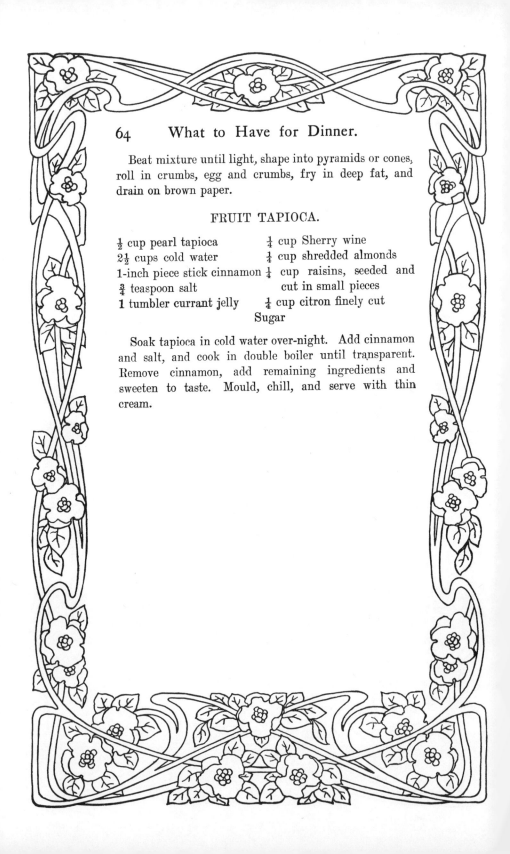

Beat mixture until light, shape into pyramids or cones, roll in crumbs, egg and crumbs, fry in deep fat, and drain on brown paper.

FRUIT TAPIOCA.

½ cup pearl tapioca	¼ cup Sherry wine
2½ cups cold water	¼ cup shredded almonds
1-inch piece stick cinnamon	¼ cup raisins, seeded and
¾ teaspoon salt	cut in small pieces
1 tumbler currant jelly	¼ cup citron finely cut

Sugar

Soak tapioca in cold water over-night. Add cinnamon and salt, and cook in double boiler until transparent. Remove cinnamon, add remaining ingredients and sweeten to taste. Mould, chill, and serve with thin cream.

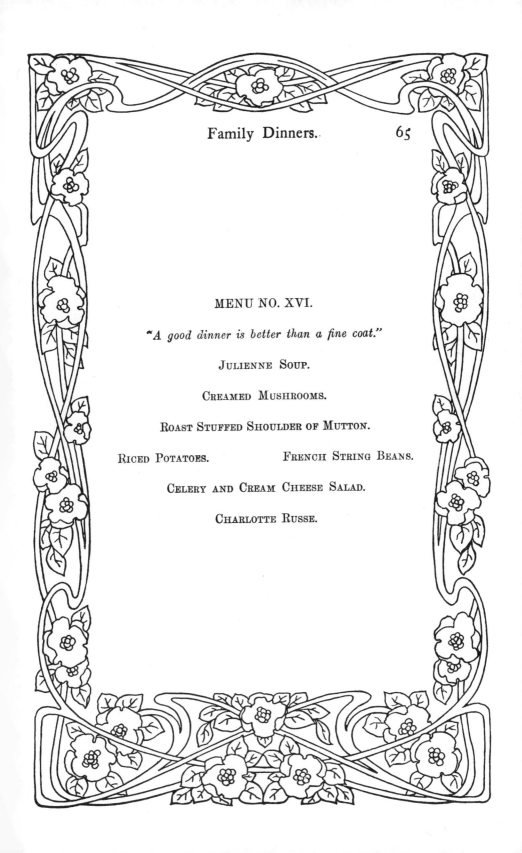

MENU NO. XVI.

"A good dinner is better than a fine coat."

JULIENNE SOUP.

CREAMED MUSHROOMS.

ROAST STUFFED SHOULDER OF MUTTON.

RICED POTATOES.   FRENCH STRING BEANS.

CELERY AND CREAM CHEESE SALAD.

CHARLOTTE RUSSE.

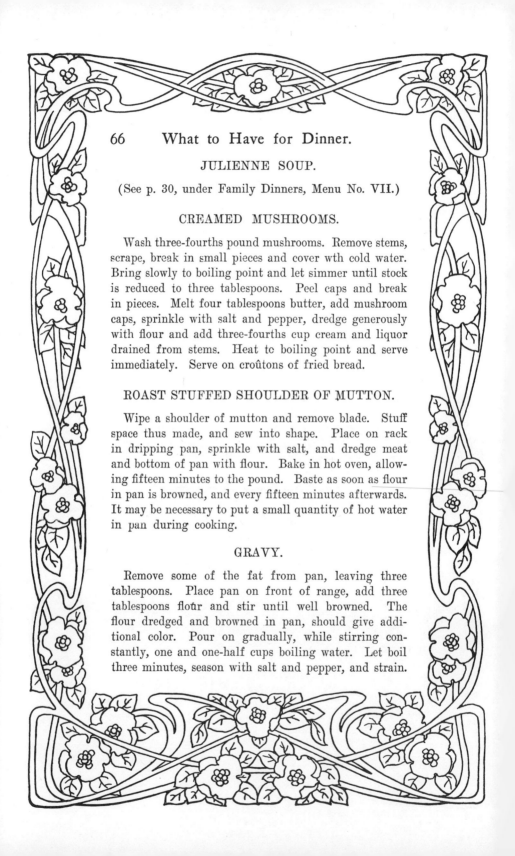

JULIENNE SOUP.

(See p. 30, under Family Dinners, Menu No. VII.)

CREAMED MUSHROOMS.

Wash three-fourths pound mushrooms. Remove stems, scrape, break in small pieces and cover wth cold water. Bring slowly to boiling point and let simmer until stock is reduced to three tablespoons. Peel caps and break in pieces. Melt four tablespoons butter, add mushroom caps, sprinkle with salt and pepper, dredge generously with flour and add three-fourths cup cream and liquor drained from stems. Heat to boiling point and serve immediately. Serve on croûtons of fried bread.

ROAST STUFFED SHOULDER OF MUTTON.

Wipe a shoulder of mutton and remove blade. Stuff space thus made, and sew into shape. Place on rack in dripping pan, sprinkle with salt, and dredge meat and bottom of pan with flour. Bake in hot oven, allowing fifteen minutes to the pound. Baste as soon as flour in pan is browned, and every fifteen minutes afterwards. It may be necessary to put a small quantity of hot water in pan during cooking.

GRAVY.

Remove some of the fat from pan, leaving three tablespoons. Place pan on front of range, add three tablespoons flour and stir until well browned. The flour dredged and browned in pan, should give additional color. Pour on gradually, while stirring constantly, one and one-half cups boiling water. Let boil three minutes, season with salt and pepper, and strain.

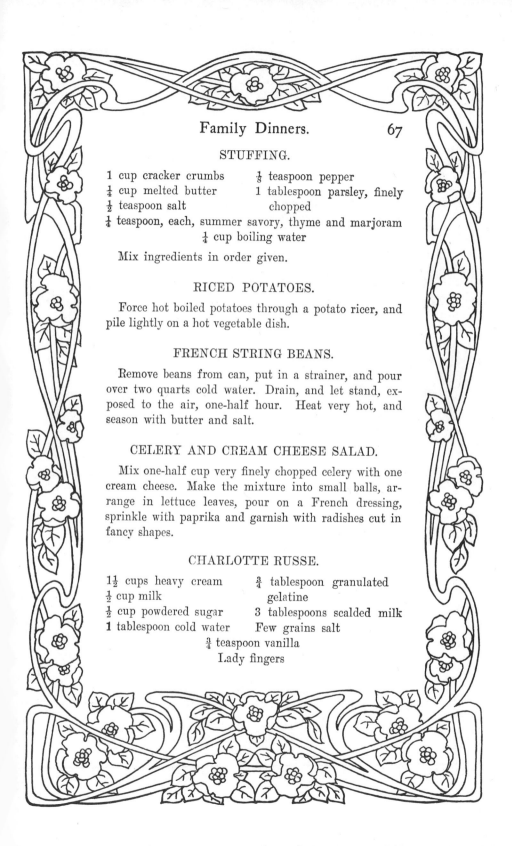

STUFFING.

1 cup cracker crumbs
¼ cup melted butter
½ teaspoon salt
¼ teaspoon, each, summer savory, thyme and marjoram

⅛ teaspoon pepper
1 tablespoon parsley, finely chopped

¼ cup boiling water

Mix ingredients in order given.

RICED POTATOES.

Force hot boiled potatoes through a potato ricer, and pile lightly on a hot vegetable dish.

FRENCH STRING BEANS.

Remove beans from can, put in a strainer, and pour over two quarts cold water. Drain, and let stand, exposed to the air, one-half hour. Heat very hot, and season with butter and salt.

CELERY AND CREAM CHEESE SALAD.

Mix one-half cup very finely chopped celery with one cream cheese. Make the mixture into small balls, arrange in lettuce leaves, pour on a French dressing, sprinkle with paprika and garnish with radishes cut in fancy shapes.

CHARLOTTE RUSSE.

1½ cups heavy cream
½ cup milk
½ cup powdered sugar
1 tablespoon cold water

¾ tablespoon granulated gelatine
3 tablespoons scalded milk
Few grains salt

¾ teaspoon vanilla
Lady fingers

Dilute cream with milk and beat until stiff, then add sugar. Soak gelatine in cold water and dissolve in scalded milk. Fold gelatine carefully into cream to prevent mixture from lumping. Add salt and flavoring. Line a mould with Lady Fingers, turn in mixture and chill.

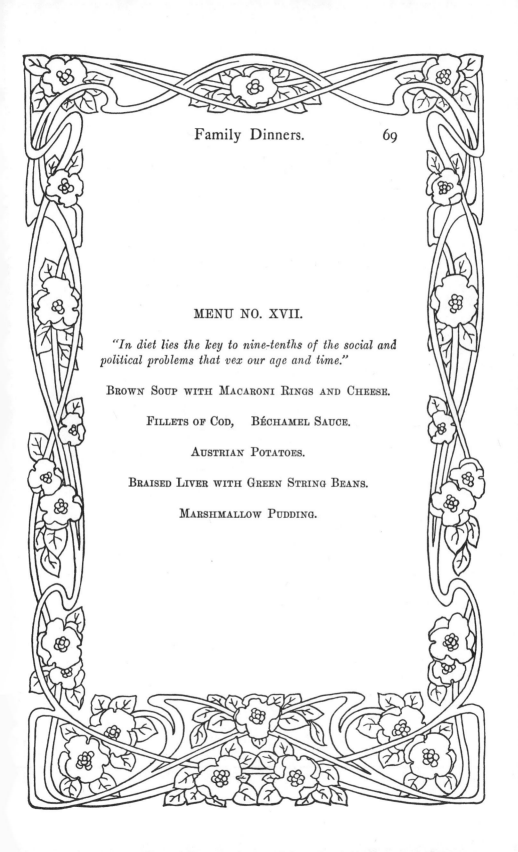

MENU NO. XVII.

"In diet lies the key to nine-tenths of the social and political problems that vex our age and time."

BROWN SOUP WITH MACARONI RINGS AND CHEESE.

FILLETS OF COD,   BÉCHAMEL SAUCE.

AUSTRIAN POTATOES.

BRAISED LIVER WITH GREEN STRING BEANS.

MARSHMALLOW PUDDING.

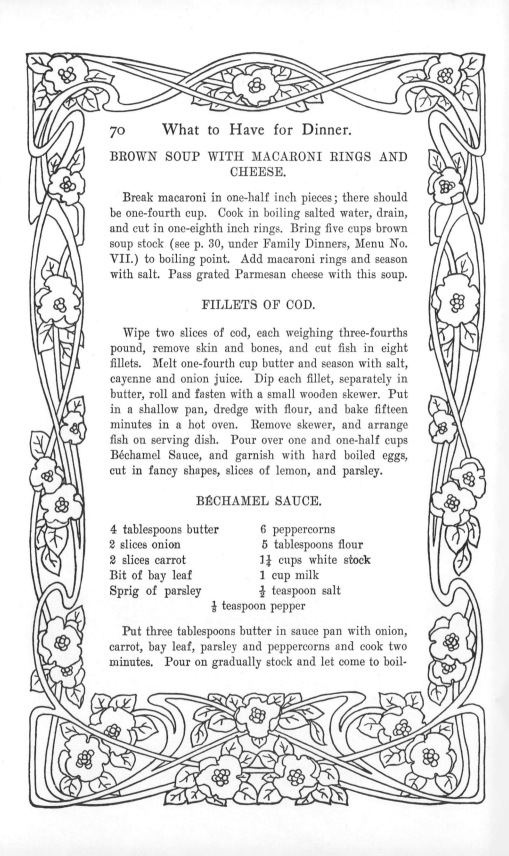

BROWN SOUP WITH MACARONI RINGS AND CHEESE.

Break macaroni in one-half inch pieces; there should be one-fourth cup. Cook in boiling salted water, drain, and cut in one-eighth inch rings. Bring five cups brown soup stock (see p. 30, under Family Dinners, Menu No. VII.) to boiling point. Add macaroni rings and season with salt. Pass grated Parmesan cheese with this soup.

FILLETS OF COD.

Wipe two slices of cod, each weighing three-fourths pound, remove skin and bones, and cut fish in eight fillets. Melt one-fourth cup butter and season with salt, cayenne and onion juice. Dip each fillet, separately in butter, roll and fasten with a small wooden skewer. Put in a shallow pan, dredge with flour, and bake fifteen minutes in a hot oven. Remove skewer, and arrange fish on serving dish. Pour over one and one-half cups Béchamel Sauce, and garnish with hard boiled eggs, cut in fancy shapes, slices of lemon, and parsley.

BÉCHAMEL SAUCE.

4 tablespoons butter	6 peppercorns
2 slices onion	5 tablespoons flour
2 slices carrot	1¼ cups white stock
Bit of bay leaf	1 cup milk
Sprig of parsley	½ teaspoon salt
⅛ teaspoon pepper	

Put three tablespoons butter in sauce pan with onion, carrot, bay leaf, parsley and peppercorns and cook two minutes. Pour on gradually stock and let come to boil-

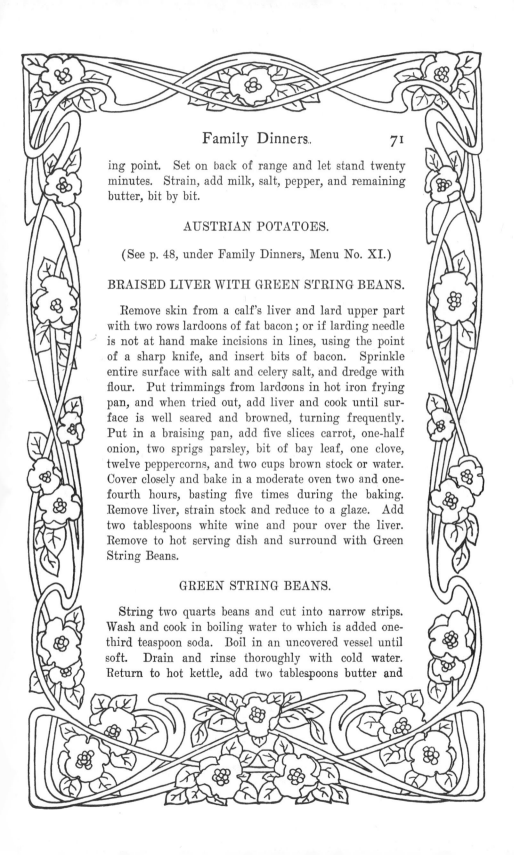

ing point. Set on back of range and let stand twenty minutes. Strain, add milk, salt, pepper, and remaining butter, bit by bit.

AUSTRIAN POTATOES.

(See p. 48, under Family Dinners, Menu No. XI.)

BRAISED LIVER WITH GREEN STRING BEANS.

Remove skin from a calf's liver and lard upper part with two rows lardoons of fat bacon; or if larding needle is not at hand make incisions in lines, using the point of a sharp knife, and insert bits of bacon. Sprinkle entire surface with salt and celery salt, and dredge with flour. Put trimmings from lardoons in hot iron frying pan, and when tried out, add liver and cook until surface is well seared and browned, turning frequently. Put in a braising pan, add five slices carrot, one-half onion, two sprigs parsley, bit of bay leaf, one clove, twelve peppercorns, and two cups brown stock or water. Cover closely and bake in a moderate oven two and one-fourth hours, basting five times during the baking. Remove liver, strain stock and reduce to a glaze. Add two tablespoons white wine and pour over the liver. Remove to hot serving dish and surround with Green String Beans.

GREEN STRING BEANS.

String two quarts beans and cut into narrow strips. Wash and cook in boiling water to which is added one-third teaspoon soda. Boil in an uncovered vessel until soft. Drain and rinse thoroughly with cold water. Return to hot kettle, add two tablespoons butter and

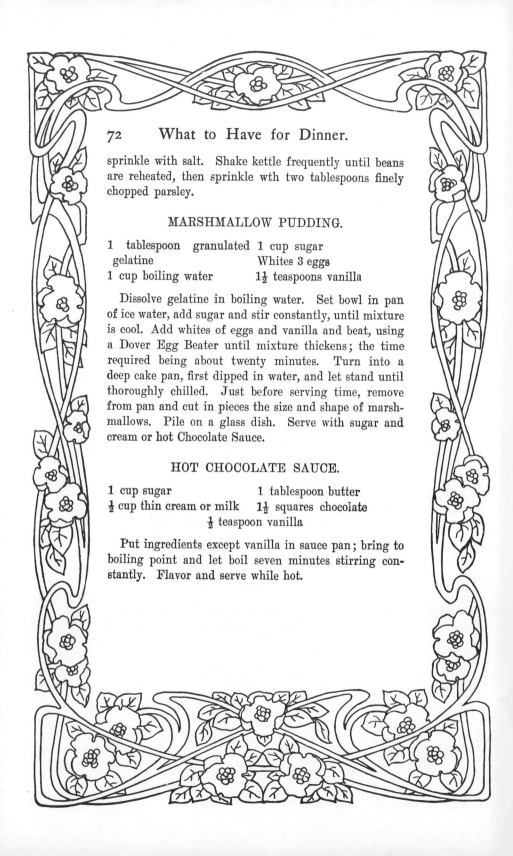

sprinkle with salt. Shake kettle frequently until beans are reheated, then sprinkle wth two tablespoons finely chopped parsley.

MARSHMALLOW PUDDING.

1 tablespoon granulated gelatine
1 cup boiling water

1 cup sugar
Whites 3 eggs
1½ teaspoons vanilla

Dissolve gelatine in boiling water. Set bowl in pan of ice water, add sugar and stir constantly, until mixture is cool. Add whites of eggs and vanilla and beat, using a Dover Egg Beater until mixture thickens; the time required being about twenty minutes. Turn into a deep cake pan, first dipped in water, and let stand until thoroughly chilled. Just before serving time, remove from pan and cut in pieces the size and shape of marshmallows. Pile on a glass dish. Serve with sugar and cream or hot Chocolate Sauce.

HOT CHOCOLATE SAUCE.

1 cup sugar
½ cup thin cream or milk
½ teaspoon vanilla

1 tablespoon butter
1½ squares chocolate

Put ingredients except vanilla in sauce pan; bring to boiling point and let boil seven minutes stirring constantly. Flavor and serve while hot.

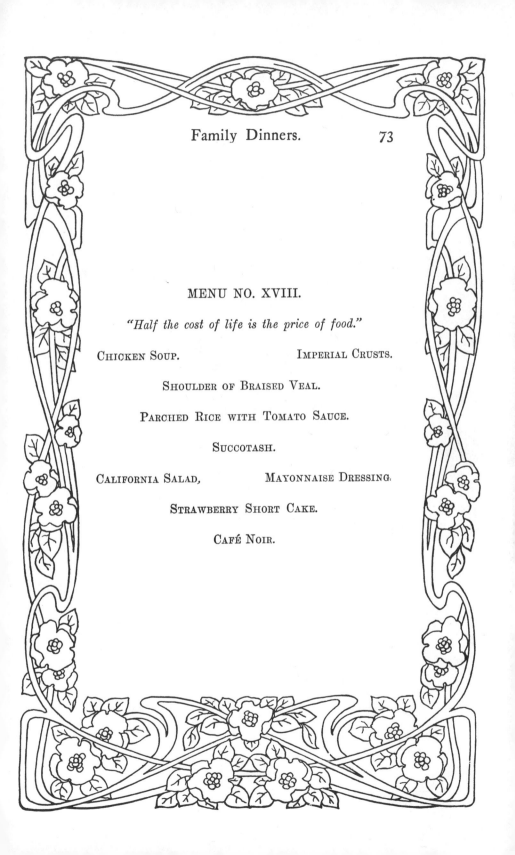

MENU NO. XVIII.

"Half the cost of life is the price of food."

CHICKEN SOUP.   IMPERIAL CRUSTS.

SHOULDER OF BRAISED VEAL.

PARCHED RICE WITH TOMATO SAUCE.

SUCCOTASH.

CALIFORNIA SALAD,   MAYONNAISE DRESSING.

STRAWBERRY SHORT CAKE.

CAFÉ NOIR.

CHICKEN SOUP.

4 cups chicken stock	1 tablespoon flour
¼ cup butter	½ cup soft bread crumbs
2 slices carrot	Salt
2 slices onion	Pepper
2 stalks celery	2 cups milk

Cook vegetables, finely cut, in three tablespoons butter, three minutes, add stock, and bread crumbs, boil ten minutes and strain. Add milk and thicken with remaining butter and flour, cooked together. Season with salt and pepper. If a richer soup is desired, use one cup, each, milk and cream, in place of all milk.

IMPERIAL CRUSTS.

Cut stale bread in one-third slices and remove crusts. Cut slices in one-third inch strips, put in pan, and bake until delicately browned. Stir occasionally, that crusts may be browned evenly.

BRAISED SHOULDER OF VEAL.

Bone, stuff, and sew in shape five pounds shoulder of veal. Try out two slices fat salt pork, and remove scraps. Sprinkle veal with salt and pepper, dredge with flour, and brown entire surface in pork fat. Place on trivet in a deep earthen pudding dish and add one-fourth cup, each, carrot, turnip and onion, cut in dice, twelve peppercorns, one sprig thyme, two sprigs marjoram, and three cups boiling water. Cover closely and cook four hours in a very slow oven, basting every half hour, and turning after the second hour. Serve with a brown sauce made from liquor remaining in pan.

PARCHED RICE WITH TOMATO SAUCE.

Pick over three-fourths cup rice and add slowly to two quarts boiling water, to which is added one tablespoon salt. Let boil twenty-five minutes, or until kernels are soft. Drain, and pour over one quart hot water; return to kettle in which it was cooked, and let stand until cool and dry, when kernels will be distinct. Heat an iron frying pan very hot, add two tablespoons butter, and when melted, add rice, and cook until rice is slightly browned, stirring lightly with a fork. Put in hot serving dish, pour over one cup hot tomato sauce and sprinkle with one-half cup grated cheese, lifting rice with fork, that sauce and cheese may coat each kernel.

TOMATO SAUCE.

2 tablespoons butter
1 slice onion
2½ tablespoons flour
Few grains paprika

1 cup stewed and strained tomatoes
¼ teaspoon salt

Cook butter with onion until slightly browned, add flour, and when well browned, pour on, gradually, while stirring constantly, tomatoes. Bring to boiling point, add seasonings and strain.

SUCCOTASH.

1 pint shell beans
1 pint green corn
1 inch cube fat salt pork
Pepper

1 tablespoon butter
⅓ cup cream
Salt

Shell and pick over beans, cover with boiling water, add pork, and let boil until nearly soft; then add green

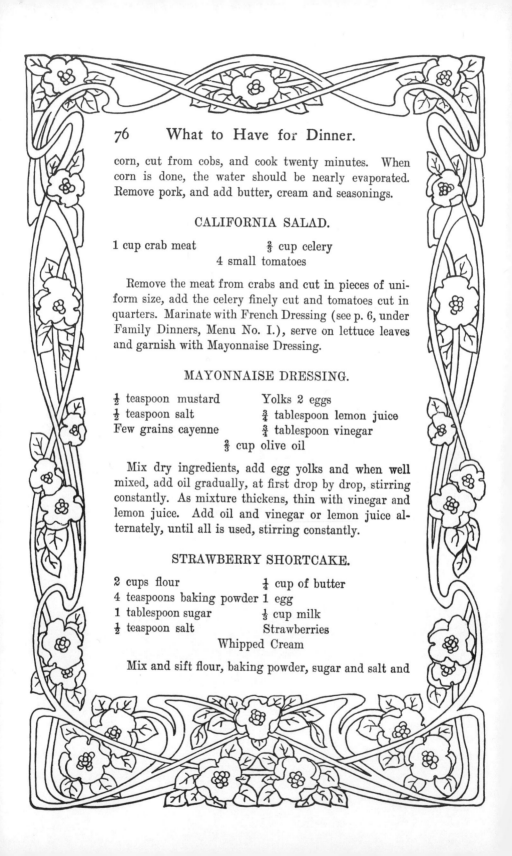

corn, cut from cobs, and cook twenty minutes. When corn is done, the water should be nearly evaporated. Remove pork, and add butter, cream and seasonings.

CALIFORNIA SALAD.

1 cup crab meat   ⅔ cup celery
4 small tomatoes

Remove the meat from crabs and cut in pieces of uniform size, add the celery finely cut and tomatoes cut in quarters. Marinate with French Dressing (see p. 6, under Family Dinners, Menu No. I.), serve on lettuce leaves and garnish with Mayonnaise Dressing.

MAYONNAISE DRESSING.

½ teaspoon mustard   Yolks 2 eggs
½ teaspoon salt   ¾ tablespoon lemon juice
Few grains cayenne   ¾ tablespoon vinegar
⅔ cup olive oil

Mix dry ingredients, add egg yolks and when well mixed, add oil gradually, at first drop by drop, stirring constantly. As mixture thickens, thin with vinegar and lemon juice. Add oil and vinegar or lemon juice alternately, until all is used, stirring constantly.

STRAWBERRY SHORTCAKE.

2 cups flour   ¼ cup of butter
4 teaspoons baking powder 1 egg
1 tablespoon sugar   ⅓ cup milk
½ teaspoon salt   Strawberries
Whipped Cream

Mix and sift flour, baking powder, sugar and salt and

work in butter, using tips of fingers. Beat egg until very light and add milk; then combine the mixtures. Toss on a slightly floured board and divide in two parts. Pat, roll out, and bake in a hot oven in round layer cake pans. Split, remove soft part, and spread with butter. Sprinkle strawberries with sugar, place on back of range until warmed, crush slightly and put between and on top of shortcakes. Cover with whipped cream sweetened and flavored, and garnish with whole berries.

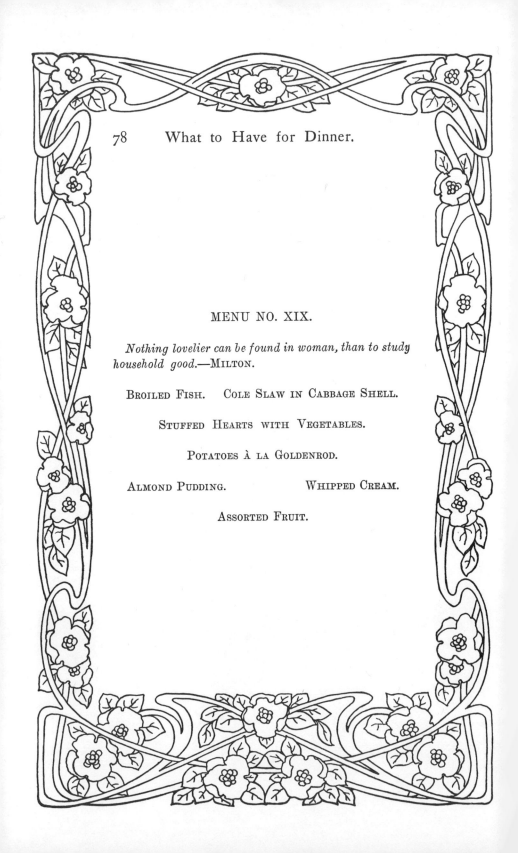

MENU NO. XIX.

Nothing lovelier can be found in woman, than to study household good.—MILTON.

BROILED FISH.   COLE SLAW IN CABBAGE SHELL.

STUFFED HEARTS WITH VEGETABLES.

POTATOES À LA GOLDENROD.

ALMOND PUDDING.   WHIPPED CREAM.

ASSORTED FRUIT.

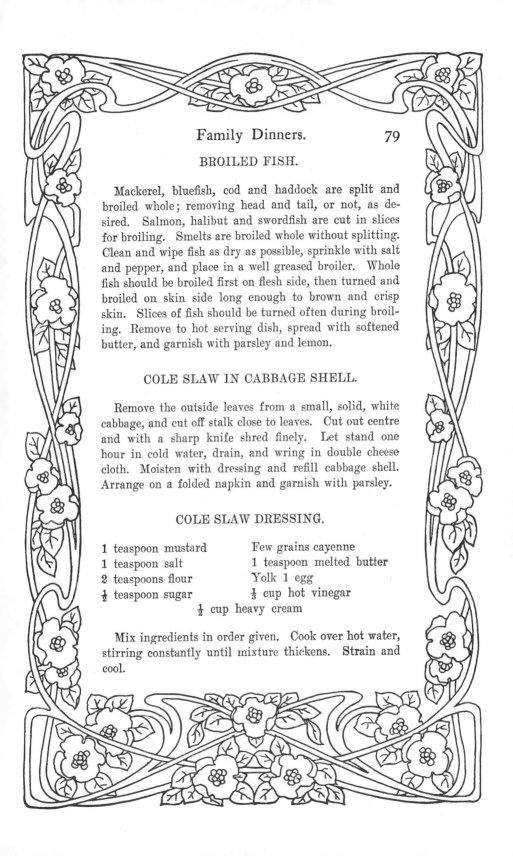

BROILED FISH.

Mackerel, bluefish, cod and haddock are split and broiled whole; removing head and tail, or not, as desired. Salmon, halibut and swordfish are cut in slices for broiling. Smelts are broiled whole without splitting. Clean and wipe fish as dry as possible, sprinkle with salt and pepper, and place in a well greased broiler. Whole fish should be broiled first on flesh side, then turned and broiled on skin side long enough to brown and crisp skin. Slices of fish should be turned often during broiling. Remove to hot serving dish, spread with softened butter, and garnish with parsley and lemon.

COLE SLAW IN CABBAGE SHELL.

Remove the outside leaves from a small, solid, white cabbage, and cut off stalk close to leaves. Cut out centre and with a sharp knife shred finely. Let stand one hour in cold water, drain, and wring in double cheese cloth. Moisten with dressing and refill cabbage shell. Arrange on a folded napkin and garnish with parsley.

COLE SLAW DRESSING.

1 teaspoon mustard	Few grains cayenne
1 teaspoon salt	1 teaspoon melted butter
2 teaspoons flour	Yolk 1 egg
$\frac{1}{4}$ teaspoon sugar	$\frac{1}{3}$ cup hot vinegar
	$\frac{1}{2}$ cup heavy cream

Mix ingredients in order given. Cook over hot water, stirring constantly until mixture thickens. Strain and cool.

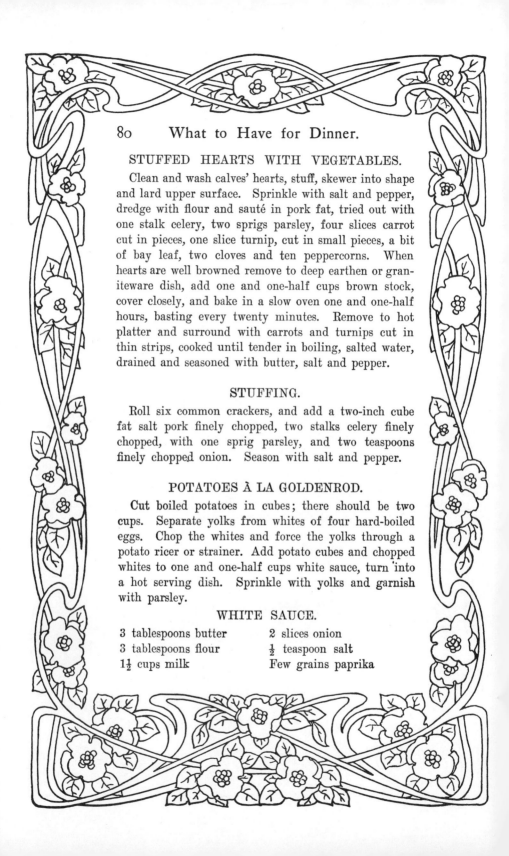

STUFFED HEARTS WITH VEGETABLES.

Clean and wash calves' hearts, stuff, skewer into shape and lard upper surface. Sprinkle with salt and pepper, dredge with flour and sauté in pork fat, tried out with one stalk celery, two sprigs parsley, four slices carrot cut in pieces, one slice turnip, cut in small pieces, a bit of bay leaf, two cloves and ten peppercorns. When hearts are well browned remove to deep earthen or graniteware dish, add one and one-half cups brown stock, cover closely, and bake in a slow oven one and one-half hours, basting every twenty minutes. Remove to hot platter and surround with carrots and turnips cut in thin strips, cooked until tender in boiling, salted water, drained and seasoned with butter, salt and pepper.

STUFFING.

Roll six common crackers, and add a two-inch cube fat salt pork finely chopped, two stalks celery finely chopped, with one sprig parsley, and two teaspoons finely chopped onion. Season with salt and pepper.

POTATOES À LA GOLDENROD.

Cut boiled potatoes in cubes; there should be two cups. Separate yolks from whites of four hard-boiled eggs. Chop the whites and force the yolks through a potato ricer or strainer. Add potato cubes and chopped whites to one and one-half cups white sauce, turn into a hot serving dish. Sprinkle with yolks and garnish with parsley.

WHITE SAUCE.

3 tablespoons butter	2 slices onion
3 tablespoons flour	½ teaspoon salt
1½ cups milk	Few grains paprika

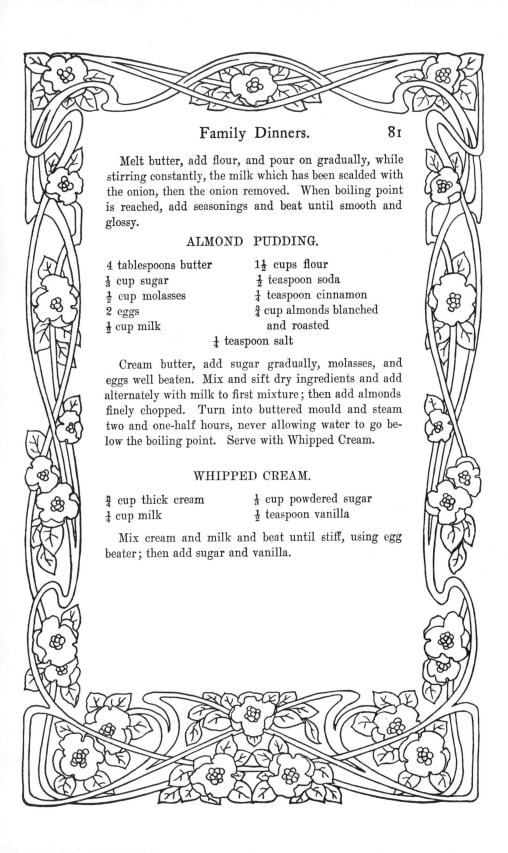

Melt butter, add flour, and pour on gradually, while stirring constantly, the milk which has been scalded with the onion, then the onion removed. When boiling point is reached, add seasonings and beat until smooth and glossy.

ALMOND PUDDING.

4 tablespoons butter
⅓ cup sugar
½ cup molasses
2 eggs
½ cup milk

1½ cups flour
½ teaspoon soda
¼ teaspoon cinnamon
¾ cup almonds blanched
    and roasted
¼ teaspoon salt

Cream butter, add sugar gradually, molasses, and eggs well beaten. Mix and sift dry ingredients and add alternately with milk to first mixture; then add almonds finely chopped. Turn into buttered mould and steam two and one-half hours, never allowing water to go below the boiling point. Serve with Whipped Cream.

WHIPPED CREAM.

¾ cup thick cream
¼ cup milk

⅓ cup powdered sugar
½ teaspoon vanilla

Mix cream and milk and beat until stiff, using egg beater; then add sugar and vanilla.

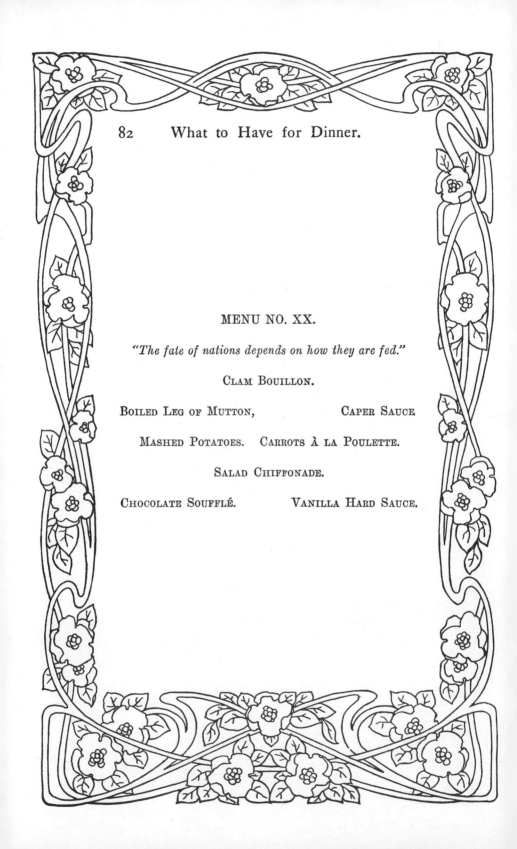

MENU NO. XX.

"The fate of nations depends on how they are fed."

CLAM BOUILLON.

BOILED LEG OF MUTTON,   CAPER SAUCE

MASHED POTATOES.   CARROTS À LA POULETTE.

SALAD CHIFFONADE.

CHOCOLATE SOUFFLÉ.   VANILLA HARD SAUCE.

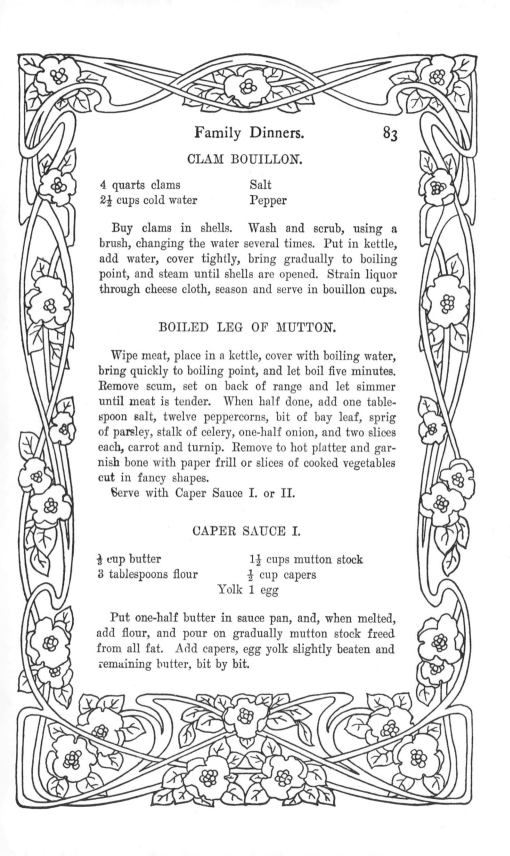

CLAM BOUILLON.

4 quarts clams	Salt
2½ cups cold water	Pepper

Buy clams in shells. Wash and scrub, using a brush, changing the water several times. Put in kettle, add water, cover tightly, bring gradually to boiling point, and steam until shells are opened. Strain liquor through cheese cloth, season and serve in bouillon cups.

BOILED LEG OF MUTTON.

Wipe meat, place in a kettle, cover with boiling water, bring quickly to boiling point, and let boil five minutes. Remove scum, set on back of range and let simmer until meat is tender. When half done, add one tablespoon salt, twelve peppercorns, bit of bay leaf, sprig of parsley, stalk of celery, one-half onion, and two slices each, carrot and turnip. Remove to hot platter and garnish bone with paper frill or slices of cooked vegetables cut in fancy shapes.

Serve with Caper Sauce I. or II.

CAPER SAUCE I.

⅓ cup butter	1½ cups mutton stock
3 tablespoons flour	½ cup capers
	Yolk 1 egg

Put one-half butter in sauce pan, and, when melted, add flour, and pour on gradually mutton stock freed from all fat. Add capers, egg yolk slightly beaten and remaining butter, bit by bit.

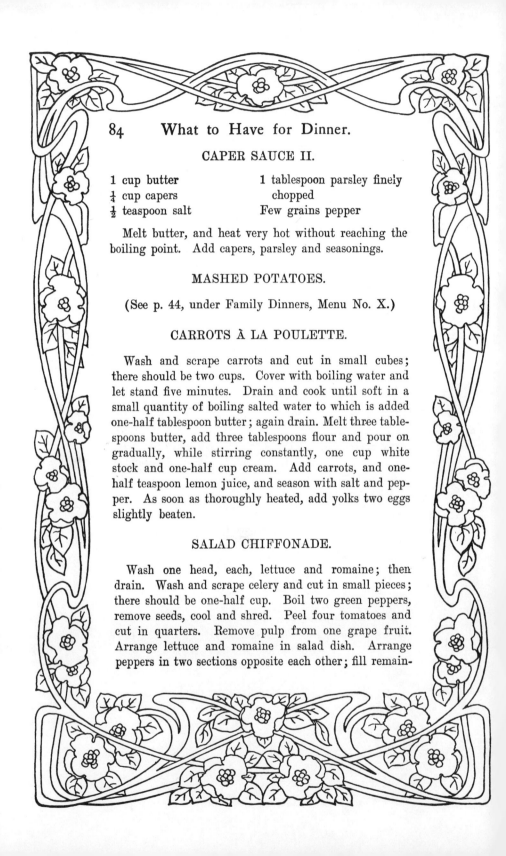

CAPER SAUCE II.

1 cup butter	1 tablespoon parsley finely
$\frac{1}{4}$ cup capers	chopped
$\frac{1}{2}$ teaspoon salt	Few grains pepper

Melt butter, and heat very hot without reaching the boiling point. Add capers, parsley and seasonings.

MASHED POTATOES.

(See p. 44, under Family Dinners, Menu No. X.)

CARROTS À LA POULETTE.

Wash and scrape carrots and cut in small cubes; there should be two cups. Cover with boiling water and let stand five minutes. Drain and cook until soft in a small quantity of boiling salted water to which is added one-half tablespoon butter; again drain. Melt three tablespoons butter, add three tablespoons flour and pour on gradually, while stirring constantly, one cup white stock and one-half cup cream. Add carrots, and one-half teaspoon lemon juice, and season with salt and pepper. As soon as thoroughly heated, add yolks two eggs slightly beaten.

SALAD CHIFFONADE.

Wash one head, each, lettuce and romaine; then drain. Wash and scrape celery and cut in small pieces; there should be one-half cup. Boil two green peppers, remove seeds, cool and shred. Peel four tomatoes and cut in quarters. Remove pulp from one grape fruit. Arrange lettuce and romaine in salad dish. Arrange peppers in two sections opposite each other; fill remain-

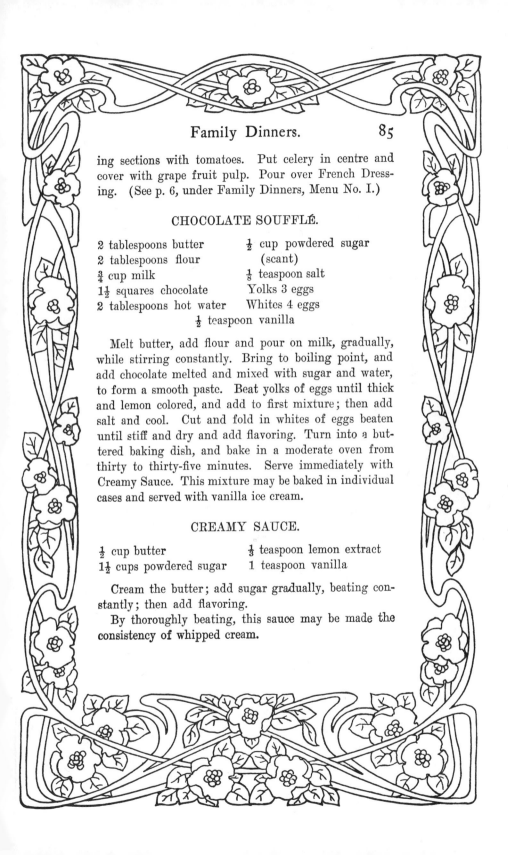

ing sections with tomatoes. Put celery in centre and cover with grape fruit pulp. Pour over French Dressing. (See p. 6, under Family Dinners, Menu No. I.)

CHOCOLATE SOUFFLÉ.

2 tablespoons butter	½ cup powdered sugar
2 tablespoons flour	(scant)
¾ cup milk	⅛ teaspoon salt
1½ squares chocolate	Yolks 3 eggs
2 tablespoons hot water	Whites 4 eggs
	½ teaspoon vanilla

Melt butter, add flour and pour on milk, gradually, while stirring constantly. Bring to boiling point, and add chocolate melted and mixed with sugar and water, to form a smooth paste. Beat yolks of eggs until thick and lemon colored, and add to first mixture; then add salt and cool. Cut and fold in whites of eggs beaten until stiff and dry and add flavoring. Turn into a buttered baking dish, and bake in a moderate oven from thirty to thirty-five minutes. Serve immediately with Creamy Sauce. This mixture may be baked in individual cases and served with vanilla ice cream.

CREAMY SAUCE.

½ cup butter	⅓ teaspoon lemon extract
1½ cups powdered sugar	1 teaspoon vanilla

Cream the butter; add sugar gradually, beating constantly; then add flavoring.

By thoroughly beating, this sauce may be made the consistency of whipped cream.

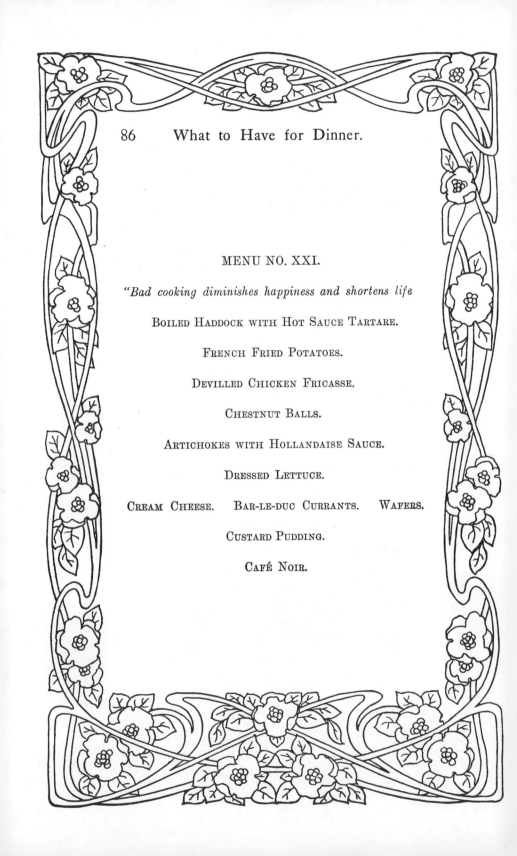

MENU NO. XXI.

"Bad cooking diminishes happiness and shortens life

BOILED HADDOCK WITH HOT SAUCE TARTARE.

FRENCH FRIED POTATOES.

DEVILLED CHICKEN FRICASSE.

CHESTNUT BALLS.

ARTICHOKES WITH HOLLANDAISE SAUCE.

DRESSED LETTUCE.

CREAM CHEESE.　　BAR-LE-DUC CURRANTS.　　WAFERS.

CUSTARD PUDDING.

CAFÉ NOIR.

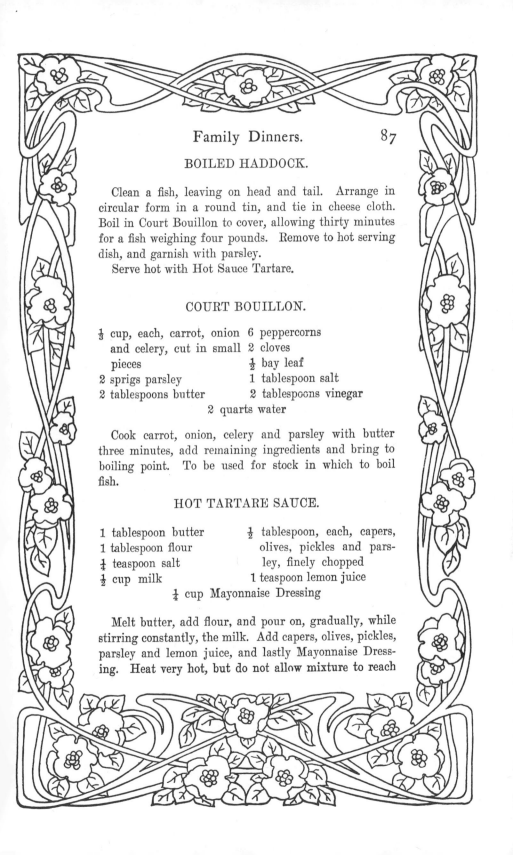

BOILED HADDOCK.

Clean a fish, leaving on head and tail. Arrange in circular form in a round tin, and tie in cheese cloth. Boil in Court Bouillon to cover, allowing thirty minutes for a fish weighing four pounds. Remove to hot serving dish, and garnish with parsley.

Serve hot with Hot Sauce Tartare.

COURT BOUILLON.

⅓ cup, each, carrot, onion and celery, cut in small pieces
2 sprigs parsley
2 tablespoons butter
6 peppercorns
2 cloves
½ bay leaf
1 tablespoon salt
2 tablespoons vinegar
2 quarts water

Cook carrot, onion, celery and parsley with butter three minutes, add remaining ingredients and bring to boiling point. To be used for stock in which to boil fish.

HOT TARTARE SAUCE.

1 tablespoon butter
1 tablespoon flour
¼ teaspoon salt
½ cup milk
½ tablespoon, each, capers, olives, pickles and parsley, finely chopped
1 teaspoon lemon juice
¼ cup Mayonnaise Dressing

Melt butter, add flour, and pour on, gradually, while stirring constantly, the milk. Add capers, olives, pickles, parsley and lemon juice, and lastly Mayonnaise Dressing. Heat very hot, but do not allow mixture to reach

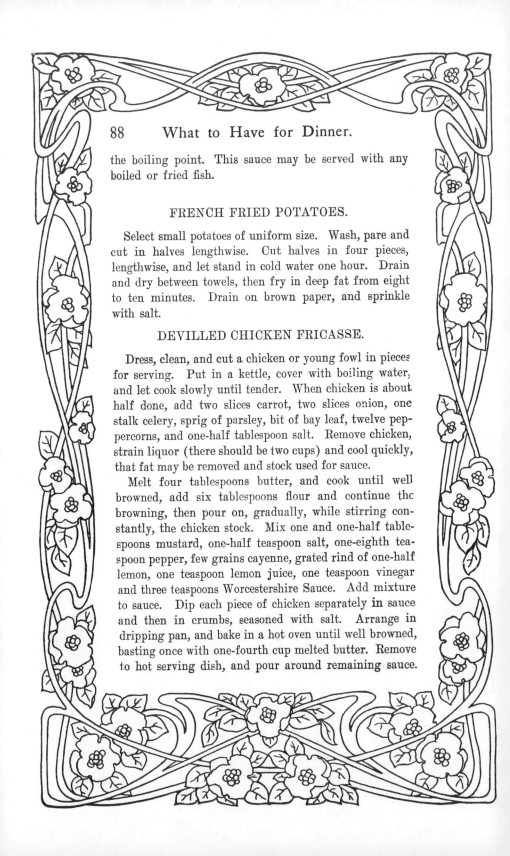

the boiling point. This sauce may be served with any boiled or fried fish.

FRENCH FRIED POTATOES.

Select small potatoes of uniform size. Wash, pare and cut in halves lengthwise. Cut halves in four pieces, lengthwise, and let stand in cold water one hour. Drain and dry between towels, then fry in deep fat from eight to ten minutes. Drain on brown paper, and sprinkle with salt.

DEVILLED CHICKEN FRICASSE.

Dress, clean, and cut a chicken or young fowl in pieces for serving. Put in a kettle, cover with boiling water, and let cook slowly until tender. When chicken is about half done, add two slices carrot, two slices onion, one stalk celery, sprig of parsley, bit of bay leaf, twelve peppercorns, and one-half tablespoon salt. Remove chicken, strain liquor (there should be two cups) and cool quickly, that fat may be removed and stock used for sauce.

Melt four tablespoons butter, and cook until well browned, add six tablespoons flour and continue the browning, then pour on, gradually, while stirring constantly, the chicken stock. Mix one and one-half tablespoons mustard, one-half teaspoon salt, one-eighth teaspoon pepper, few grains cayenne, grated rind of one-half lemon, one teaspoon lemon juice, one teaspoon vinegar and three teaspoons Worcestershire Sauce. Add mixture to sauce. Dip each piece of chicken separately in sauce and then in crumbs, seasoned with salt. Arrange in dripping pan, and bake in a hot oven until well browned, basting once with one-fourth cup melted butter. Remove to hot serving dish, and pour around remaining sauce.

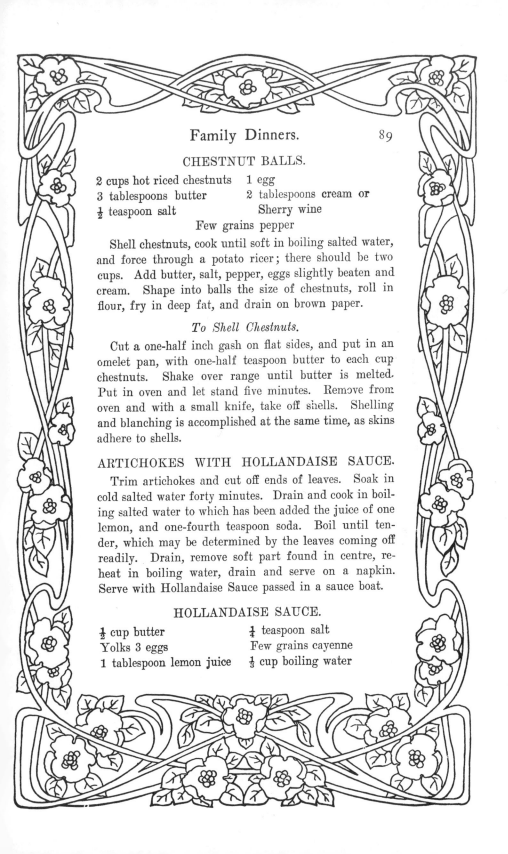

CHESTNUT BALLS.

2 cups hot riced chestnuts   1 egg
3 tablespoons butter   2 tablespoons cream or
½ teaspoon salt   Sherry wine
Few grains pepper

Shell chestnuts, cook until soft in boiling salted water, and force through a potato ricer; there should be two cups. Add butter, salt, pepper, eggs slightly beaten and cream. Shape into balls the size of chestnuts, roll in flour, fry in deep fat, and drain on brown paper.

To Shell Chestnuts.

Cut a one-half inch gash on flat sides, and put in an omelet pan, with one-half teaspoon butter to each cup chestnuts. Shake over range until butter is melted. Put in oven and let stand five minutes. Remove from oven and with a small knife, take off shells. Shelling and blanching is accomplished at the same time, as skins adhere to shells.

ARTICHOKES WITH HOLLANDAISE SAUCE.

Trim artichokes and cut off ends of leaves. Soak in cold salted water forty minutes. Drain and cook in boiling salted water to which has been added the juice of one lemon, and one-fourth teaspoon soda. Boil until tender, which may be determined by the leaves coming off readily. Drain, remove soft part found in centre, reheat in boiling water, drain and serve on a napkin. Serve with Hollandaise Sauce passed in a sauce boat.

HOLLANDAISE SAUCE.

½ cup butter   ¼ teaspoon salt
Yolks 3 eggs   Few grains cayenne
1 tablespoon lemon juice   ⅓ cup boiling water

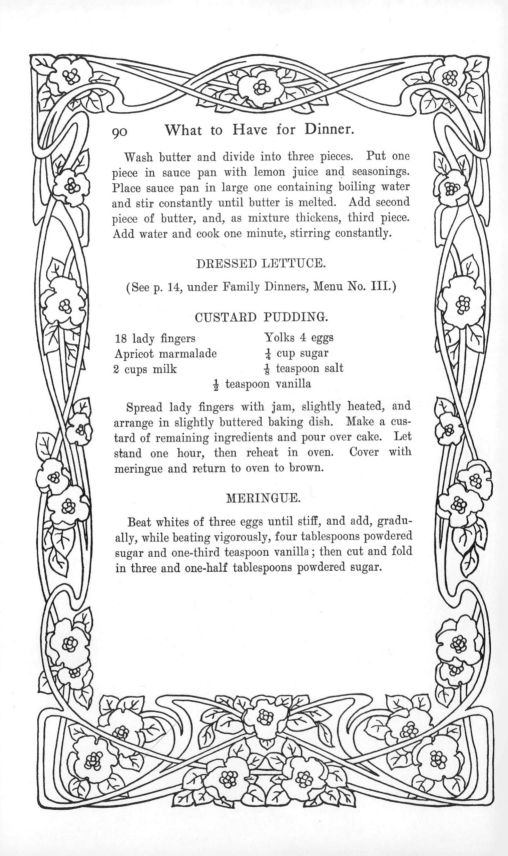

Wash butter and divide into three pieces. Put one piece in sauce pan with lemon juice and seasonings. Place sauce pan in large one containing boiling water and stir constantly until butter is melted. Add second piece of butter, and, as mixture thickens, third piece. Add water and cook one minute, stirring constantly.

DRESSED LETTUCE.

(See p. 14, under Family Dinners, Menu No. III.)

CUSTARD PUDDING.

18 lady fingers	Yolks 4 eggs
Apricot marmalade	$\frac{1}{4}$ cup sugar
2 cups milk	$\frac{1}{8}$ teaspoon salt

$\frac{1}{2}$ teaspoon vanilla

Spread lady fingers with jam, slightly heated, and arrange in slightly buttered baking dish. Make a custard of remaining ingredients and pour over cake. Let stand one hour, then reheat in oven. Cover with meringue and return to oven to brown.

MERINGUE.

Beat whites of three eggs until stiff, and add, gradually, while beating vigorously, four tablespoons powdered sugar and one-third teaspoon vanilla; then cut and fold in three and one-half tablespoons powdered sugar.

MENU NO. XXII.

"Preserve and treat food as you would your body, remembering that in time food will be your body."

OYSTER SOUP.

BREADED LAMB FILLETS.

MASHED POTATOES.   FRIED CUCUMBERS.

PEACH CABINET PUDDING.

CRACKERS.   CHEESE.

CAFÉ NOIR.

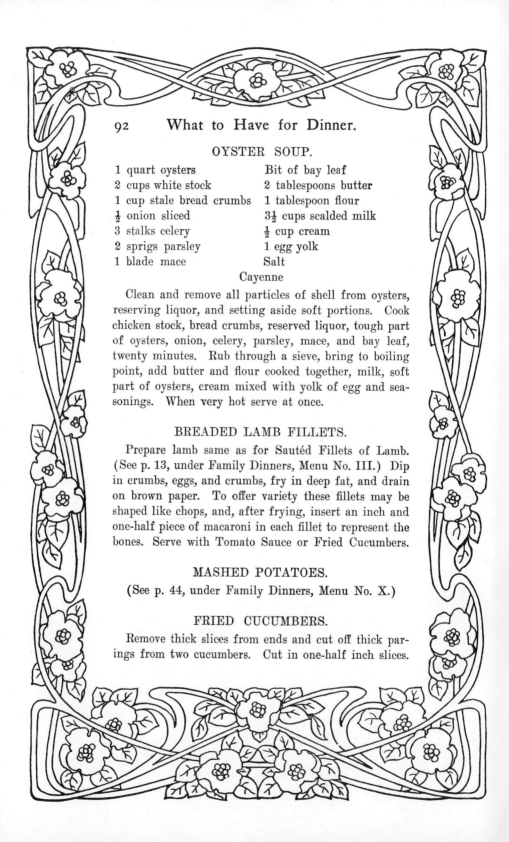

OYSTER SOUP.

1 quart oysters	Bit of bay leaf
2 cups white stock	2 tablespoons butter
1 cup stale bread crumbs	1 tablespoon flour
½ onion sliced	3½ cups scalded milk
3 stalks celery	½ cup cream
2 sprigs parsley	1 egg yolk
1 blade mace	Salt

Cayenne

Clean and remove all particles of shell from oysters, reserving liquor, and setting aside soft portions. Cook chicken stock, bread crumbs, reserved liquor, tough part of oysters, onion, celery, parsley, mace, and bay leaf, twenty minutes. Rub through a sieve, bring to boiling point, add butter and flour cooked together, milk, soft part of oysters, cream mixed with yolk of egg and seasonings. When very hot serve at once.

BREADED LAMB FILLETS.

Prepare lamb same as for Sautéd Fillets of Lamb. (See p. 13, under Family Dinners, Menu No. III.) Dip in crumbs, eggs, and crumbs, fry in deep fat, and drain on brown paper. To offer variety these fillets may be shaped like chops, and, after frying, insert an inch and one-half piece of macaroni in each fillet to represent the bones. Serve with Tomato Sauce or Fried Cucumbers.

MASHED POTATOES.

(See p. 44, under Family Dinners, Menu No. X.)

FRIED CUCUMBERS.

Remove thick slices from ends and cut off thick parings from two cucumbers. Cut in one-half inch slices.

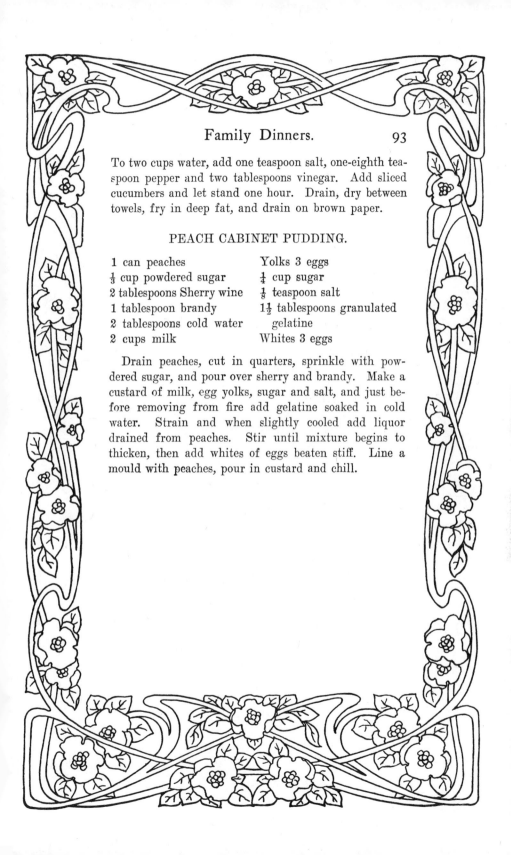

To two cups water, add one teaspoon salt, one-eighth teaspoon pepper and two tablespoons vinegar. Add sliced cucumbers and let stand one hour. Drain, dry between towels, fry in deep fat, and drain on brown paper.

PEACH CABINET PUDDING.

1 can peaches	Yolks 3 eggs
$\frac{1}{3}$ cup powdered sugar	$\frac{1}{4}$ cup sugar
2 tablespoons Sherry wine	$\frac{1}{8}$ teaspoon salt
1 tablespoon brandy	$1\frac{1}{2}$ tablespoons granulated
2 tablespoons cold water	gelatine
2 cups milk	Whites 3 eggs

Drain peaches, cut in quarters, sprinkle with powdered sugar, and pour over sherry and brandy. Make a custard of milk, egg yolks, sugar and salt, and just before removing from fire add gelatine soaked in cold water. Strain and when slightly cooled add liquor drained from peaches. Stir until mixture begins to thicken, then add whites of eggs beaten stiff. Line a mould with peaches, pour in custard and chill.

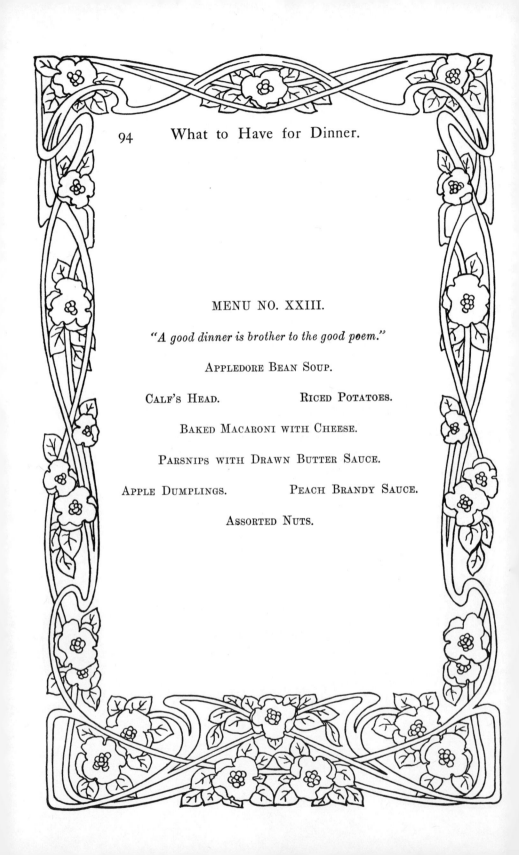

MENU NO. XXIII.

"A good dinner is brother to the good poem."

APPLEDORE BEAN SOUP.

CALF'S HEAD.   RICED POTATOES.

BAKED MACARONI WITH CHEESE.

PARSNIPS WITH DRAWN BUTTER SAUCE.

APPLE DUMPLINGS.   PEACH BRANDY SAUCE.

ASSORTED NUTS.

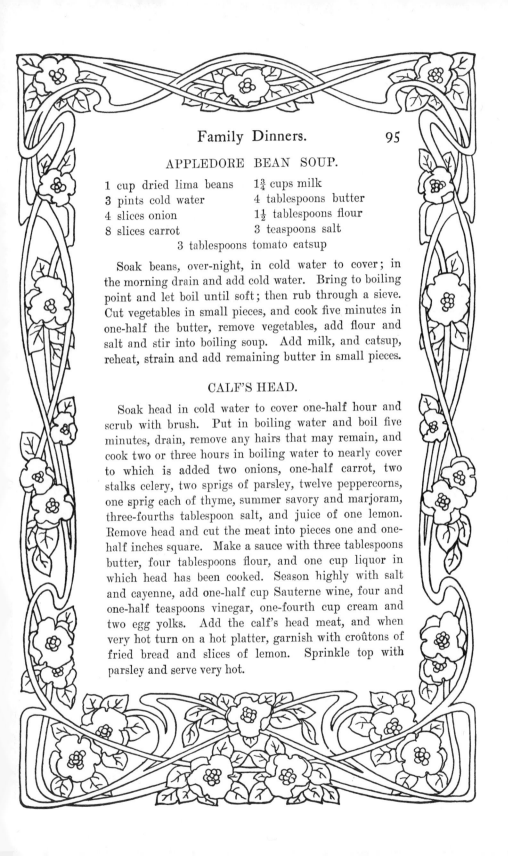

APPLEDORE BEAN SOUP.

1 cup dried lima beans   1¾ cups milk
3 pints cold water   4 tablespoons butter
4 slices onion   1½ tablespoons flour
8 slices carrot   3 teaspoons salt
3 tablespoons tomato catsup

Soak beans, over-night, in cold water to cover; in the morning drain and add cold water. Bring to boiling point and let boil until soft; then rub through a sieve. Cut vegetables in small pieces, and cook five minutes in one-half the butter, remove vegetables, add flour and salt and stir into boiling soup. Add milk, and catsup, reheat, strain and add remaining butter in small pieces.

CALF'S HEAD.

Soak head in cold water to cover one-half hour and scrub with brush. Put in boiling water and boil five minutes, drain, remove any hairs that may remain, and cook two or three hours in boiling water to nearly cover to which is added two onions, one-half carrot, two stalks celery, two sprigs of parsley, twelve peppercorns, one sprig each of thyme, summer savory and marjoram, three-fourths tablespoon salt, and juice of one lemon. Remove head and cut the meat into pieces one and one-half inches square. Make a sauce with three tablespoons butter, four tablespoons flour, and one cup liquor in which head has been cooked. Season highly with salt and cayenne, add one-half cup Sauterne wine, four and one-half teaspoons vinegar, one-fourth cup cream and two egg yolks. Add the calf's head meat, and when very hot turn on a hot platter, garnish with croûtons of fried bread and slices of lemon. Sprinkle top with parsley and serve very hot.

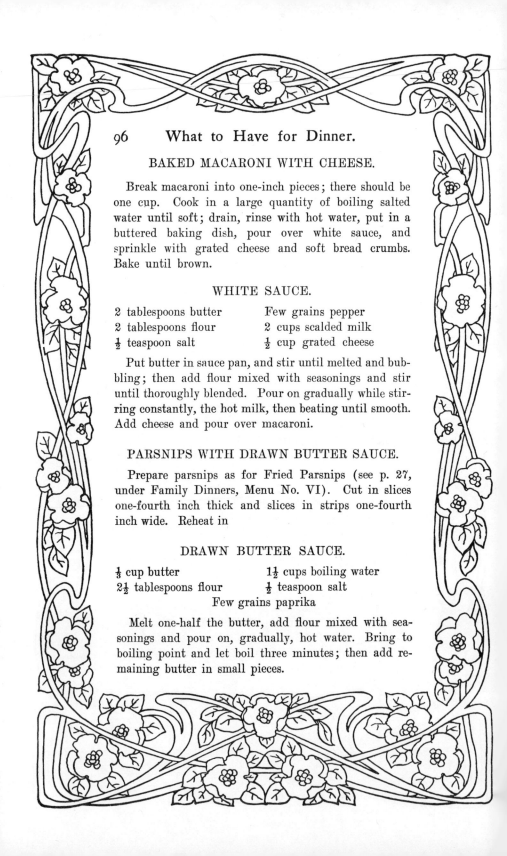

BAKED MACARONI WITH CHEESE.

Break macaroni into one-inch pieces; there should be one cup. Cook in a large quantity of boiling salted water until soft; drain, rinse with hot water, put in a buttered baking dish, pour over white sauce, and sprinkle with grated cheese and soft bread crumbs. Bake until brown.

WHITE SAUCE.

2 tablespoons butter	Few grains pepper
2 tablespoons flour	2 cups scalded milk
$\frac{1}{2}$ teaspoon salt	$\frac{1}{2}$ cup grated cheese

Put butter in sauce pan, and stir until melted and bubbling; then add flour mixed with seasonings and stir until thoroughly blended. Pour on gradually while stirring constantly, the hot milk, then beating until smooth. Add cheese and pour over macaroni.

PARSNIPS WITH DRAWN BUTTER SAUCE.

Prepare parsnips as for Fried Parsnips (see p. 27, under Family Dinners, Menu No. VI). Cut in slices one-fourth inch thick and slices in strips one-fourth inch wide. Reheat in

DRAWN BUTTER SAUCE.

$\frac{1}{3}$ cup butter	$1\frac{1}{2}$ cups boiling water
$2\frac{1}{2}$ tablespoons flour	$\frac{1}{2}$ teaspoon salt
Few grains paprika	

Melt one-half the butter, add flour mixed with seasonings and pour on, gradually, hot water. Bring to boiling point and let boil three minutes; then add remaining butter in small pieces.

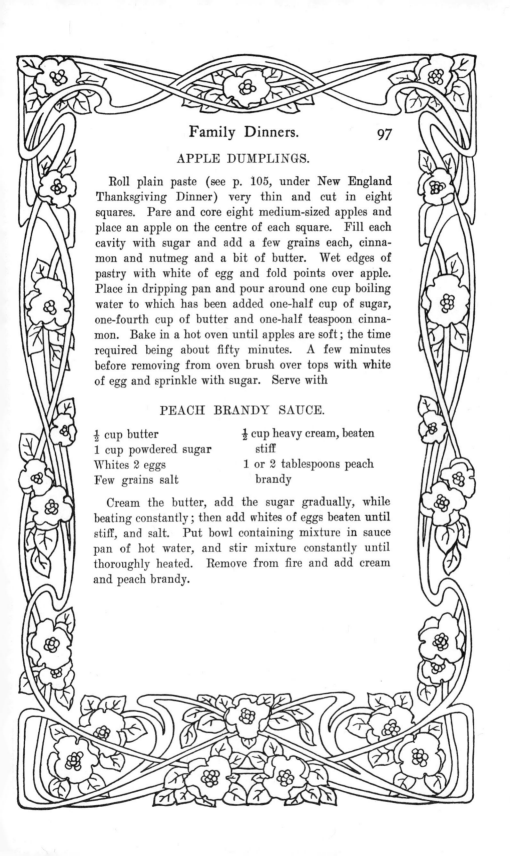

APPLE DUMPLINGS.

Roll plain paste (see p. 105, under New England Thanksgiving Dinner) very thin and cut in eight squares. Pare and core eight medium-sized apples and place an apple on the centre of each square. Fill each cavity with sugar and add a few grains each, cinnamon and nutmeg and a bit of butter. Wet edges of pastry with white of egg and fold points over apple. Place in dripping pan and pour around one cup boiling water to which has been added one-half cup of sugar, one-fourth cup of butter and one-half teaspoon cinnamon. Bake in a hot oven until apples are soft; the time required being about fifty minutes. A few minutes before removing from oven brush over tops with white of egg and sprinkle with sugar. Serve with

PEACH BRANDY SAUCE.

$\frac{1}{2}$ cup butter
1 cup powdered sugar
Whites 2 eggs
Few grains salt

$\frac{1}{2}$ cup heavy cream, beaten stiff
1 or 2 tablespoons peach brandy

Cream the butter, add the sugar gradually, while beating constantly; then add whites of eggs beaten until stiff, and salt. Put bowl containing mixture in sauce pan of hot water, and stir mixture constantly until thoroughly heated. Remove from fire and add cream and peach brandy.

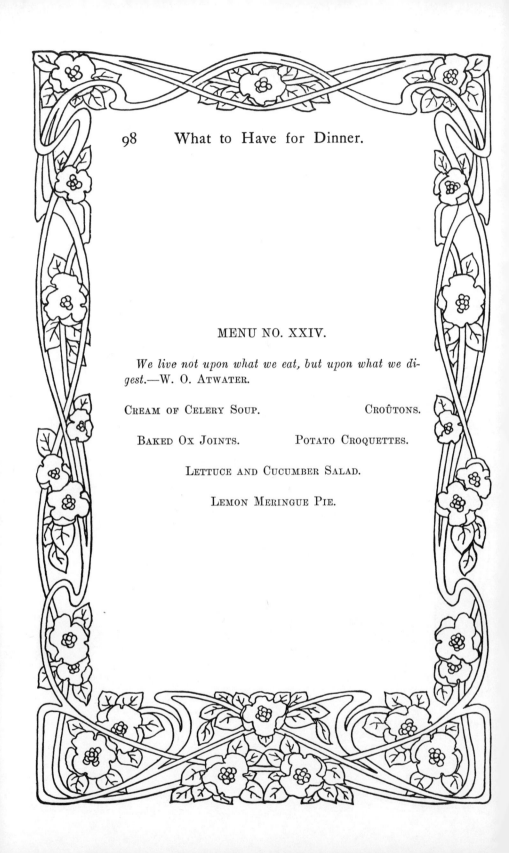

MENU NO. XXIV.

We live not upon what we eat, but upon what we digest.—W. O. ATWATER.

CREAM OF CELERY SOUP.   CROÛTONS.

BAKED OX JOINTS.   POTATO CROQUETTES.

LETTUCE AND CUCUMBER SALAD.

LEMON MERINGUE PIE.

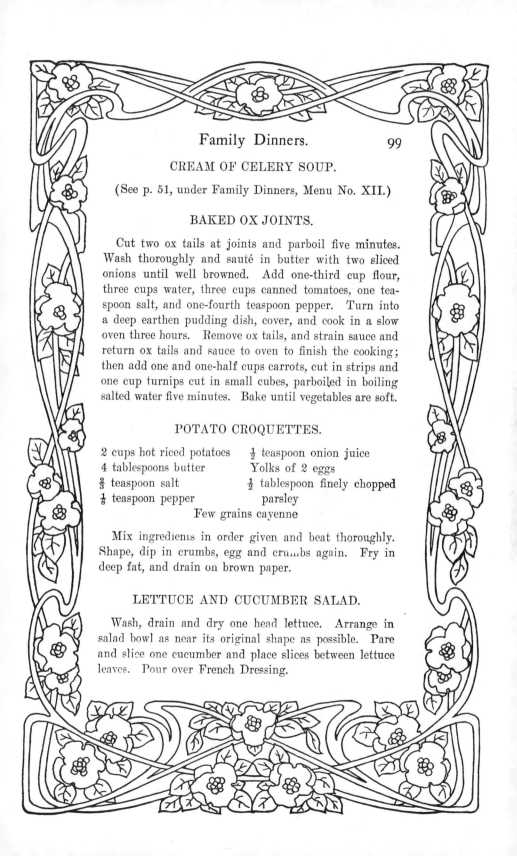

CREAM OF CELERY SOUP.

(See p. 51, under Family Dinners, Menu No. XII.)

BAKED OX JOINTS.

Cut two ox tails at joints and parboil five minutes. Wash thoroughly and sauté in butter with two sliced onions until well browned. Add one-third cup flour, three cups water, three cups canned tomatoes, one teaspoon salt, and one-fourth teaspoon pepper. Turn into a deep earthen pudding dish, cover, and cook in a slow oven three hours. Remove ox tails, and strain sauce and return ox tails and sauce to oven to finish the cooking; then add one and one-half cups carrots, cut in strips and one cup turnips cut in small cubes, parboiled in boiling salted water five minutes. Bake until vegetables are soft.

POTATO CROQUETTES.

2 cups hot riced potatoes	$\frac{1}{2}$ teaspoon onion juice
4 tablespoons butter	Yolks of 2 eggs
$\frac{2}{3}$ teaspoon salt	$\frac{1}{2}$ tablespoon finely chopped
$\frac{1}{8}$ teaspoon pepper	parsley
Few grains cayenne	

Mix ingredients in order given and beat thoroughly. Shape, dip in crumbs, egg and crumbs again. Fry in deep fat, and drain on brown paper.

LETTUCE AND CUCUMBER SALAD.

Wash, drain and dry one head lettuce. Arrange in salad bowl as near its original shape as possible. Pare and slice one cucumber and place slices between lettuce leaves. Pour over French Dressing.

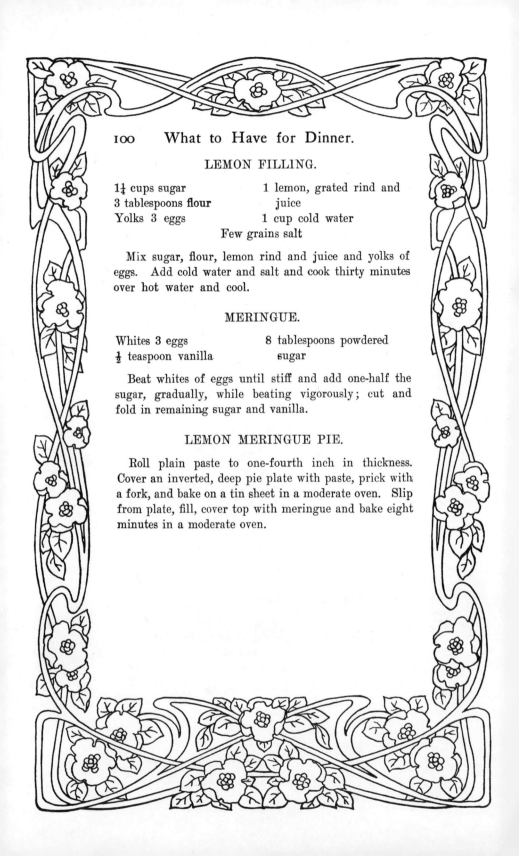

LEMON FILLING.

1¼ cups sugar
3 tablespoons **flour**
Yolks 3 eggs
Few grains salt

1 lemon, grated rind and juice
1 cup cold water

Mix sugar, flour, lemon rind and juice and yolks of eggs. Add cold water and salt and cook thirty minutes over hot water and cool.

MERINGUE.

Whites 3 eggs
½ teaspoon vanilla

8 tablespoons powdered sugar

Beat whites of eggs until stiff and add one-half the sugar, gradually, while beating vigorously; cut and fold in remaining sugar and vanilla.

LEMON MERINGUE PIE.

Roll plain paste to one-fourth inch in thickness. Cover an inverted, deep pie plate with paste, prick with a fork, and bake on a tin sheet in a moderate oven. Slip from plate, fill, cover top with meringue and bake eight minutes in a moderate oven.

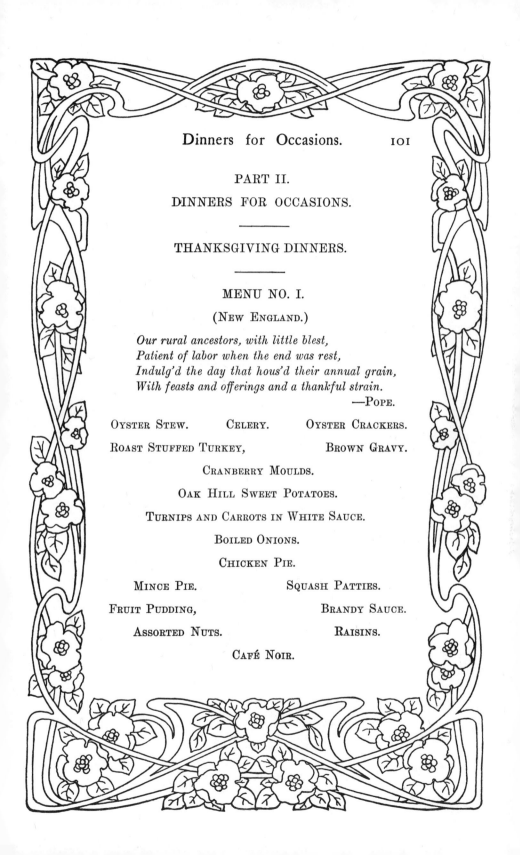

PART II.
DINNERS FOR OCCASIONS.

THANKSGIVING DINNERS.

MENU NO. I.
(NEW ENGLAND.)

Our rural ancestors, with little blest,
Patient of labor when the end was rest,
Indulg'd the day that hous'd their annual grain,
With feasts and offerings and a thankful strain.
                                        —POPE.

OYSTER STEW.   CELERY.   OYSTER CRACKERS.

ROAST STUFFED TURKEY,   BROWN GRAVY.

CRANBERRY MOULDS.

OAK HILL SWEET POTATOES.

TURNIPS AND CARROTS IN WHITE SAUCE.

BOILED ONIONS.

CHICKEN PIE.

MINCE PIE.   SQUASH PATTIES.

FRUIT PUDDING,   BRANDY SAUCE.

ASSORTED NUTS.   RAISINS.

CAFÉ NOIR.

OYSTER STEW.

1 quart oysters	1 blade mace
1 cup water	$\frac{1}{3}$ cup butter
3 cups milk	$\frac{1}{2}$ tablespoon salt

$\frac{1}{8}$ teaspoon pepper

Clean oysters by placing in a colander and pouring over cold water. Carefully pick over oysters, reserve liquor and heat to boiling point; strain through double cheese cloth, add oysters and cook until oysters are plump and edges begin to curl. Remove oysters with skimmer and put in tureen with butter, salt and pepper. Add oyster liquor, strained a second time, and milk which has been scalded with mace, then mace removed. Serve with oyster crackers.

ROAST TURKEY.

Dress, clean, stuff and truss a turkey and rub over with salt. Place on back on rack in dripping pan and spread breast, legs and wings with one-fourth cup butter rubbed until creamy and mixed with one-fourth cup flour. Dredge bottom of pan with flour. Place in hot oven, and when surface is browned reduce heat and baste with fat in pan. Turn bird on breast to complete the roasting, and baste every fifteen minutes with one-half cup butter, dissolved in two cups boiling water; and after this is used, with fat in pan.

STUFFING.

$3\frac{1}{2}$ cups stale bread	$\frac{1}{8}$ teaspoon pepper
1 cup boiling water	2 teaspoons poultry season-
$\frac{1}{2}$ cup butter	ing
1 teaspoon salt	$\frac{1}{2}$ cup finely chopped celery

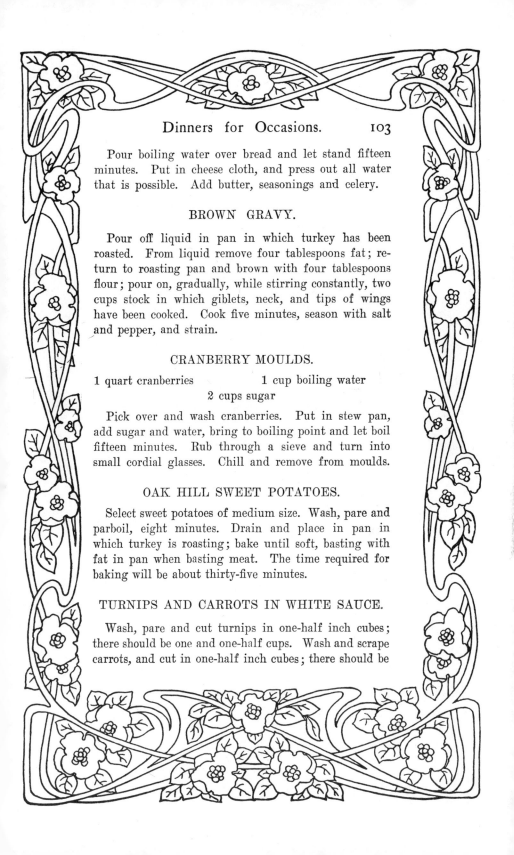

Pour boiling water over bread and let stand fifteen minutes. Put in cheese cloth, and press out all water that is possible. Add butter, seasonings and celery.

BROWN GRAVY.

Pour off liquid in pan in which turkey has been roasted. From liquid remove four tablespoons fat; return to roasting pan and brown with four tablespoons flour; pour on, gradually, while stirring constantly, two cups stock in which giblets, neck, and tips of wings have been cooked. Cook five minutes, season with salt and pepper, and strain.

CRANBERRY MOULDS.

1 quart cranberries   1 cup boiling water
2 cups sugar

Pick over and wash cranberries. Put in stew pan, add sugar and water, bring to boiling point and let boil fifteen minutes. Rub through a sieve and turn into small cordial glasses. Chill and remove from moulds.

OAK HILL SWEET POTATOES.

Select sweet potatoes of medium size. Wash, pare and parboil, eight minutes. Drain and place in pan in which turkey is roasting; bake until soft, basting with fat in pan when basting meat. The time required for baking will be about thirty-five minutes.

TURNIPS AND CARROTS IN WHITE SAUCE.

Wash, pare and cut turnips in one-half inch cubes; there should be one and one-half cups. Wash and scrape carrots, and cut in one-half inch cubes; there should be

one cup. Cook in boiling salted water until soft. Drain
and add one cup White Sauce.

WHITE SAUCE.

2½ tablespoons butter   1 cup milk
3 tablespoons flour   ¼ teaspoon salt
               ⅛ teaspoon pepper

Melt butter, add flour, and pour on, gradually, while
stirring constantly, hot milk. Add seasonings, bring to
boiling point and beat until smooth and glossy.

BOILED ONIONS.

Remove skins from ten medium-sized onions, cover
with boiling water, and let boil ten minutes; drain,
again cover with boiling salted water and cook until tender. Drain, add two tablespoons butter, and sprinkle
with salt.

CHICKEN PIE.

Dress, clean and cut up two fowls in pieces for
serving. Put in stew pan, cover with boiling water,
and cook until chicken is tender, adding one teaspoon
salt, and one-eighth teaspoon pepper when chicken is
half cooked. Remove chicken, and strain stock. Skim
off fat and reduce stock to three and one-half cups.
Melt four tablespoons butter, add one-third cup flour,
and pour on gradually, while stirring constantly, reduced stock. Remove larger bones from fowls and add
meat to gravy, allowing it to stand several hours that
chicken may absorb as much gravy as possible. Turn
in large pudding dish, and cover with plain paste in
which several incisions have been made that there may
be an outlet for escape of steam and gases. Wet edge

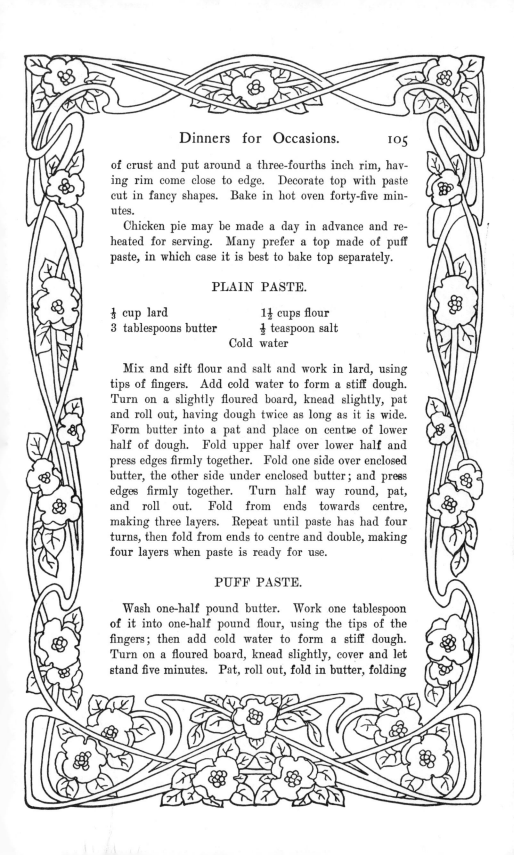

of crust and put around a three-fourths inch rim, having rim come close to edge. Decorate top with paste cut in fancy shapes. Bake in hot oven forty-five minutes.

Chicken pie may be made a day in advance and reheated for serving. Many prefer a top made of puff paste, in which case it is best to bake top separately.

PLAIN PASTE.

$\frac{1}{3}$ cup lard 1$\frac{1}{2}$ cups flour
3 tablespoons butter $\frac{1}{2}$ teaspoon salt
Cold water

Mix and sift flour and salt and work in lard, using tips of fingers. Add cold water to form a stiff dough. Turn on a slightly floured board, knead slightly, pat and roll out, having dough twice as long as it is wide. Form butter into a pat and place on centre of lower half of dough. Fold upper half over lower half and press edges firmly together. Fold one side over enclosed butter, the other side under enclosed butter; and press edges firmly together. Turn half way round, pat, and roll out. Fold from ends towards centre, making three layers. Repeat until paste has had four turns, then fold from ends to centre and double, making four layers when paste is ready for use.

PUFF PASTE.

Wash one-half pound butter. Work one tablespoon of it into one-half pound flour, using the tips of the fingers; then add cold water to form a stiff dough. Turn on a floured board, knead slightly, cover and let stand five minutes. Pat, roll out, fold in butter, folding first from the ends and then from the sides, cover and again let stand five minutes. Pat, roll, and fold to make three layers. Roll and fold five times for patties, pie crust, fancy desserts, etc. Seven times for vol-au-vents, allowing it to stand one minute between each rolling and folding.

MINCE MEAT.

5 cups chopped cooked beef   Juice 2 lemons
2½ cups chopped beef suet   Juice 2 oranges
7½ cups chopped apples   1 tablespoon mace
3 cups cider   2 tablespoons cinnamon
½ cup vinegar   2 tablespoons cloves
1 cup molasses   2 tablespoons allspice
5 cups sugar   2 nutmegs, grated
¾ lb. citron, finely chopped   2 tablespoons lemon extract
2½ cups whole seedless   1 teaspoon almond extract
   raisins   1 cup brandy
1½ cups raisins, finely   Salt
   chopped
        Liquor in which meat was cooked

Mix ingredients in order given, and season with salt. Reduce liquor in which meat was cooked to three cups. Add to mixture, bring to boiling point and let simmer one and one-half hours.

MINCE PIE.

Line a perforated tin pie plate with plain paste and fill with mince meat. Wet edges of under crust with cold water, cover with upper crust of puff paste and press edges together. Ornament with a rim and perforate upper crust that steam may escape.

SQUASH PATTIES.

1 cup steamed and sifted squash	1 teaspoon nutmeg
	$\frac{3}{4}$ teaspoon ginger
1 cup sugar	$\frac{3}{4}$ teaspoon salt
3 eggs, slightly beaten	$\frac{1}{4}$ teaspoon mace
1 teaspoon cinnamon	4 tablespoons brandy

1 cup heavy cream

Line fluted patty pans with plain paste, brush paste with white of egg, sprinkle with stale bread crumbs and fill pans two-thirds full of squash mixture. Bake in quick oven at first, and then decrease heat and complete the cooking.

Squash patties, when eaten at their best, should be freshly baked and served warm.

FRUIT PUDDING.

$\frac{1}{4}$ lb. suet	$\frac{1}{2}$ teaspoon nutmeg
$\frac{1}{2}$ lb. figs	$\frac{1}{4}$ teaspoon clove
2$\frac{1}{2}$ cups stale bread crumbs	$\frac{1}{2}$ cup English walnut meats
$\frac{3}{4}$ cup of milk	
3 eggs	$\frac{1}{2}$ cup raisins, seeded and cut in pieces
1 cup brown sugar	
1 teaspoon salt	2 tablespoons flour
$\frac{1}{2}$ teaspoon cinnamon	2$\frac{1}{2}$ teaspoons baking powder

Chop suet and work until creamy, using the hand. Chop figs and work into the suet. Soak bread crumbs in milk, add eggs well beaten, sugar, salt and spices. Combine mixtures, and add raisins mixed with nut meats broken in pieces and dredged with flour mixed with baking powder. Turn into a buttered mould, cover and steam three hours. Serve with Brandy Sauce.

BRANDY SAUCE.

1¼ cups brown sugar ⅓ cup heavy cream
⅓ cup water 2 tablespoons brandy
Yolks 2 eggs Few grains salt

Put sugar and water in sauce pan, bring to boiling point, and let boil until syrup will thread. Pour syrup gradually on yolks of eggs beaten until thick and lemon colored. Beat until mixture is cool and thick, then add cream, beaten until stiff, brandy and salt.

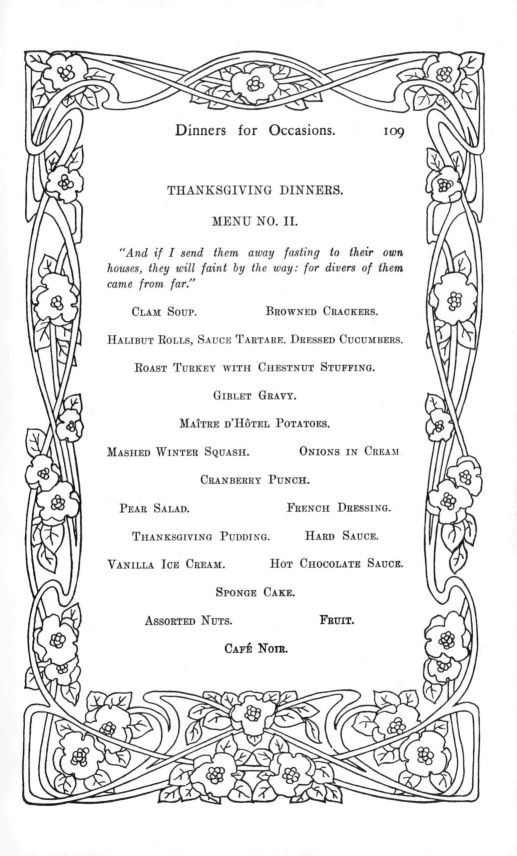

THANKSGIVING DINNERS.

MENU NO. II.

"And if I send them away fasting to their own houses, they will faint by the way: for divers of them came from far."

CLAM SOUP.   BROWNED CRACKERS.

HALIBUT ROLLS, SAUCE TARTARE. DRESSED CUCUMBERS.

ROAST TURKEY WITH CHESTNUT STUFFING.

GIBLET GRAVY.

MAÎTRE D'HÔTEL POTATOES.

MASHED WINTER SQUASH.   ONIONS IN CREAM.

CRANBERRY PUNCH.

PEAR SALAD.   FRENCH DRESSING.

THANKSGIVING PUDDING.   HARD SAUCE.

VANILLA ICE CREAM.   HOT CHOCOLATE SAUCE.

SPONGE CAKE.

ASSORTED NUTS.   FRUIT.

CAFÉ NOIR.

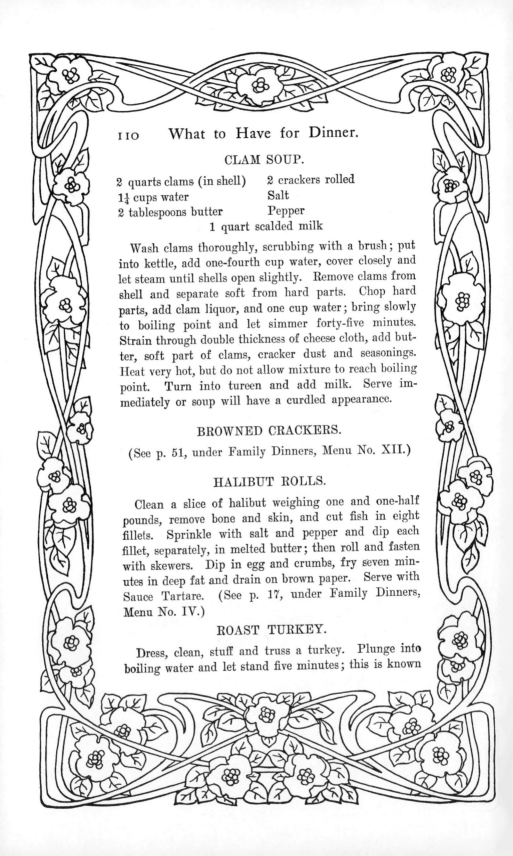

CLAM SOUP.

2 quarts clams (in shell)	2 crackers rolled
1¼ cups water	Salt
2 tablespoons butter	Pepper
1 quart scalded milk	

Wash clams thoroughly, scrubbing with a brush; put into kettle, add one-fourth cup water, cover closely and let steam until shells open slightly. Remove clams from shell and separate soft from hard parts. Chop hard parts, add clam liquor, and one cup water; bring slowly to boiling point and let simmer forty-five minutes. Strain through double thickness of cheese cloth, add butter, soft part of clams, cracker dust and seasonings. Heat very hot, but do not allow mixture to reach boiling point. Turn into tureen and add milk. Serve immediately or soup will have a curdled appearance.

BROWNED CRACKERS.

(See p. 51, under Family Dinners, Menu No. XII.)

HALIBUT ROLLS.

Clean a slice of halibut weighing one and one-half pounds, remove bone and skin, and cut fish in eight fillets. Sprinkle with salt and pepper and dip each fillet, separately, in melted butter; then roll and fasten with skewers. Dip in egg and crumbs, fry seven minutes in deep fat and drain on brown paper. Serve with Sauce Tartare. (See p. 17, under Family Dinners, Menu No. IV.)

ROAST TURKEY.

Dress, clean, stuff and truss a turkey. Plunge into boiling water and let stand five minutes; this is known

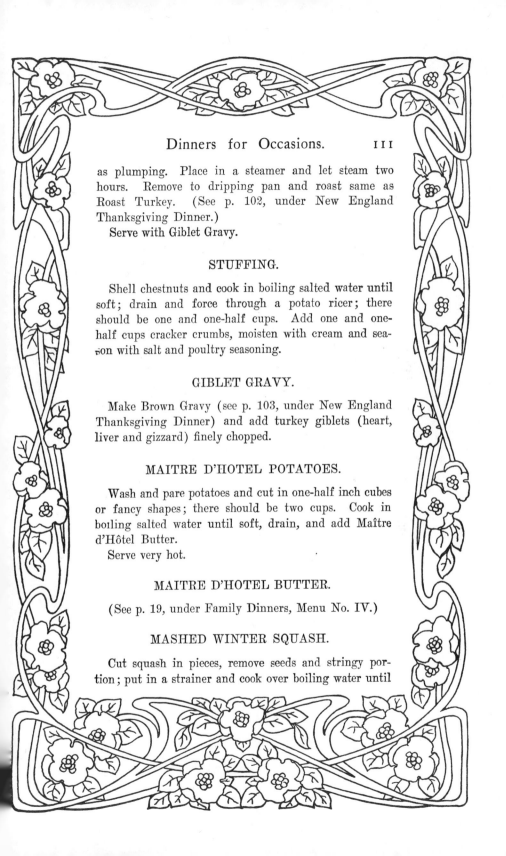

as plumping. Place in a steamer and let steam two hours. Remove to dripping pan and roast same as Roast Turkey. (See p. 102, under New England Thanksgiving Dinner.)

Serve with Giblet Gravy.

STUFFING.

Shell chestnuts and cook in boiling salted water until soft; drain and force through a potato ricer; there should be one and one-half cups. Add one and one-half cups cracker crumbs, moisten with cream and season with salt and poultry seasoning.

GIBLET GRAVY.

Make Brown Gravy (see p. 103, under New England Thanksgiving Dinner) and add turkey giblets (heart, liver and gizzard) finely chopped.

MAITRE D'HOTEL POTATOES.

Wash and pare potatoes and cut in one-half inch cubes or fancy shapes; there should be two cups. Cook in boiling salted water until soft, drain, and add Maître d'Hôtel Butter.

Serve very hot.

MAITRE D'HOTEL BUTTER.

(See p. 19, under Family Dinners, Menu No. IV.)

MASHED WINTER SQUASH.

Cut squash in pieces, remove seeds and stringy portion; put in a strainer and cook over boiling water until

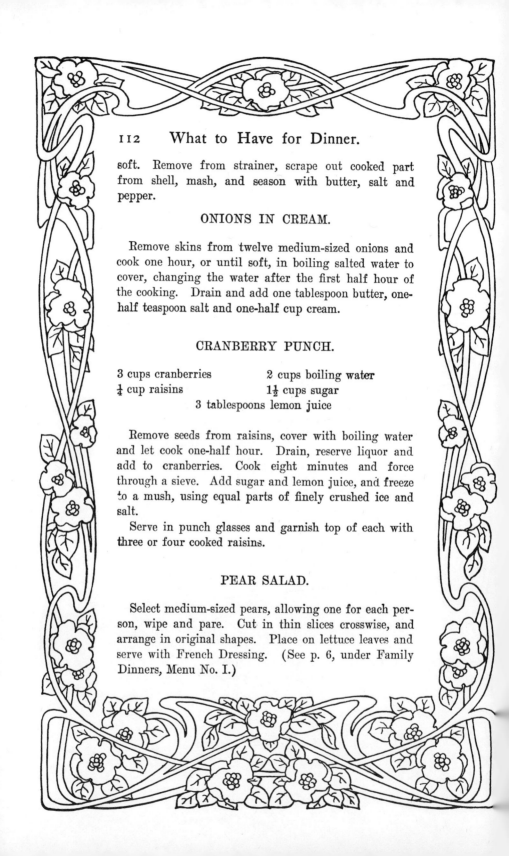

soft. Remove from strainer, scrape out cooked part from shell, mash, and season with butter, salt and pepper.

ONIONS IN CREAM.

Remove skins from twelve medium-sized onions and cook one hour, or until soft, in boiling salted water to cover, changing the water after the first half hour of the cooking. Drain and add one tablespoon butter, one-half teaspoon salt and one-half cup cream.

CRANBERRY PUNCH.

3 cups cranberries	2 cups boiling water
$\frac{1}{4}$ cup raisins	$1\frac{1}{2}$ cups sugar
3 tablespoons lemon juice	

Remove seeds from raisins, cover with boiling water and let cook one-half hour. Drain, reserve liquor and add to cranberries. Cook eight minutes and force through a sieve. Add sugar and lemon juice, and freeze to a mush, using equal parts of finely crushed ice and salt.

Serve in punch glasses and garnish top of each with three or four cooked raisins.

PEAR SALAD.

Select medium-sized pears, allowing one for each person, wipe and pare. Cut in thin slices crosswise, and arrange in original shapes. Place on lettuce leaves and serve with French Dressing. (See p. 6, under Family Dinners, Menu No. I.)

THANKSGIVING PUDDING.

3½ cups milk
1⅓ cups rolled crackers
1 cup sugar
¼ cup melted **butter**
5 eggs
½ cup cream

½ grated nutmeg
¼ teaspoon cinnamon
1 teaspoon salt
1 cup raisins, seeded
¼ cup citron, finely cut
¼ cup currants

Scald milk, pour over crackers and let stand one hour. Add sugar, butter, eggs, well beaten, cream, spices, and fruits. Turn into a buttered mould, set in pan of hot water, and bake in a slow oven three hours, stirring after the first half hour of the cooking to prevent fruit from settling. Remove from mould and serve with Hard Sauce. This pudding may be baked the day before it is needed and reheated for serving. If a convenient sized mould is not at hand, a deep bread pan will serve as a desirable substitute.

HARD SAUCE.

½ cup butter
1 cup powdered sugar

3 tablespoons milk or cream
½ teaspoon vanilla

Cream the butter, add sugar gradually, continuing the beating; then milk, drop by drop. Beat until very light and add flavoring.

VANILLA ICE CREAM,
HOT CHOCOLATE SAUCE.

1½ pints heavy cream
2 cups milk

1 cup sugar
2 tablespoons vanilla

Mix ingredients and freeze. Serve with Hot Chocolate Sauce. (See p. 72, under Family Dinners, Menu No. XVII.)

SPONGE CAKE.

Yolks 6 eggs	Whites 6 eggs
1⅔ cups powdered sugar	1 cup flour
Juice of ½ lemon	1 teaspoon baking powder
Grated rind of ½ lemon	¼ teaspoon salt

Beat yolks of eggs until thick and lemon colored and add sugar gradually, while continuing the beating; then add juice and rind of lemon. Beat whites of eggs until stiff and dry and add to fruit mixture; then cut and fold in flour mixed and sifted with salt and baking powder. Bake in an unbuttered pan in a slow oven, one hour.

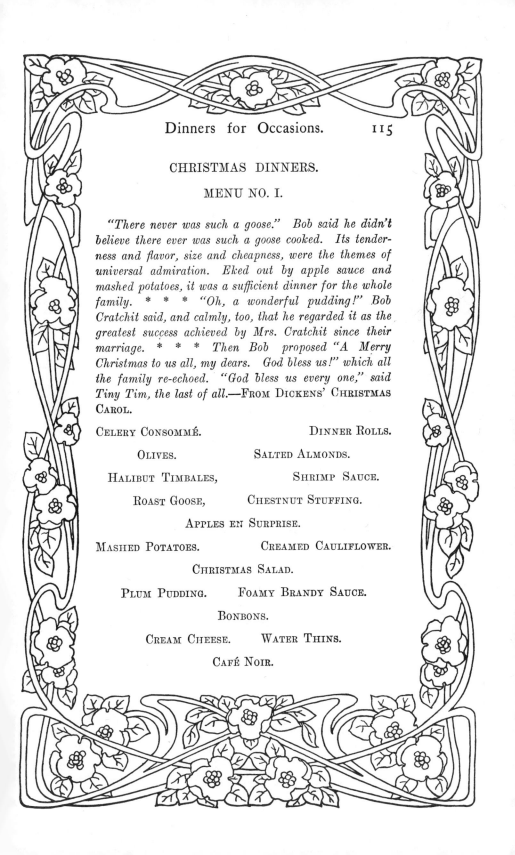

CHRISTMAS DINNERS.

MENU NO. I.

*"There never was such a goose." Bob said he didn't believe there ever was such a goose cooked. Its tenderness and flavor, size and cheapness, were the themes of universal admiration. Eked out by apple sauce and mashed potatoes, it was a sufficient dinner for the whole family. * * * "Oh, a wonderful pudding!" Bob Cratchit said, and calmly, too, that he regarded it as the greatest success achieved by Mrs. Cratchit since their marriage. * * * Then Bob proposed "A Merry Christmas to us all, my dears. God bless us!" which all the family re-echoed. "God bless us every one," said Tiny Tim, the last of all.—*FROM DICKENS' CHRISTMAS CAROL.

CELERY CONSOMMÉ.   DINNER ROLLS.

OLIVES.   SALTED ALMONDS.

HALIBUT TIMBALES,   SHRIMP SAUCE.

ROAST GOOSE,   CHESTNUT STUFFING.

APPLES EN SURPRISE.

MASHED POTATOES.   CREAMED CAULIFLOWER.

CHRISTMAS SALAD.

PLUM PUDDING.   FOAMY BRANDY SAUCE.

BONBONS.

CREAM CHEESE.   WATER THINS.

CAFÉ NOIR.

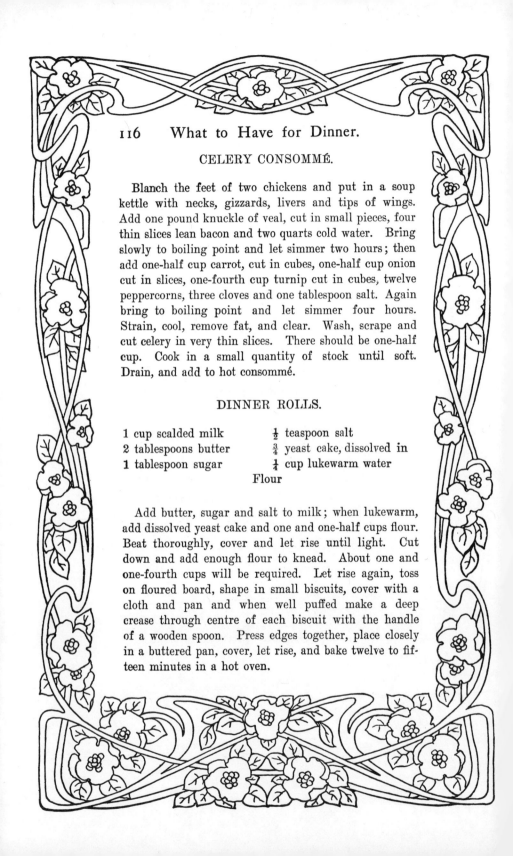

CELERY CONSOMMÉ.

Blanch the feet of two chickens and put in a soup kettle with necks, gizzards, livers and tips of wings. Add one pound knuckle of veal, cut in small pieces, four thin slices lean bacon and two quarts cold water. Bring slowly to boiling point and let simmer two hours; then add one-half cup carrot, cut in cubes, one-half cup onion cut in slices, one-fourth cup turnip cut in cubes, twelve peppercorns, three cloves and one tablespoon salt. Again bring to boiling point and let simmer four hours. Strain, cool, remove fat, and clear. Wash, scrape and cut celery in very thin slices. There should be one-half cup. Cook in a small quantity of stock until soft. Drain, and add to hot consommé.

DINNER ROLLS.

1 cup scalded milk	$\frac{1}{2}$ teaspoon salt
2 tablespoons butter	$\frac{3}{4}$ yeast cake, dissolved in
1 tablespoon sugar	$\frac{1}{4}$ cup lukewarm water
	Flour

Add butter, sugar and salt to milk; when lukewarm, add dissolved yeast cake and one and one-half cups flour. Beat thoroughly, cover and let rise until light. Cut down and add enough flour to knead. About one and one-fourth cups will be required. Let rise again, toss on floured board, shape in small biscuits, cover with a cloth and pan and when well puffed make a deep crease through centre of each biscuit with the handle of a wooden spoon. Press edges together, place closely in a buttered pan, cover, let rise, and bake twelve to fifteen minutes in a hot oven.

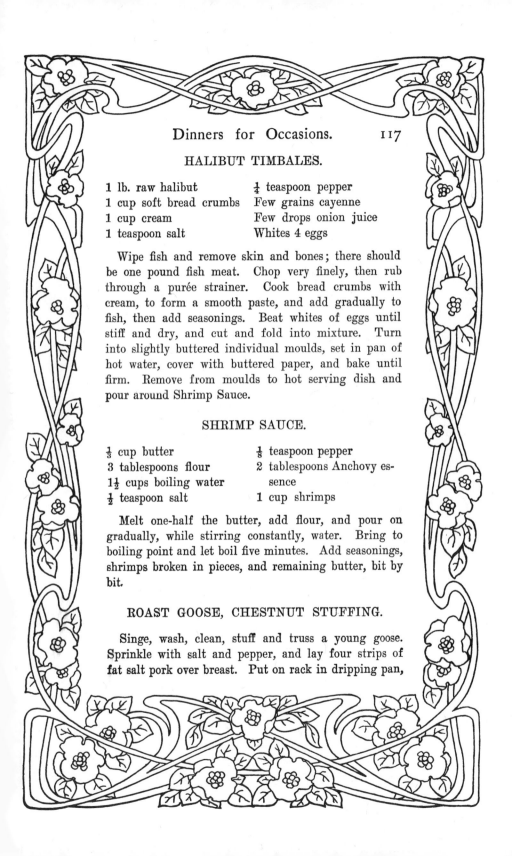

HALIBUT TIMBALES.

1 lb. raw halibut	$\frac{1}{4}$ teaspoon pepper
1 cup soft bread crumbs	Few grains cayenne
1 cup cream	Few drops onion juice
1 teaspoon salt	Whites 4 eggs

Wipe fish and remove skin and bones; there should be one pound fish meat. Chop very finely, then rub through a purée strainer. Cook bread crumbs with cream, to form a smooth paste, and add gradually to fish, then add seasonings. Beat whites of eggs until stiff and dry, and cut and fold into mixture. Turn into slightly buttered individual moulds, set in pan of hot water, cover with buttered paper, and bake until firm. Remove from moulds to hot serving dish and pour around Shrimp Sauce.

SHRIMP SAUCE.

$\frac{1}{3}$ cup butter	$\frac{1}{8}$ teaspoon pepper
3 tablespoons flour	2 tablespoons Anchovy es-
$1\frac{1}{2}$ cups boiling water	sence
$\frac{1}{2}$ teaspoon salt	1 cup shrimps

Melt one-half the butter, add flour, and pour on gradually, while stirring constantly, water. Bring to boiling point and let boil five minutes. Add seasonings, shrimps broken in pieces, and remaining butter, bit by bit.

ROAST GOOSE, CHESTNUT STUFFING.

Singe, wash, clean, stuff and truss a young goose. Sprinkle with salt and pepper, and lay four strips of fat salt pork over breast. Put on rack in dripping pan,

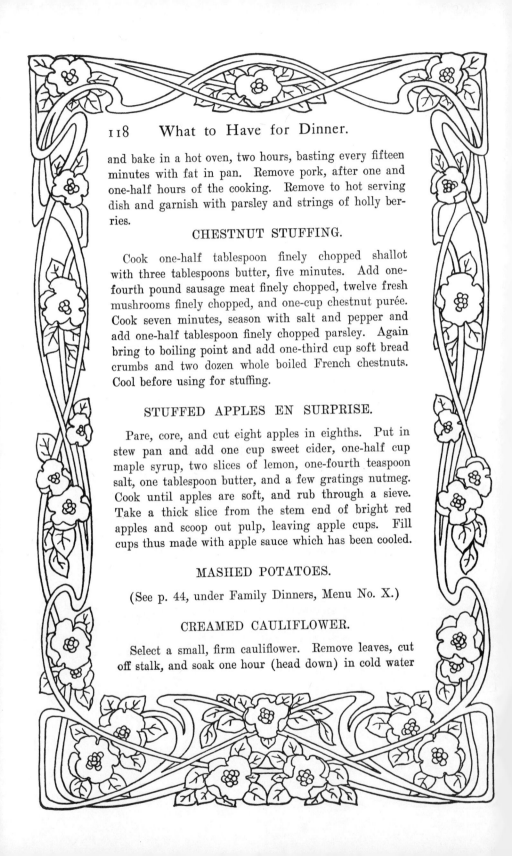

and bake in a hot oven, two hours, basting every fifteen minutes with fat in pan. Remove pork, after one and one-half hours of the cooking. Remove to hot serving dish and garnish with parsley and strings of holly berries.

CHESTNUT STUFFING.

Cook one-half tablespoon finely chopped shallot with three tablespoons butter, five minutes. Add one-fourth pound sausage meat finely chopped, twelve fresh mushrooms finely chopped, and one-cup chestnut purée. Cook seven minutes, season with salt and pepper and add one-half tablespoon finely chopped parsley. Again bring to boiling point and add one-third cup soft bread crumbs and two dozen whole boiled French chestnuts. Cool before using for stuffing.

STUFFED APPLES EN SURPRISE.

Pare, core, and cut eight apples in eighths. Put in stew pan and add one cup sweet cider, one-half cup maple syrup, two slices of lemon, one-fourth teaspoon salt, one tablespoon butter, and a few gratings nutmeg. Cook until apples are soft, and rub through a sieve. Take a thick slice from the stem end of bright red apples and scoop out pulp, leaving apple cups. Fill cups thus made with apple sauce which has been cooled.

MASHED POTATOES.

(See p. 44, under Family Dinners, Menu No. X.)

CREAMED CAULIFLOWER.

Select a small, firm cauliflower. Remove leaves, cut off stalk, and soak one hour (head down) in cold water

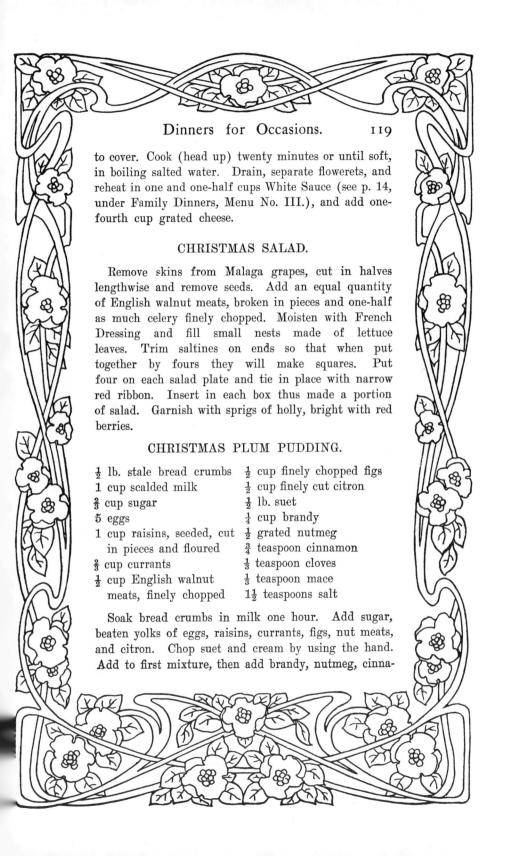

to cover. Cook (head up) twenty minutes or until soft, in boiling salted water. Drain, separate flowerets, and reheat in one and one-half cups White Sauce (see p. 14, under Family Dinners, Menu No. III.), and add one-fourth cup grated cheese.

CHRISTMAS SALAD.

Remove skins from Malaga grapes, cut in halves lengthwise and remove seeds. Add an equal quantity of English walnut meats, broken in pieces and one-half as much celery finely chopped. Moisten with French Dressing and fill small nests made of lettuce leaves. Trim saltines on ends so that when put together by fours they will make squares. Put four on each salad plate and tie in place with narrow red ribbon. Insert in each box thus made a portion of salad. Garnish with sprigs of holly, bright with red berries.

CHRISTMAS PLUM PUDDING.

$\frac{1}{2}$ lb. stale bread crumbs	$\frac{1}{2}$ cup finely chopped figs
1 cup scalded milk	$\frac{1}{2}$ cup finely cut citron
$\frac{2}{3}$ cup sugar	$\frac{1}{2}$ lb. suet
5 eggs	$\frac{1}{4}$ cup brandy
1 cup raisins, seeded, cut in pieces and floured	$\frac{1}{2}$ grated nutmeg
	$\frac{3}{4}$ teaspoon cinnamon
$\frac{2}{3}$ cup currants	$\frac{1}{3}$ teaspoon cloves
$\frac{1}{2}$ cup English walnut meats, finely chopped	$\frac{1}{3}$ teaspoon mace
	$1\frac{1}{2}$ teaspoons salt

Soak bread crumbs in milk one hour. Add sugar, beaten yolks of eggs, raisins, currants, figs, nut meats, and citron. Chop suet and cream by using the hand. Add to first mixture, then add brandy, nutmeg, cinna-

mon, cloves, mace, salt and white of eggs beaten stiff.
Turn into a buttered bomb-shaped mould and steam
six hours.   Garnish with holly, and send to the table
surrounded with burning brandy.   Serve with Foamy
Brandy Sauce.

FOAMY BRANDY SAUCE.

½ cup butter   Few grains salt
1 cup powdered sugar   ½ cup heavy cream, beaten
Whites two eggs   stiff
              2 tablespoons brandy

Cream the butter and add sugar, gradually, continuing the beating.   Put over hot water, add eggs beaten
until stiff, and beat until well blended, using a wire
whisk.   Cool, and add brandy, salt and cream.

SALTED ALMONDS.

Blanch one-fourth pound almonds, and dry on a
towel. Put one and one-half tablespoons, each, butter
and lard, in a sauce pan, and when melted and well
heated add almonds and fry until delicately browned,
stirring constantly, that nuts may brown evenly.   Remove with a spoon or small skimmer, taking up as little
fat as possible. Drain on brown paper, and sprinkle
with salt.

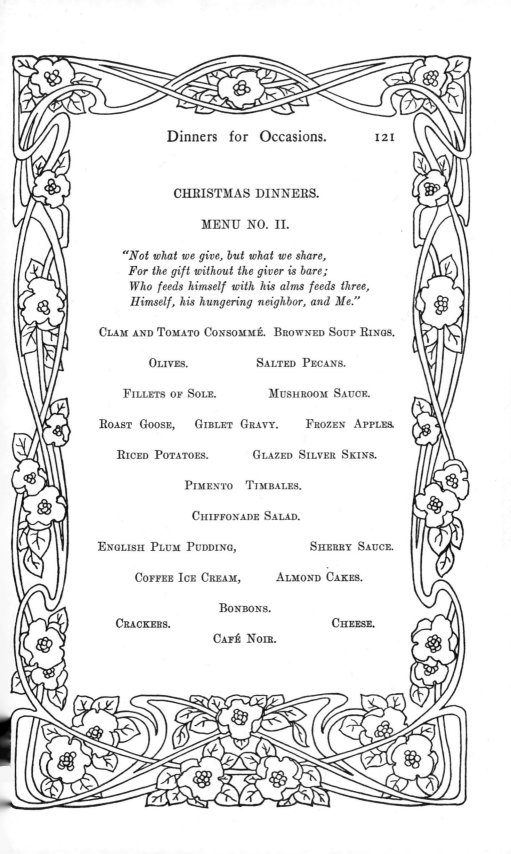

CHRISTMAS DINNERS.

MENU NO. II.

"Not what we give, but what we share,
For the gift without the giver is bare;
Who feeds himself with his alms feeds three,
Himself, his hungering neighbor, and Me."

CLAM AND TOMATO CONSOMMÉ. BROWNED SOUP RINGS.

OLIVES. SALTED PECANS.

FILLETS OF SOLE. MUSHROOM SAUCE.

ROAST GOOSE, GIBLET GRAVY. FROZEN APPLES.

RICED POTATOES. GLAZED SILVER SKINS.

PIMENTO TIMBALES.

CHIFFONADE SALAD.

ENGLISH PLUM PUDDING, SHERRY SAUCE.

COFFEE ICE CREAM, ALMOND CAKES.

BONBONS.

CRACKERS. CHEESE.

CAFÉ NOIR.

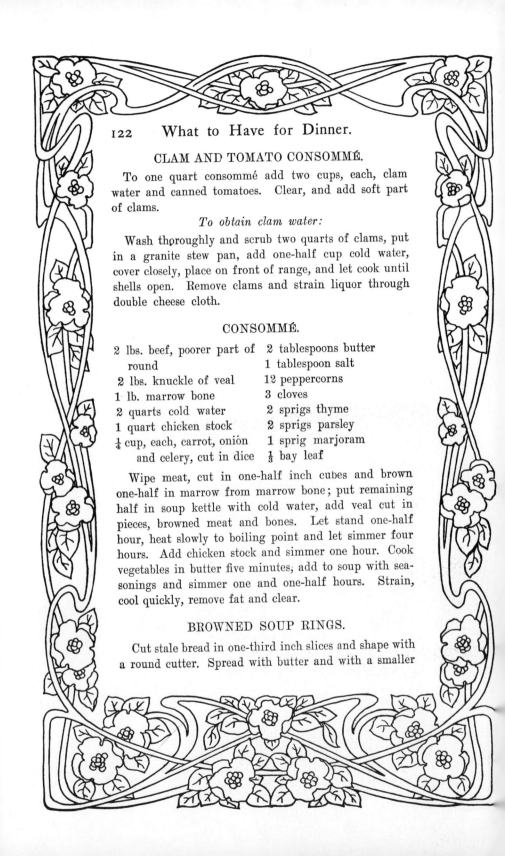

CLAM AND TOMATO CONSOMMÉ.

To one quart consommé add two cups, each, clam water and canned tomatoes. Clear, and add soft part of clams.

To obtain clam water:

Wash thoroughly and scrub two quarts of clams, put in a granite stew pan, add one-half cup cold water, cover closely, place on front of range, and let cook until shells open. Remove clams and strain liquor through double cheese cloth.

CONSOMMÉ.

2 lbs. beef, poorer part of round	2 tablespoons butter
2 lbs. knuckle of veal	1 tablespoon salt
1 lb. marrow bone	12 peppercorns
2 quarts cold water	3 cloves
1 quart chicken stock	2 sprigs thyme
¼ cup, each, carrot, onion and celery, cut in dice	2 sprigs parsley
	1 sprig marjoram
	⅓ bay leaf

Wipe meat, cut in one-half inch cubes and brown one-half in marrow from marrow bone; put remaining half in soup kettle with cold water, add veal cut in pieces, browned meat and bones. Let stand one-half hour, heat slowly to boiling point and let simmer four hours. Add chicken stock and simmer one hour. Cook vegetables in butter five minutes; add to soup with seasonings and simmer one and one-half hours. Strain, cool quickly, remove fat and clear.

BROWNED SOUP RINGS.

Cut stale bread in one-third inch slices and shape with a round cutter. Spread with butter and with a smaller

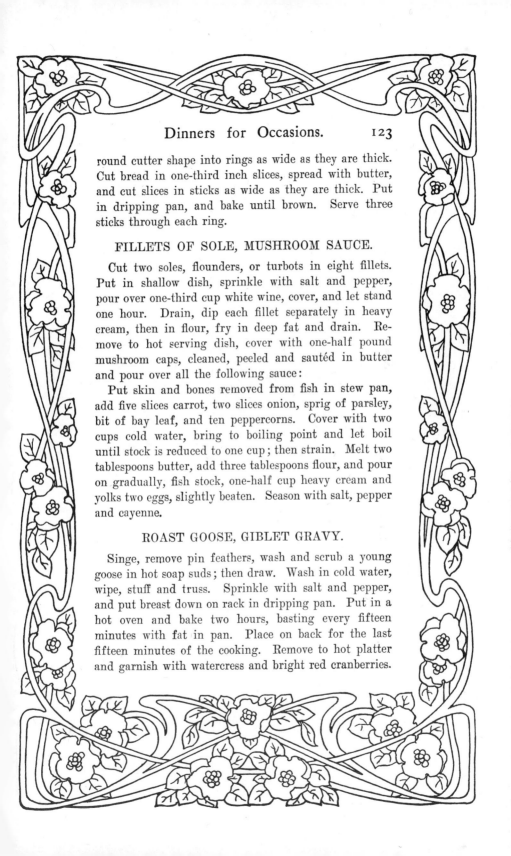

round cutter shape into rings as wide as they are thick. Cut bread in one-third inch slices, spread with butter, and cut slices in sticks as wide as they are thick. Put in dripping pan, and bake until brown. Serve three sticks through each ring.

FILLETS OF SOLE, MUSHROOM SAUCE.

Cut two soles, flounders, or turbots in eight fillets. Put in shallow dish, sprinkle with salt and pepper, pour over one-third cup white wine, cover, and let stand one hour. Drain, dip each fillet separately in heavy cream, then in flour, fry in deep fat and drain. Remove to hot serving dish, cover with one-half pound mushroom caps, cleaned, peeled and sautéd in butter and pour over all the following sauce:

Put skin and bones removed from fish in stew pan, add five slices carrot, two slices onion, sprig of parsley, bit of bay leaf, and ten peppercorns. Cover with two cups cold water, bring to boiling point and let boil until stock is reduced to one cup; then strain. Melt two tablespoons butter, add three tablespoons flour, and pour on gradually, fish stock, one-half cup heavy cream and yolks two eggs, slightly beaten. Season with salt, pepper and cayenne.

ROAST GOOSE, GIBLET GRAVY.

Singe, remove pin feathers, wash and scrub a young goose in hot soap suds; then draw. Wash in cold water, wipe, stuff and truss. Sprinkle with salt and pepper, and put breast down on rack in dripping pan. Put in a hot oven and bake two hours, basting every fifteen minutes with fat in pan. Place on back for the last fifteen minutes of the cooking. Remove to hot platter and garnish with watercress and bright red cranberries.

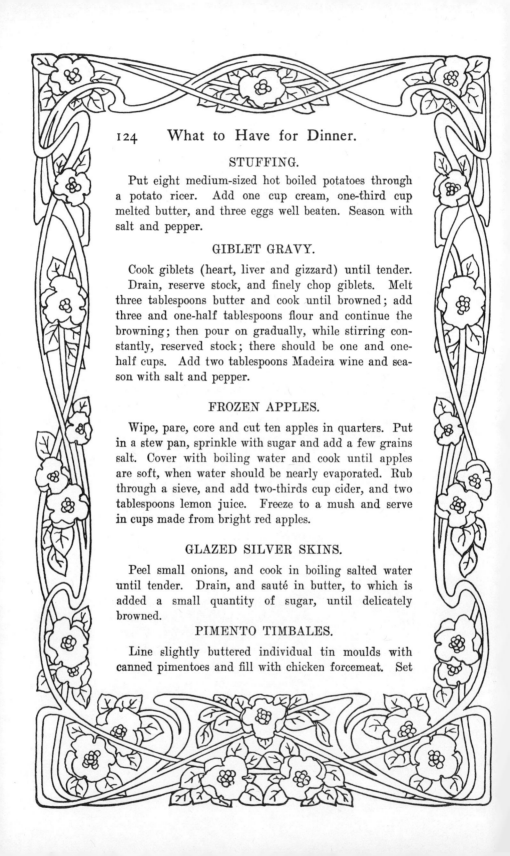

STUFFING.

Put eight medium-sized hot boiled potatoes through a potato ricer. Add one cup cream, one-third cup melted butter, and three eggs well beaten. Season with salt and pepper.

GIBLET GRAVY.

Cook giblets (heart, liver and gizzard) until tender. Drain, reserve stock, and finely chop giblets. Melt three tablespoons butter and cook until browned; add three and one-half tablespoons flour and continue the browning; then pour on gradually, while stirring constantly, reserved stock; there should be one and one-half cups. Add two tablespoons Madeira wine and season with salt and pepper.

FROZEN APPLES.

Wipe, pare, core and cut ten apples in quarters. Put in a stew pan, sprinkle with sugar and add a few grains salt. Cover with boiling water and cook until apples are soft, when water should be nearly evaporated. Rub through a sieve, and add two-thirds cup cider, and two tablespoons lemon juice. Freeze to a mush and serve in cups made from bright red apples.

GLAZED SILVER SKINS.

Peel small onions, and cook in boiling salted water until tender. Drain, and sauté in butter, to which is added a small quantity of sugar, until delicately browned.

PIMENTO TIMBALES.

Line slightly buttered individual tin moulds with canned pimentoes and fill with chicken forcemeat. Set

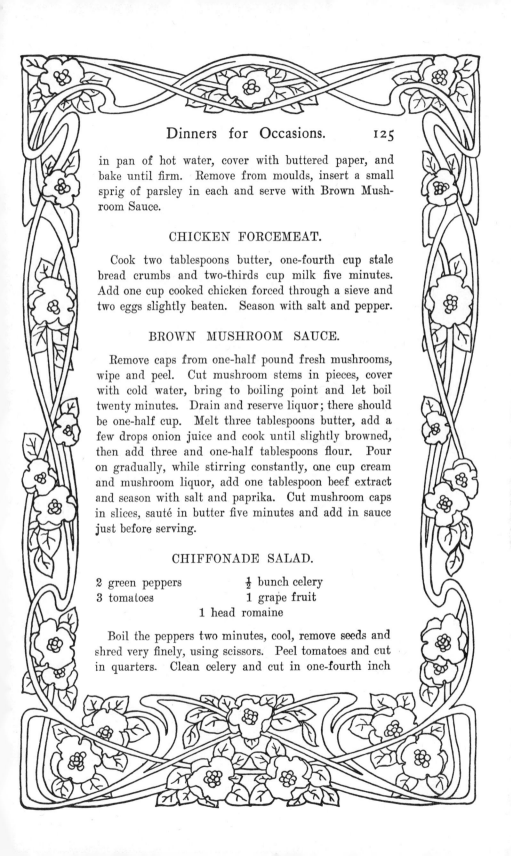

in pan of hot water, cover with buttered paper, and bake until firm. Remove from moulds, insert a small sprig of parsley in each and serve with Brown Mushroom Sauce.

CHICKEN FORCEMEAT.

Cook two tablespoons butter, one-fourth cup stale bread crumbs and two-thirds cup milk five minutes. Add one cup cooked chicken forced through a sieve and two eggs slightly beaten. Season with salt and pepper.

BROWN MUSHROOM SAUCE.

Remove caps from one-half pound fresh mushrooms, wipe and peel. Cut mushroom stems in pieces, cover with cold water, bring to boiling point and let boil twenty minutes. Drain and reserve liquor; there should be one-half cup. Melt three tablespoons butter, add a few drops onion juice and cook until slightly browned, then add three and one-half tablespoons flour. Pour on gradually, while stirring constantly, one cup cream and mushroom liquor, add one tablespoon beef extract and season with salt and paprika. Cut mushroom caps in slices, sauté in butter five minutes and add in sauce just before serving.

CHIFFONADE SALAD.

2 green peppers	½ bunch celery
3 tomatoes	1 grape fruit
1 head romaine	

Boil the peppers two minutes, cool, remove seeds and shred very finely, using scissors. Peel tomatoes and cut in quarters. Clean celery and cut in one-fourth inch

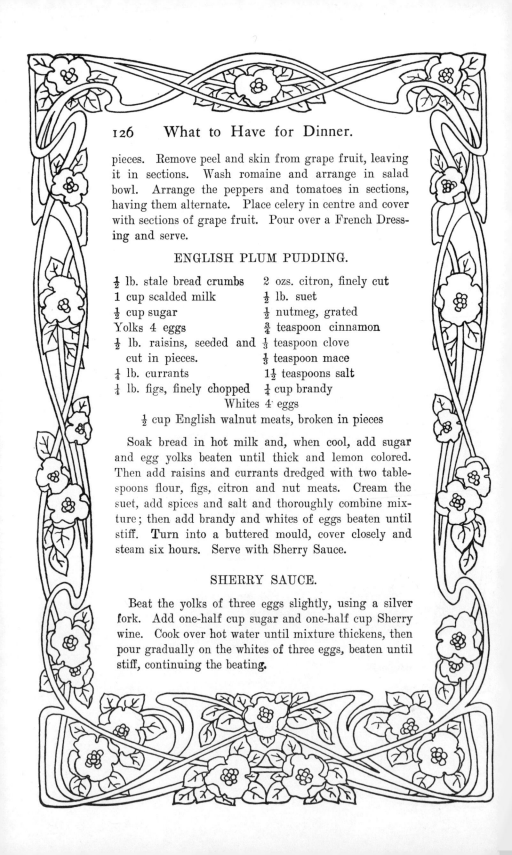

pieces. Remove peel and skin from grape fruit, leaving it in sections. Wash romaine and arrange in salad bowl. Arrange the peppers and tomatoes in sections, having them alternate. Place celery in centre and cover with sections of grape fruit. Pour over a French Dressing and serve.

ENGLISH PLUM PUDDING.

$\frac{1}{2}$ lb. stale bread crumbs	2 ozs. citron, finely cut
1 cup scalded milk	$\frac{1}{2}$ lb. suet
$\frac{1}{2}$ cup sugar	$\frac{1}{2}$ nutmeg, grated
Yolks 4 eggs	$\frac{3}{4}$ teaspoon cinnamon
$\frac{1}{2}$ lb. raisins, seeded and cut in pieces.	$\frac{1}{3}$ teaspoon clove
	$\frac{1}{3}$ teaspoon mace
$\frac{1}{4}$ lb. currants	$1\frac{1}{2}$ teaspoons salt
$\frac{1}{4}$ lb. figs, finely chopped	$\frac{1}{4}$ cup brandy
Whites 4 eggs	

$\frac{1}{2}$ cup English walnut meats, broken in pieces

Soak bread in hot milk and, when cool, add sugar and egg yolks beaten until thick and lemon colored. Then add raisins and currants dredged with two tablespoons flour, figs, citron and nut meats. Cream the suet, add spices and salt and thoroughly combine mixture; then add brandy and whites of eggs beaten until stiff. Turn into a buttered mould, cover closely and steam six hours. Serve with Sherry Sauce.

SHERRY SAUCE.

Beat the yolks of three eggs slightly, using a silver fork. Add one-half cup sugar and one-half cup Sherry wine. Cook over hot water until mixture thickens, then pour gradually on the whites of three eggs, beaten until stiff, continuing the beating.

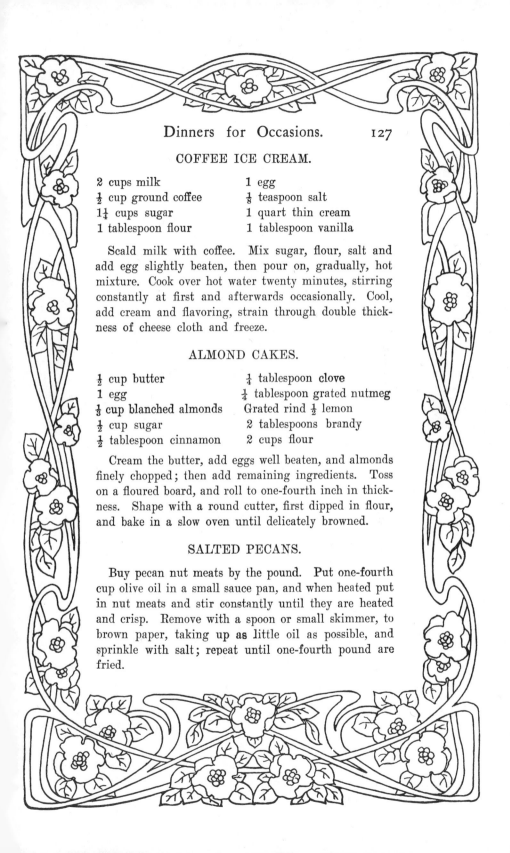

COFFEE ICE CREAM.

2 cups milk	1 egg
½ cup ground coffee	⅛ teaspoon salt
1¼ cups sugar	1 quart thin cream
1 tablespoon flour	1 tablespoon vanilla

Scald milk with coffee. Mix sugar, flour, salt and add egg slightly beaten, then pour on, gradually, hot mixture. Cook over hot water twenty minutes, stirring constantly at first and afterwards occasionally. Cool, add cream and flavoring, strain through double thickness of cheese cloth and freeze.

ALMOND CAKES.

½ cup butter	¼ tablespoon clove
1 egg	¼ tablespoon grated nutmeg
⅓ cup blanched almonds	Grated rind ½ lemon
½ cup sugar	2 tablespoons brandy
½ tablespoon cinnamon	2 cups flour

Cream the butter, add eggs well beaten, and almonds finely chopped; then add remaining ingredients. Toss on a floured board, and roll to one-fourth inch in thickness. Shape with a round cutter, first dipped in flour, and bake in a slow oven until delicately browned.

SALTED PECANS.

Buy pecan nut meats by the pound. Put one-fourth cup olive oil in a small sauce pan, and when heated put in nut meats and stir constantly until they are heated and crisp. Remove with a spoon or small skimmer, to brown paper, taking up as little oil as possible, and sprinkle with salt; repeat until one-fourth pound are fried.

It may be necessary to remove some of the salt by wiping nuts with a piece of cheese cloth.

Pecan nut meats, having a dark skin, are somewhat difficult to fry, as the color does not determine when they are sufficiently cooked. There is great danger of allowing them to remain in the oil for too long a time.

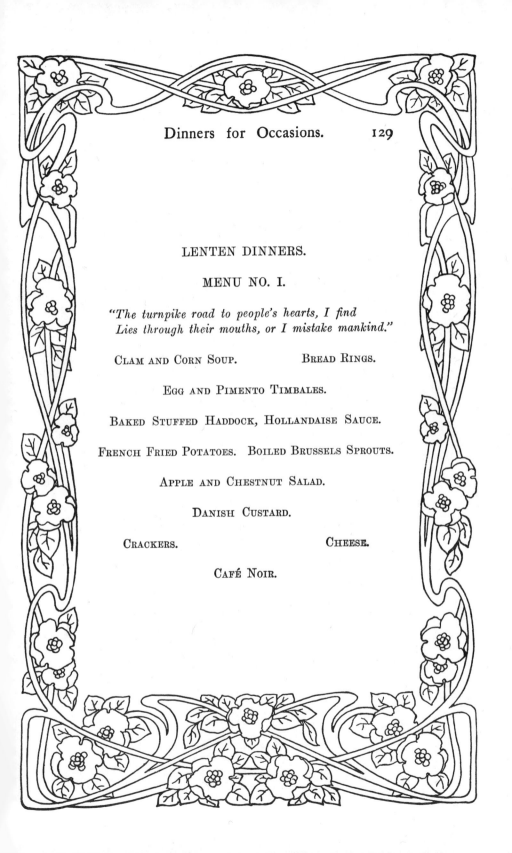

LENTEN DINNERS.

MENU NO. I.

"The turnpike road to people's hearts, I find
Lies through their mouths, or I mistake mankind."

CLAM AND CORN SOUP.　　　　BREAD RINGS.

EGG AND PIMENTO TIMBALES.

BAKED STUFFED HADDOCK, HOLLANDAISE SAUCE.

FRENCH FRIED POTATOES.　BOILED BRUSSELS SPROUTS.

APPLE AND CHESTNUT SALAD.

DANISH CUSTARD.

CRACKERS.　　　　　　　CHEESE.

CAFÉ NOIR.

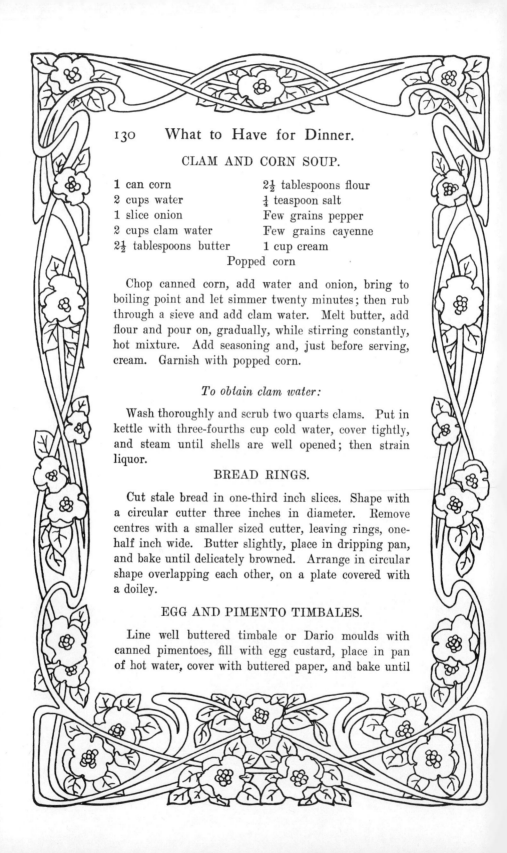

CLAM AND CORN SOUP.

1 can corn	2½ tablespoons flour
2 cups water	¼ teaspoon salt
1 slice onion	Few grains pepper
2 cups clam water	Few grains cayenne
2½ tablespoons butter	1 cup cream

Popped corn

Chop canned corn, add water and onion, bring to boiling point and let simmer twenty minutes; then rub through a sieve and add clam water. Melt butter, add flour and pour on, gradually, while stirring constantly, hot mixture. Add seasoning and, just before serving, cream. Garnish with popped corn.

To obtain clam water:

Wash thoroughly and scrub two quarts clams. Put in kettle with three-fourths cup cold water, cover tightly, and steam until shells are well opened; then strain liquor.

BREAD RINGS.

Cut stale bread in one-third inch slices. Shape with a circular cutter three inches in diameter. Remove centres with a smaller sized cutter, leaving rings, one-half inch wide. Butter slightly, place in dripping pan, and bake until delicately browned. Arrange in circular shape overlapping each other, on a plate covered with a doiley.

EGG AND PIMENTO TIMBALES.

Line well buttered timbale or Dario moulds with canned pimentoes, fill with egg custard, place in pan of hot water, cover with buttered paper, and bake until

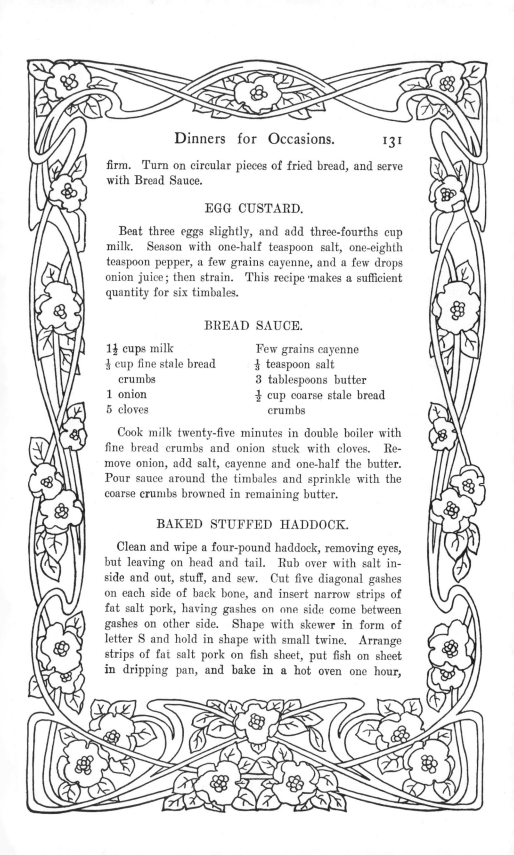

firm. Turn on circular pieces of fried bread, and serve with Bread Sauce.

EGG CUSTARD.

Beat three eggs slightly, and add three-fourths cup milk. Season with one-half teaspoon salt, one-eighth teaspoon pepper, a few grains cayenne, and a few drops onion juice; then strain. This recipe makes a sufficient quantity for six timbales.

BREAD SAUCE.

1½ cups milk	Few grains cayenne
⅓ cup fine stale bread crumbs	⅓ teaspoon salt
	3 tablespoons butter
1 onion	½ cup coarse stale bread
5 cloves	crumbs

Cook milk twenty-five minutes in double boiler with fine bread crumbs and onion stuck with cloves. Remove onion, add salt, cayenne and one-half the butter. Pour sauce around the timbales and sprinkle with the coarse crumbs browned in remaining butter.

BAKED STUFFED HADDOCK.

Clean and wipe a four-pound haddock, removing eyes, but leaving on head and tail. Rub over with salt inside and out, stuff, and sew. Cut five diagonal gashes on each side of back bone, and insert narrow strips of fat salt pork, having gashes on one side come between gashes on other side. Shape with skewer in form of letter S and hold in shape with small twine. Arrange strips of fat salt pork on fish sheet, put fish on sheet in dripping pan, and bake in a hot oven one hour,

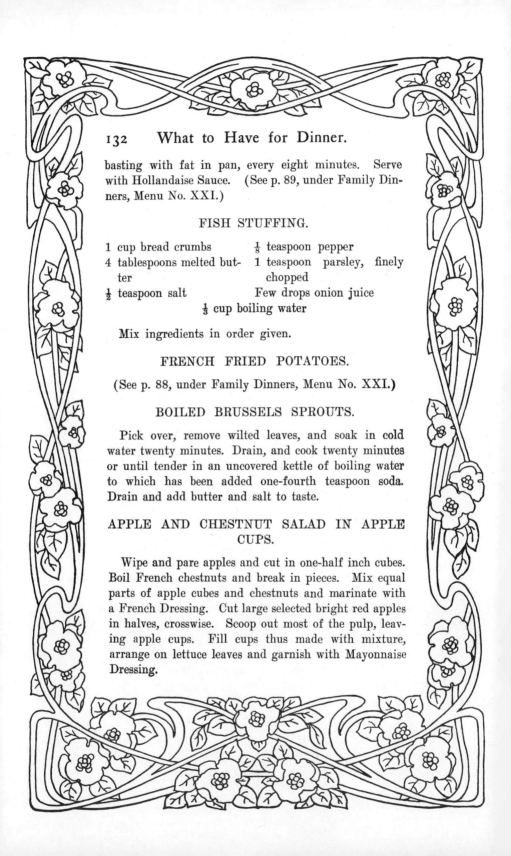

basting with fat in pan, every eight minutes. Serve with Hollandaise Sauce. (See p. 89, under Family Dinners, Menu No. XXI.)

FISH STUFFING.

1 cup bread crumbs	$\frac{1}{8}$ teaspoon pepper
4 tablespoons melted butter	1 teaspoon parsley, finely chopped
$\frac{1}{2}$ teaspoon salt	Few drops onion juice

$\frac{1}{3}$ cup boiling water

Mix ingredients in order given.

FRENCH FRIED POTATOES.

(See p. 88, under Family Dinners, Menu No. XXI.)

BOILED BRUSSELS SPROUTS.

Pick over, remove wilted leaves, and soak in cold water twenty minutes. Drain, and cook twenty minutes or until tender in an uncovered kettle of boiling water to which has been added one-fourth teaspoon soda. Drain and add butter and salt to taste.

APPLE AND CHESTNUT SALAD IN APPLE CUPS.

Wipe and pare apples and cut in one-half inch cubes. Boil French chestnuts and break in pieces. Mix equal parts of apple cubes and chestnuts and marinate with a French Dressing. Cut large selected bright red apples in halves, crosswise. Scoop out most of the pulp, leaving apple cups. Fill cups thus made with mixture, arrange on lettuce leaves and garnish with Mayonnaise Dressing.

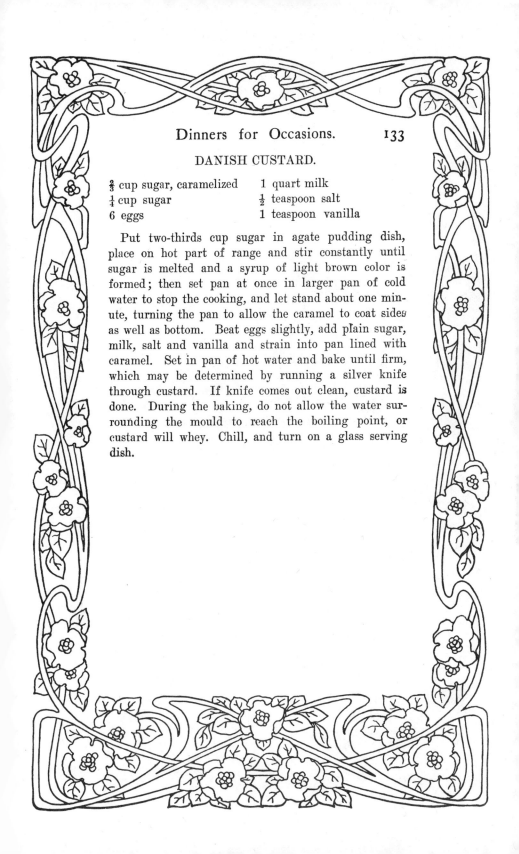

DANISH CUSTARD.

⅔ cup sugar, caramelized 1 quart milk
¼ cup sugar ½ teaspoon salt
6 eggs 1 teaspoon vanilla

Put two-thirds cup sugar in agate pudding dish, place on hot part of range and stir constantly until sugar is melted and a syrup of light brown color is formed; then set pan at once in larger pan of cold water to stop the cooking, and let stand about one minute, turning the pan to allow the caramel to coat sides as well as bottom. Beat eggs slightly, add plain sugar, milk, salt and vanilla and strain into pan lined with caramel. Set in pan of hot water and bake until firm, which may be determined by running a silver knife through custard. If knife comes out clean, custard is done. During the baking, do not allow the water surrounding the mould to reach the boiling point, or custard will whey. Chill, and turn on a glass serving dish.

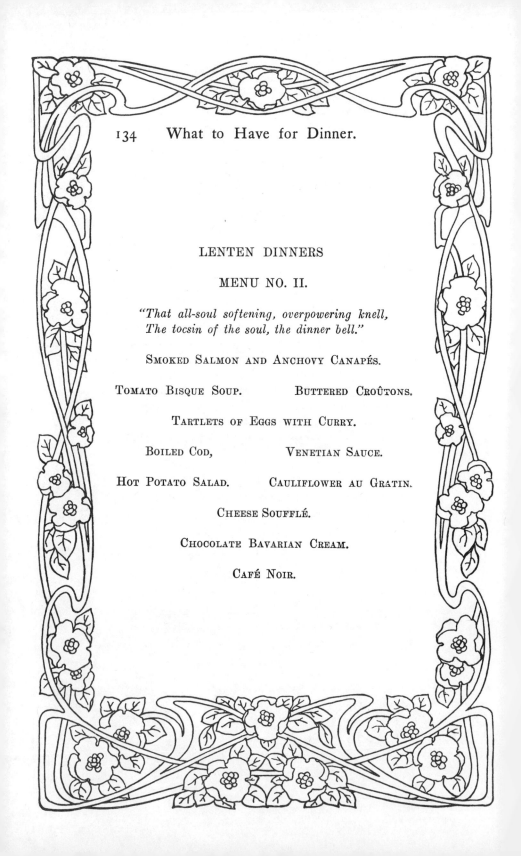

LENTEN DINNERS

MENU NO. II.

*"That all-soul softening, overpowering knell,
The tocsin of the soul, the dinner bell."*

SMOKED SALMON AND ANCHOVY CANAPÉS.

TOMATO BISQUE SOUP.   BUTTERED CROÛTONS.

TARTLETS OF EGGS WITH CURRY.

BOILED COD,   VENETIAN SAUCE.

HOT POTATO SALAD.   CAULIFLOWER AU GRATIN.

CHEESE SOUFFLÉ.

CHOCOLATE BAVARIAN CREAM.

CAFÉ NOIR.

SMOKED SALMON AND ANCHOVY CANAPÉS.

Cut stale bread in one-fourth inch slices, remove crusts and cut slices in fancy shapes—squares, rounds, or triangles—then sauté in butter. Spread with anchovies pounded in a mortar and mixed with butter. Arrange flaked smoked salmon, whites of "hard-boiled" eggs finely chopped, and yolks of eggs forced through a purée strainer in fancy forms on canapés. Garnish with pimolas or olives stuffed with anchovies.

TOMATO BISQUE SOUP.

½ can tomatoes	Bit of bay leaf
½ onion (sliced)	1 teaspoon sugar
4 cloves	⅓ teaspoon soda
8 peppercorns	1 teaspoon salt
1 sprig parsley	3 tablespoons flour
1 stalk celery	3 tablespoons butter
1 quart milk	

Mix first seven ingredients, bring to boiling point, let simmer twenty minutes, then rub through a sieve. Add sugar, soda and salt. Melt butter, add flour, and pour on gradually, while stirring constantly, hot mixture. Add to scalded milk and serve immediately. Whipped Cream used as a garnish is an improvement to this soup.

BUTTERED CROÛTONS.

Cut stale bread in one-third or one-half inch slices, and remove crusts. Spread sparingly with butter and cut in strips, one-third or one-half inch wide and cut strips in cubes. Put in pan, and bake until delicately browned.

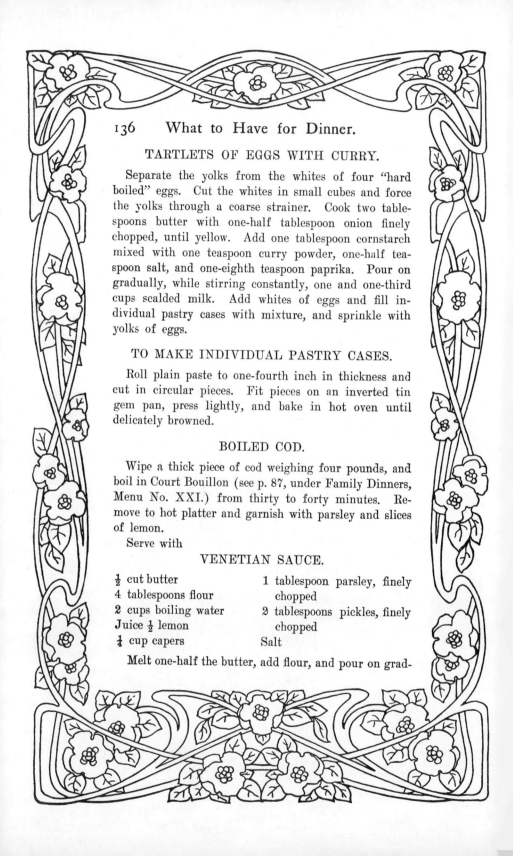

TARTLETS OF EGGS WITH CURRY.

Separate the yolks from the whites of four "hard boiled" eggs. Cut the whites in small cubes and force the yolks through a coarse strainer. Cook two tablespoons butter with one-half tablespoon onion finely chopped, until yellow. Add one tablespoon cornstarch mixed with one teaspoon curry powder, one-half teaspoon salt, and one-eighth teaspoon paprika. Pour on gradually, while stirring constantly, one and one-third cups scalded milk. Add whites of eggs and fill individual pastry cases with mixture, and sprinkle with yolks of eggs.

TO MAKE INDIVIDUAL PASTRY CASES.

Roll plain paste to one-fourth inch in thickness and cut in circular pieces. Fit pieces on an inverted tin gem pan, press lightly, and bake in hot oven until delicately browned.

BOILED COD.

Wipe a thick piece of cod weighing four pounds, and boil in Court Bouillon (see p. 87, under Family Dinners, Menu No. XXI.) from thirty to forty minutes. Remove to hot platter and garnish with parsley and slices of lemon.

Serve with

VENETIAN SAUCE.

½ cut butter	1 tablespoon parsley, finely
4 tablespoons flour	chopped
2 cups boiling water	2 tablespoons pickles, finely
Juice ½ lemon	chopped
¼ cup capers	Salt

Melt one-half the butter, add flour, and pour on grad-

ually, while stirring constantly, boiling water. Bring to boiling point and add seasonings and remaining butter, bit by bit.

HOT POTATO SALAD.

Wash and pare potatoes and cut into balls, using a French vegetable cutter; there should be two cups. Cook in boiling salted water, until soft, drain, pour over dressing and sprinkle with two tablespoons chopped parsley.

HOT POTATO SALAD DRESSING.

$\frac{1}{2}$ teaspoon salt
$\frac{1}{4}$ teaspoon pepper
4 tablespoons olive oil
$\frac{1}{2}$ cup celery, finely cut
2 slices lemon

2 tablespoons Tarragon vinegar
2 tablespoons chopped onion
1 tablespoon chopped parsley

1 tablespoon cider vinegar

Mix ingredients, heat to boiling point, remove lemon and pour mixture over potatoes. Serve at once.

CREAMED CAULIFLOWER.

Remove leaves, cut off stalks and soak thirty minutes (head down) in cold water to cover. Cook (head up) in an uncovered kettle, until tender, in a large quantity of boiling salted water, to which has been added one-eighth teaspoon soda. Drain, separate flowerets, arrange in serving dish and pour over one and one-half cups

WHITE SAUCE.

3 tablespoons butter
3 tablespoons flour
$1\frac{1}{2}$ cups scalded milk

1 slice onion
$\frac{1}{4}$ teaspoon salt
$\frac{1}{8}$ teaspoon pepper

Melt butter, add flour and pour on gradually, while

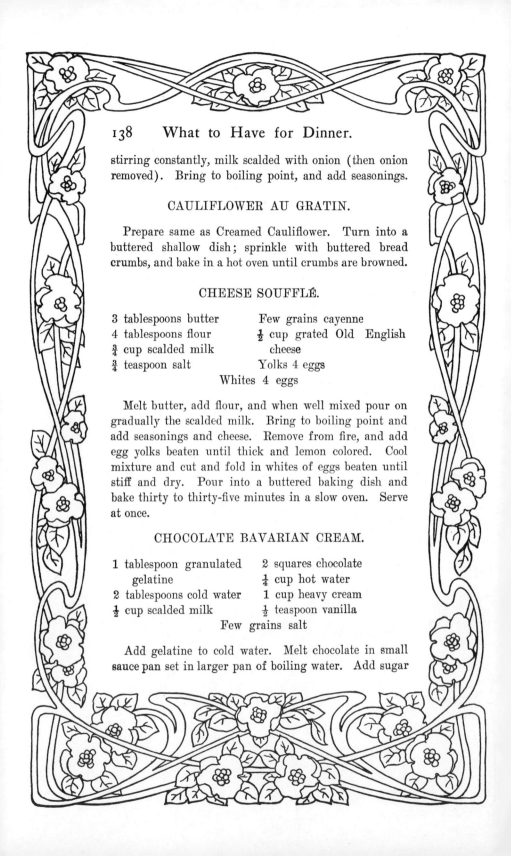

stirring constantly, milk scalded with onion (then onion removed). Bring to boiling point, and add seasonings.

CAULIFLOWER AU GRATIN.

Prepare same as Creamed Cauliflower. Turn into a buttered shallow dish; sprinkle with buttered bread crumbs, and bake in a hot oven until crumbs are browned.

CHEESE SOUFFLÉ.

3 tablespoons butter	Few grains cayenne
4 tablespoons flour	$\frac{1}{2}$ cup grated Old English
$\frac{3}{4}$ cup scalded milk	cheese
$\frac{3}{4}$ teaspoon salt	Yolks 4 eggs
Whites 4 eggs	

Melt butter, add flour, and when well mixed pour on gradually the scalded milk. Bring to boiling point and add seasonings and cheese. Remove from fire, and add egg yolks beaten until thick and lemon colored. Cool mixture and cut and fold in whites of eggs beaten until stiff and dry. Pour into a buttered baking dish and bake thirty to thirty-five minutes in a slow oven. Serve at once.

CHOCOLATE BAVARIAN CREAM.

1 tablespoon granulated gelatine	2 squares chocolate
	$\frac{1}{4}$ cup hot water
2 tablespoons cold water	1 cup heavy cream
$\frac{1}{2}$ cup scalded milk	$\frac{1}{2}$ teaspoon vanilla
Few grains salt	

Add gelatine to cold water. Melt chocolate in small sauce pan set in larger pan of boiling water. Add sugar

and hot water and stir until smooth, then add gelatine.
Add mixture to hot milk, strain into bowl, and set in
pan of ice water. Beat until mixture begins to thicken,
then add cream beaten until stiff, vanilla and salt. Turn
into moulds and chill.

EASTER DINNERS.

MENU NO. I.

"New occasions teach new duties,
Time makes ancient good uncouth."

FROZEN EGG NOG IN EGG CUPS.

POTAGE D'AVIGNON.   BREAD STICKS.

CELERY.   OLIVES.

SLICED CUCUMBERS.

BROILED TROUT, MAÎTRE D'HÔTEL BUTTER.

BOUCHÉES OF LAMBS' SWEETBREADS.

ROAST SPRING LAMB,   MINT SAUCE.

NEW POTATOES.   BOILED GREEN PEAS.

EGG PLANT AU GRATIN.

QUAIL, EPICUREAN STYLE.   DRESSED LETTUCE.

ORANGE ICE CREAM, WITH CRUSHED STRAWBERRIES.

CURRANT WAFERS.

CRACKERS.   CHEESE.

BONBONS.

CAFÉ NOIR.

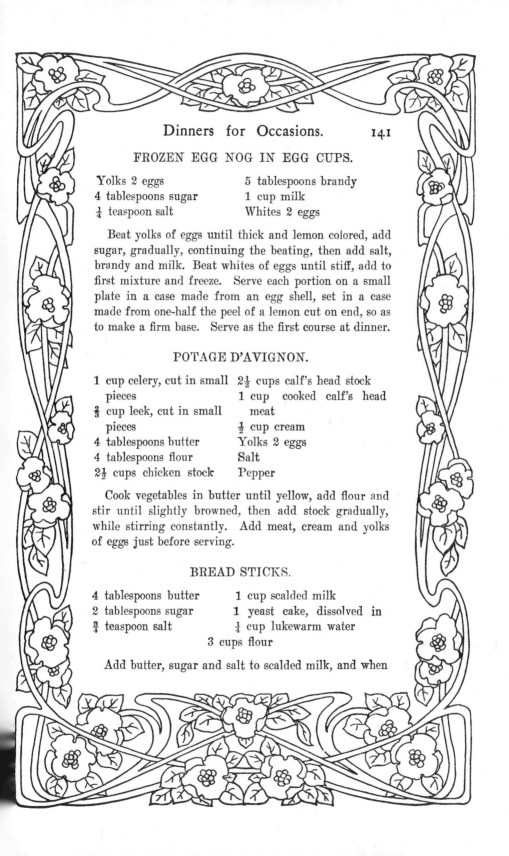

FROZEN EGG NOG IN EGG CUPS.

Yolks 2 eggs
4 tablespoons sugar
¼ teaspoon salt

5 tablespoons brandy
1 cup milk
Whites 2 eggs

Beat yolks of eggs until thick and lemon colored, add sugar, gradually, continuing the beating, then add salt, brandy and milk. Beat whites of eggs until stiff, add to first mixture and freeze. Serve each portion on a small plate in a case made from an egg shell, set in a case made from one-half the peel of a lemon cut on end, so as to make a firm base. Serve as the first course at dinner.

POTAGE D'AVIGNON.

1 cup celery, cut in small pieces
⅔ cup leek, cut in small pieces
4 tablespoons butter
4 tablespoons flour
2½ cups chicken stock

2½ cups calf's head stock
1 cup cooked calf's head meat
½ cup cream
Yolks 2 eggs
Salt
Pepper

Cook vegetables in butter until yellow, add flour and stir until slightly browned, then add stock gradually, while stirring constantly. Add meat, cream and yolks of eggs just before serving.

BREAD STICKS.

4 tablespoons butter
2 tablespoons sugar
¾ teaspoon salt

1 cup scalded milk
1 yeast cake, dissolved in
¼ cup lukewarm water
3 cups flour

Add butter, sugar and salt to scalded milk, and when

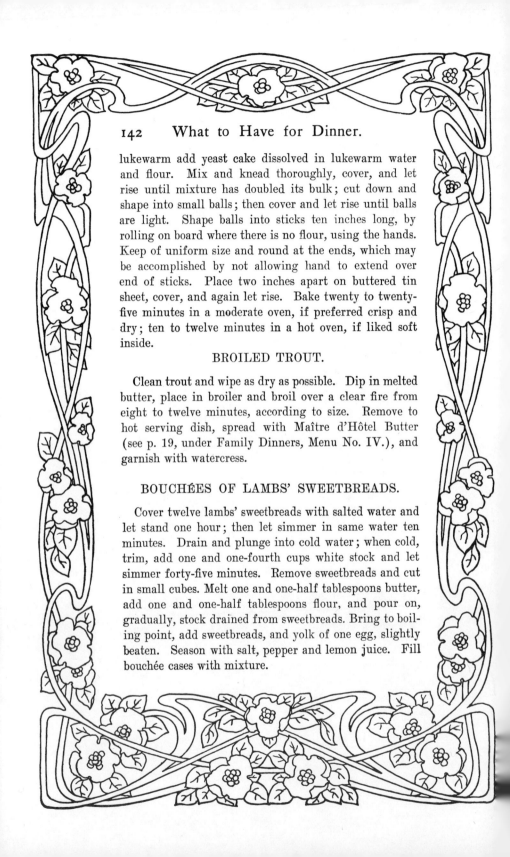

lukewarm add yeast cake dissolved in lukewarm water and flour. Mix and knead thoroughly, cover, and let rise until mixture has doubled its bulk; cut down and shape into small balls; then cover and let rise until balls are light. Shape balls into sticks ten inches long, by rolling on board where there is no flour, using the hands. Keep of uniform size and round at the ends, which may be accomplished by not allowing hand to extend over end of sticks. Place two inches apart on buttered tin sheet, cover, and again let rise. Bake twenty to twenty-five minutes in a moderate oven, if preferred crisp and dry; ten to twelve minutes in a hot oven, if liked soft inside.

BROILED TROUT.

Clean trout and wipe as dry as possible. Dip in melted butter, place in broiler and broil over a clear fire from eight to twelve minutes, according to size. Remove to hot serving dish, spread with Maître d'Hôtel Butter (see p. 19, under Family Dinners, Menu No. IV.), and garnish with watercress.

BOUCHÉES OF LAMBS' SWEETBREADS.

Cover twelve lambs' sweetbreads with salted water and let stand one hour; then let simmer in same water ten minutes. Drain and plunge into cold water; when cold, trim, add one and one-fourth cups white stock and let simmer forty-five minutes. Remove sweetbreads and cut in small cubes. Melt one and one-half tablespoons butter, add one and one-half tablespoons flour, and pour on, gradually, stock drained from sweetbreads. Bring to boiling point, add sweetbreads, and yolk of one egg, slightly beaten. Season with salt, pepper and lemon juice. Fill bouchée cases with mixture.

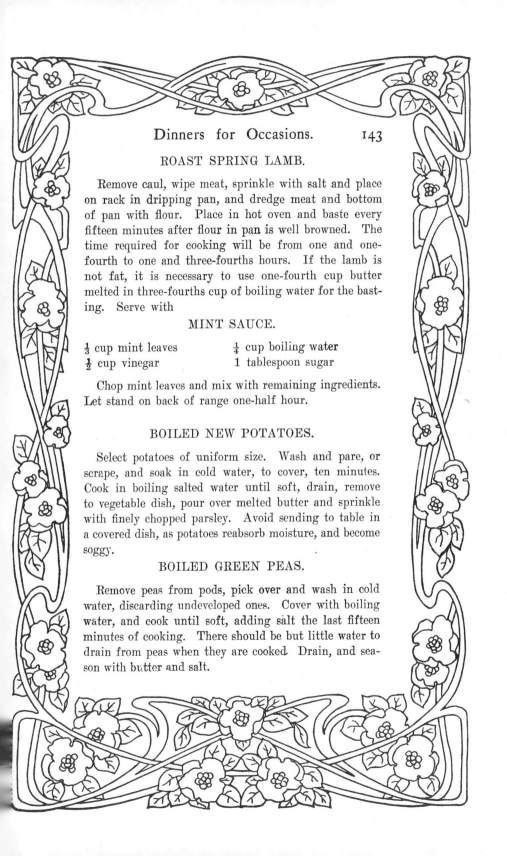

ROAST SPRING LAMB.

Remove caul, wipe meat, sprinkle with salt and place on rack in dripping pan, and dredge meat and bottom of pan with flour. Place in hot oven and baste every fifteen minutes after flour in pan is well browned. The time required for cooking will be from one and one-fourth to one and three-fourths hours. If the lamb is not fat, it is necessary to use one-fourth cup butter melted in three-fourths cup of boiling water for the basting. Serve with

MINT SAUCE.

⅓ cup mint leaves
½ cup vinegar
¼ cup boiling water
1 tablespoon sugar

Chop mint leaves and mix with remaining ingredients. Let stand on back of range one-half hour.

BOILED NEW POTATOES.

Select potatoes of uniform size. Wash and pare, or scrape, and soak in cold water, to cover, ten minutes. Cook in boiling salted water until soft, drain, remove to vegetable dish, pour over melted butter and sprinkle with finely chopped parsley. Avoid sending to table in a covered dish, as potatoes reabsorb moisture, and become soggy.

BOILED GREEN PEAS.

Remove peas from pods, pick over and wash in cold water, discarding undeveloped ones. Cover with boiling water, and cook until soft, adding salt the last fifteen minutes of cooking. There should be but little water to drain from peas when they are cooked. Drain, and season with butter and salt.

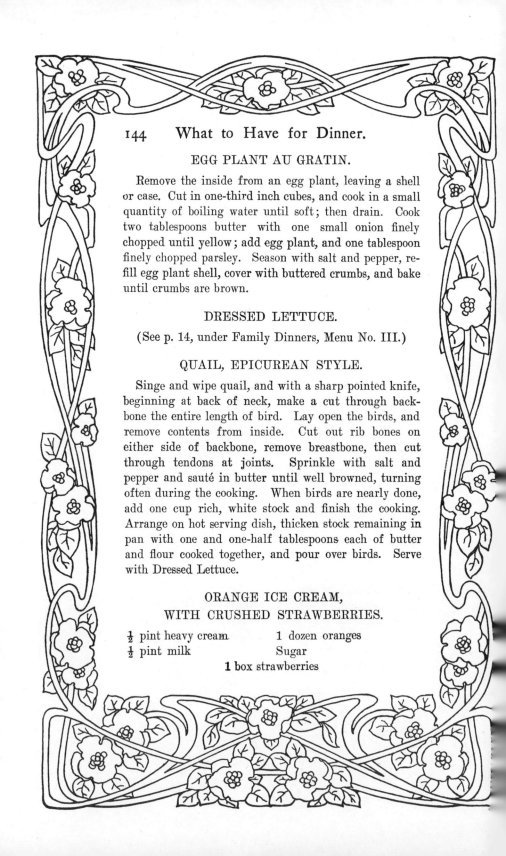

EGG PLANT AU GRATIN.

Remove the inside from an egg plant, leaving a shell or case. Cut in one-third inch cubes, and cook in a small quantity of boiling water until soft; then drain. Cook two tablespoons butter with one small onion finely chopped until yellow; add egg plant, and one tablespoon finely chopped parsley. Season with salt and pepper, refill egg plant shell, cover with buttered crumbs, and bake until crumbs are brown.

DRESSED LETTUCE.

(See p. 14, under Family Dinners, Menu No. III.)

QUAIL, EPICUREAN STYLE.

Singe and wipe quail, and with a sharp pointed knife, beginning at back of neck, make a cut through backbone the entire length of bird. Lay open the birds, and remove contents from inside. Cut out rib bones on either side of backbone, remove breastbone, then cut through tendons at joints. Sprinkle with salt and pepper and sauté in butter until well browned, turning often during the cooking. When birds are nearly done, add one cup rich, white stock and finish the cooking. Arrange on hot serving dish, thicken stock remaining in pan with one and one-half tablespoons each of butter and flour cooked together, and pour over birds. Serve with Dressed Lettuce.

ORANGE ICE CREAM, WITH CRUSHED STRAWBERRIES.

½ pint heavy cream	1 dozen oranges
½ pint milk	Sugar
1 box strawberries	

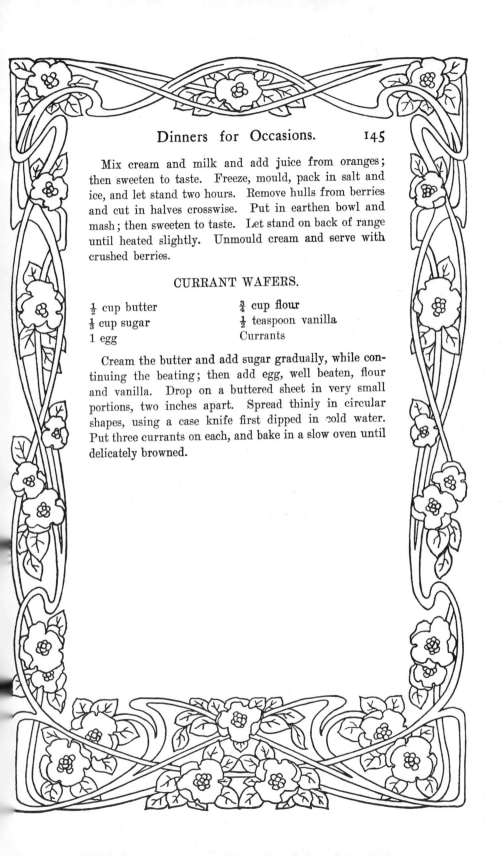

Mix cream and milk and add juice from oranges; then sweeten to taste. Freeze, mould, pack in salt and ice, and let stand two hours. Remove hulls from berries and cut in halves crosswise. Put in earthen bowl and mash; then sweeten to taste. Let stand on back of range until heated slightly. Unmould cream and serve with crushed berries.

CURRANT WAFERS.

½ cup butter
⅓ cup sugar
1 egg
¾ cup flour
½ teaspoon vanilla
Currants

Cream the butter and add sugar gradually, while continuing the beating; then add egg, well beaten, flour and vanilla. Drop on a buttered sheet in very small portions, two inches apart. Spread thinly in circular shapes, using a case knife first dipped in cold water. Put three currants on each, and bake in a slow oven until delicately browned.

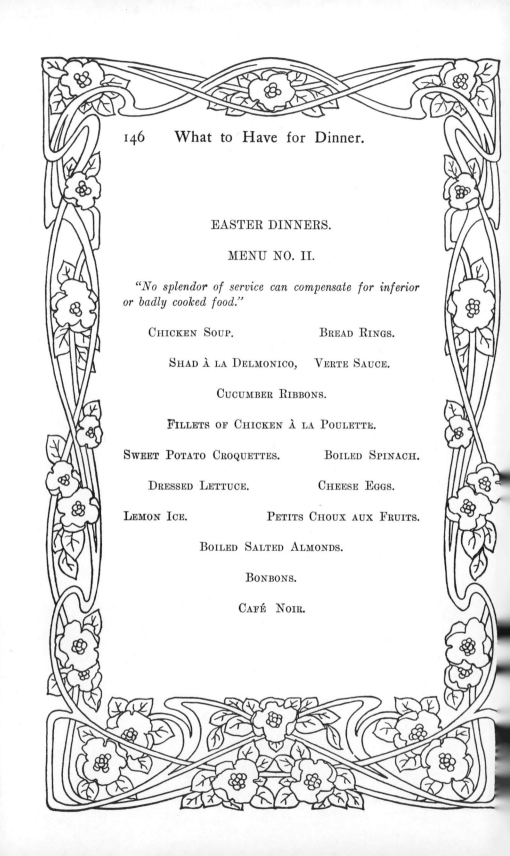

EASTER DINNERS.

MENU NO. II.

"No splendor of service can compensate for inferior or badly cooked food."

CHICKEN SOUP.   BREAD RINGS.

SHAD À LA DELMONICO,   VERTE SAUCE.

CUCUMBER RIBBONS.

FILLETS OF CHICKEN À LA POULETTE.

SWEET POTATO CROQUETTES.   BOILED SPINACH.

DRESSED LETTUCE.   CHEESE EGGS.

LEMON ICE.   PETITS CHOUX AUX FRUITS.

BOILED SALTED ALMONDS.

BONBONS.

CAFÉ NOIR.

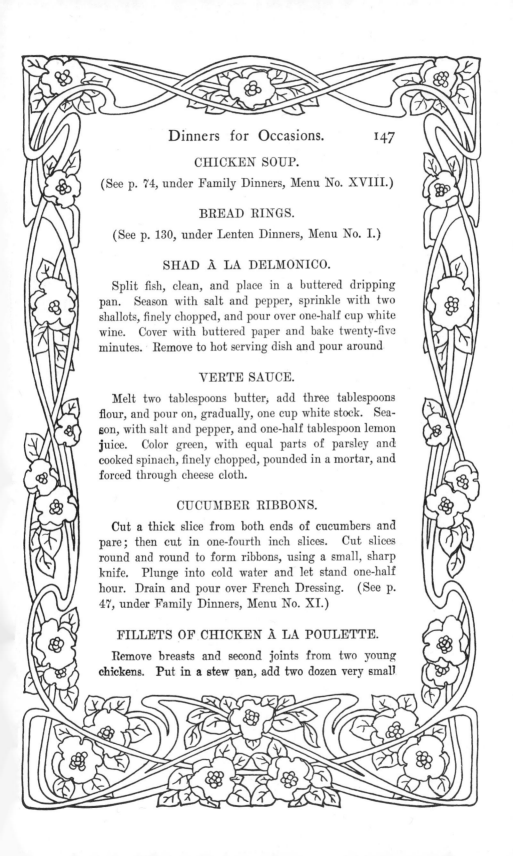

CHICKEN SOUP.

(See p. 74, under Family Dinners, Menu No. XVIII.)

BREAD RINGS.

(See p. 130, under Lenten Dinners, Menu No. I.)

SHAD À LA DELMONICO.

Split fish, clean, and place in a buttered dripping pan. Season with salt and pepper, sprinkle with two shallots, finely chopped, and pour over one-half cup white wine. Cover with buttered paper and bake twenty-five minutes. Remove to hot serving dish and pour around

VERTE SAUCE.

Melt two tablespoons butter, add three tablespoons flour, and pour on, gradually, one cup white stock. Season, with salt and pepper, and one-half tablespoon lemon juice. Color green, with equal parts of parsley and cooked spinach, finely chopped, pounded in a mortar, and forced through cheese cloth.

CUCUMBER RIBBONS.

Cut a thick slice from both ends of cucumbers and pare; then cut in one-fourth inch slices. Cut slices round and round to form ribbons, using a small, sharp knife. Plunge into cold water and let stand one-half hour. Drain and pour over French Dressing. (See p. 47, under Family Dinners, Menu No. XI.)

FILLETS OF CHICKEN À LA POULETTE.

Remove breasts and second joints from two young chickens. Put in a stew pan, add two dozen very small

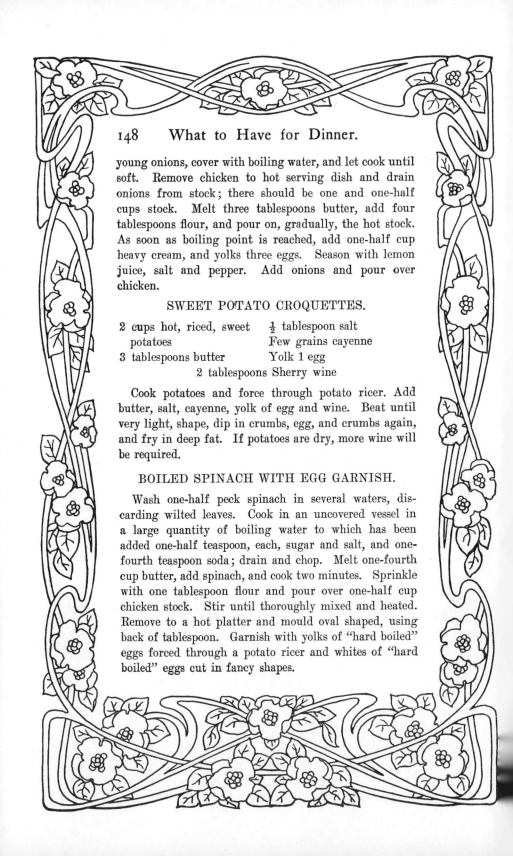

young onions, cover with boiling water, and let cook until
soft. Remove chicken to hot serving dish and drain
onions from stock; there should be one and one-half
cups stock. Melt three tablespoons butter, add four
tablespoons flour, and pour on, gradually, the hot stock.
As soon as boiling point is reached, add one-half cup
heavy cream, and yolks three eggs. Season with lemon
juice, salt and pepper. Add onions and pour over
chicken.

SWEET POTATO CROQUETTES.

2 cups hot, riced, sweet potatoes	$\frac{1}{2}$ tablespoon salt
3 tablespoons butter	Few grains cayenne
	Yolk 1 egg
2 tablespoons Sherry wine	

Cook potatoes and force through potato ricer. Add
butter, salt, cayenne, yolk of egg and wine. Beat until
very light, shape, dip in crumbs, egg, and crumbs again,
and fry in deep fat. If potatoes are dry, more wine will
be required.

BOILED SPINACH WITH EGG GARNISH.

Wash one-half peck spinach in several waters, discarding wilted leaves. Cook in an uncovered vessel in
a large quantity of boiling water to which has been
added one-half teaspoon, each, sugar and salt, and one-
fourth teaspoon soda; drain and chop. Melt one-fourth
cup butter, add spinach, and cook two minutes. Sprinkle
with one tablespoon flour and pour over one-half cup
chicken stock. Stir until thoroughly mixed and heated.
Remove to a hot platter and mould oval shaped, using
back of tablespoon. Garnish with yolks of "hard boiled"
eggs forced through a potato ricer and whites of "hard
boiled" eggs cut in fancy shapes.

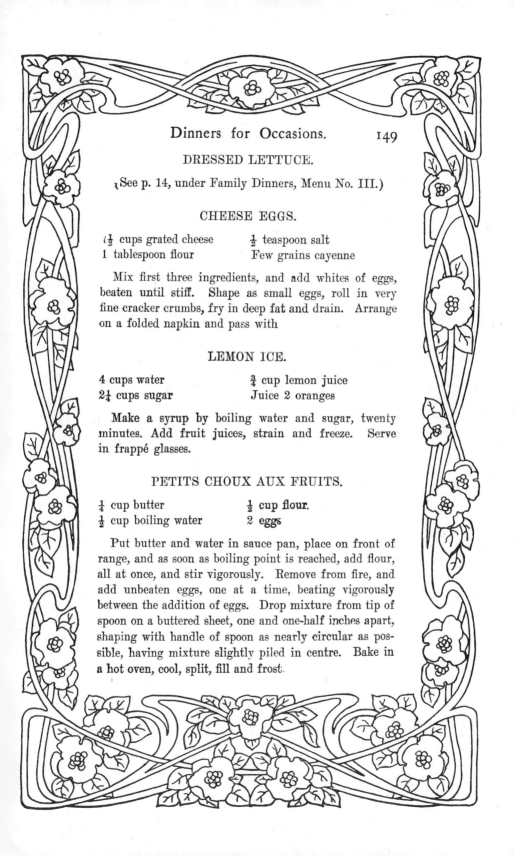

DRESSED LETTUCE.

(See p. 14, under Family Dinners, Menu No. III.)

CHEESE EGGS.

1½ cups grated cheese	½ teaspoon salt
1 tablespoon flour	Few grains cayenne

Mix first three ingredients, and add whites of eggs, beaten until stiff. Shape as small eggs, roll in very fine cracker crumbs, fry in deep fat and drain. Arrange on a folded napkin and pass with

LEMON ICE.

4 cups water	¾ cup lemon juice
2¼ cups sugar	Juice 2 oranges

Make a syrup by boiling water and sugar, twenty minutes. Add fruit juices, strain and freeze. Serve in frappé glasses.

PETITS CHOUX AUX FRUITS.

¼ cup butter	½ cup flour.
½ cup boiling water	2 eggs

Put butter and water in sauce pan, place on front of range, and as soon as boiling point is reached, add flour, all at once, and stir vigorously. Remove from fire, and add unbeaten eggs, one at a time, beating vigorously between the addition of eggs. Drop mixture from tip of spoon on a buttered sheet, one and one-half inches apart, shaping with handle of spoon as nearly circular as possible, having mixture slightly piled in centre. Bake in a hot oven, cool, split, fill and frost.

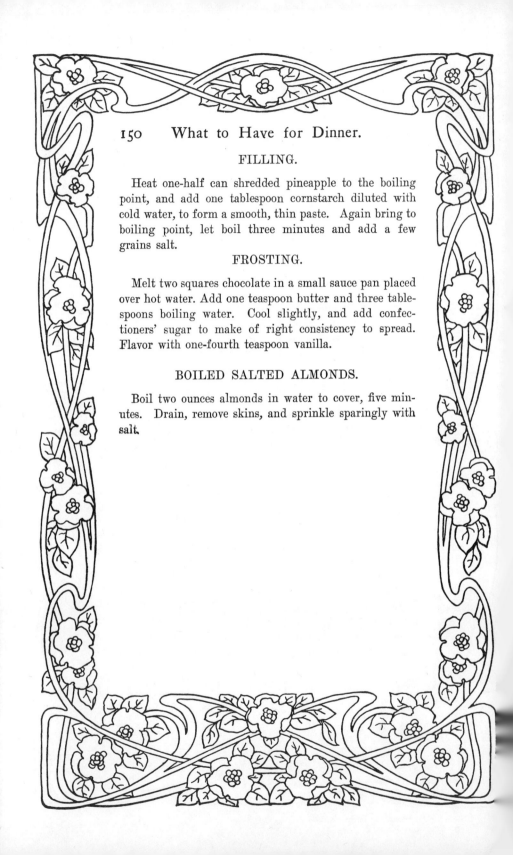

FILLING.

Heat one-half can shredded pineapple to the boiling point, and add one tablespoon cornstarch diluted with cold water, to form a smooth, thin paste. Again bring to boiling point, let boil three minutes and add a few grains salt.

FROSTING.

Melt two squares chocolate in a small sauce pan placed over hot water. Add one teaspoon butter and three tablespoons boiling water. Cool slightly, and add confectioners' sugar to make of right consistency to spread. Flavor with one-fourth teaspoon vanilla.

BOILED SALTED ALMONDS.

Boil two ounces almonds in water to cover, five minutes. Drain, remove skins, and sprinkle sparingly with salt.

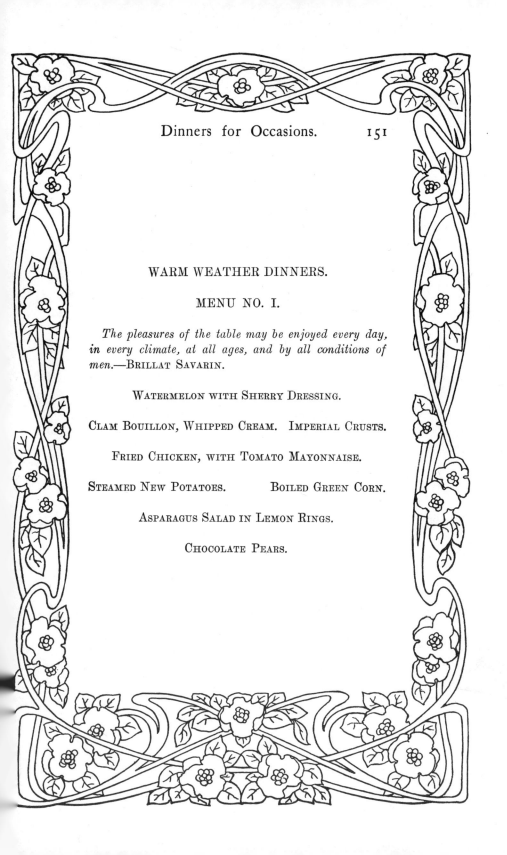

WARM WEATHER DINNERS.

MENU NO. I.

The pleasures of the table may be enjoyed every day, in every climate, at all ages, and by all conditions of men.—BRILLAT SAVARIN.

WATERMELON WITH SHERRY DRESSING.

CLAM BOUILLON, WHIPPED CREAM. IMPERIAL CRUSTS.

FRIED CHICKEN, WITH TOMATO MAYONNAISE.

STEAMED NEW POTATOES.   BOILED GREEN CORN.

ASPARAGUS SALAD IN LEMON RINGS.

CHOCOLATE PEARS.

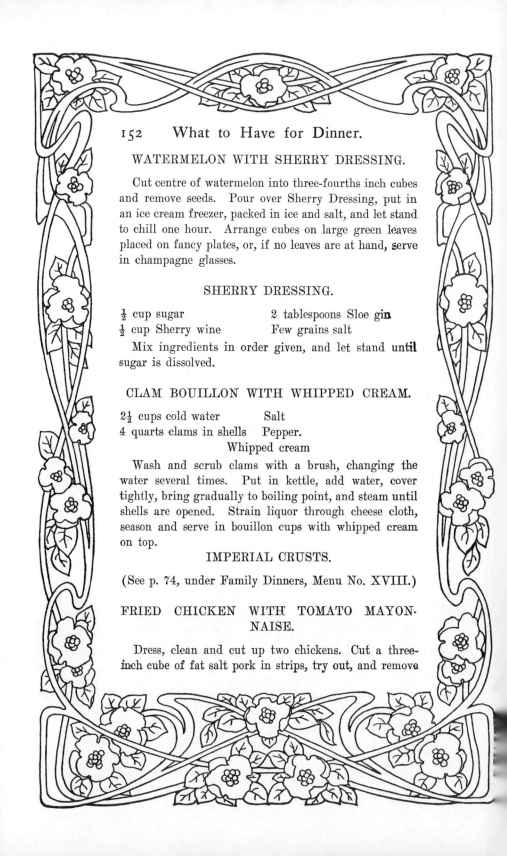

WATERMELON WITH SHERRY DRESSING.

Cut centre of watermelon into three-fourths inch cubes and remove seeds. Pour over Sherry Dressing, put in an ice cream freezer, packed in ice and salt, and let stand to chill one hour. Arrange cubes on large green leaves placed on fancy plates, or, if no leaves are at hand, serve in champagne glasses.

SHERRY DRESSING.

$\frac{1}{2}$ cup sugar	2 tablespoons Sloe gin
$\frac{1}{2}$ cup Sherry wine	Few grains salt

Mix ingredients in order given, and let stand until sugar is dissolved.

CLAM BOUILLON WITH WHIPPED CREAM.

$2\frac{1}{2}$ cups cold water	Salt
4 quarts clams in shells	Pepper.

Whipped cream

Wash and scrub clams with a brush, changing the water several times. Put in kettle, add water, cover tightly, bring gradually to boiling point, and steam until shells are opened. Strain liquor through cheese cloth, season and serve in bouillon cups with whipped cream on top.

IMPERIAL CRUSTS.

(See p. 74, under Family Dinners, Menu No. XVIII.)

FRIED CHICKEN WITH TOMATO MAYON-NAISE.

Dress, clean and cut up two chickens. Cut a three-inch cube of fat salt pork in strips, try out, and remove

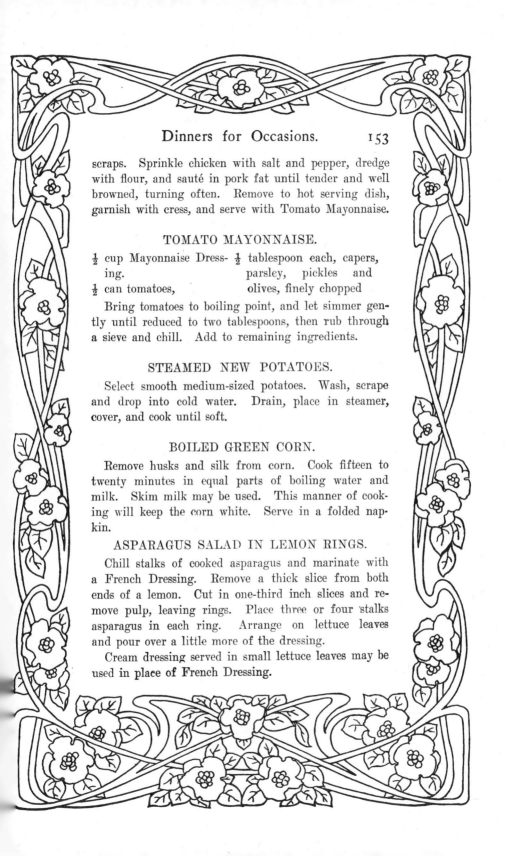

scraps. Sprinkle chicken with salt and pepper, dredge with flour, and sauté in pork fat until tender and well browned, turning often. Remove to hot serving dish, garnish with cress, and serve with Tomato Mayonnaise.

TOMATO MAYONNAISE.

½ cup Mayonnaise Dress-   ½ tablespoon each, capers,
  ing.   parsley, pickles and
½ can tomatoes,   olives, finely chopped

Bring tomatoes to boiling point, and let simmer gently until reduced to two tablespoons, then rub through a sieve and chill. Add to remaining ingredients.

STEAMED NEW POTATOES.

Select smooth medium-sized potatoes. Wash, scrape and drop into cold water. Drain, place in steamer, cover, and cook until soft.

BOILED GREEN CORN.

Remove husks and silk from corn. Cook fifteen to twenty minutes in equal parts of boiling water and milk. Skim milk may be used. This manner of cooking will keep the corn white. Serve in a folded napkin.

ASPARAGUS SALAD IN LEMON RINGS.

Chill stalks of cooked asparagus and marinate with a French Dressing. Remove a thick slice from both ends of a lemon. Cut in one-third inch slices and remove pulp, leaving rings. Place three or four stalks asparagus in each ring. Arrange on lettuce leaves and pour over a little more of the dressing.

Cream dressing served in small lettuce leaves may be used in place of French Dressing.

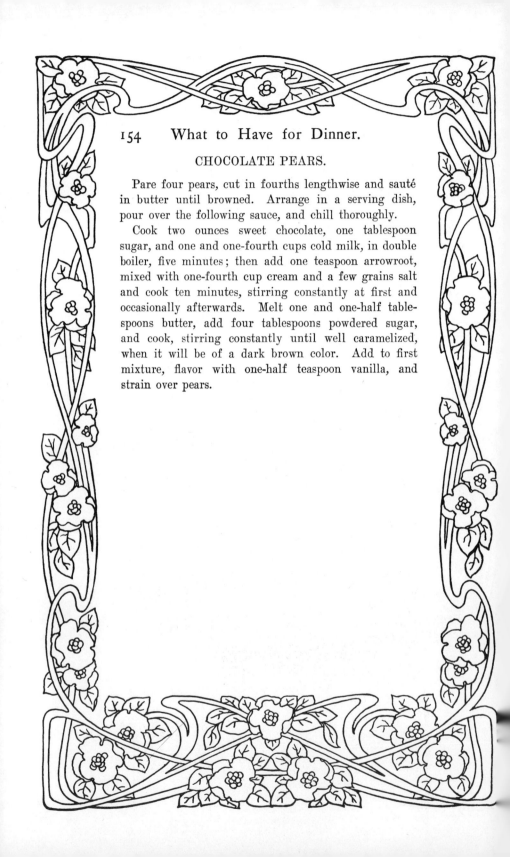

CHOCOLATE PEARS.

Pare four pears, cut in fourths lengthwise and sauté in butter until browned. Arrange in a serving dish, pour over the following sauce, and chill thoroughly.

Cook two ounces sweet chocolate, one tablespoon sugar, and one and one-fourth cups cold milk, in double boiler, five minutes; then add one teaspoon arrowroot, mixed with one-fourth cup cream and a few grains salt and cook ten minutes, stirring constantly at first and occasionally afterwards. Melt one and one-half tablespoons butter, add four tablespoons powdered sugar, and cook, stirring constantly until well caramelized, when it will be of a dark brown color. Add to first mixture, flavor with one-half teaspoon vanilla, and strain over pears.

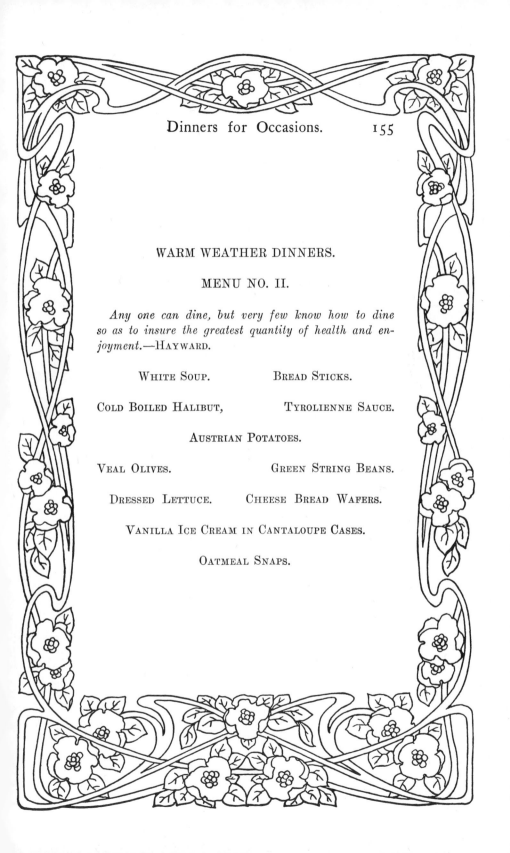

WARM WEATHER DINNERS.

MENU NO. II.

Any one can dine, but very few know how to dine so as to insure the greatest quantity of health and enjoyment.—HAYWARD.

WHITE SOUP.   BREAD STICKS.

COLD BOILED HALIBUT,   TYROLIENNE SAUCE.

AUSTRIAN POTATOES.

VEAL OLIVES.   GREEN STRING BEANS.

DRESSED LETTUCE.   CHEESE BREAD WAFERS.

VANILLA ICE CREAM IN CANTALOUPE CASES.

OATMEAL SNAPS.

WHITE SOUP.

Knuckle of veal	½ tablespoon salt
2 slices turnip	2 tablespoons farina
1 slice carrot	2 quarts cold water
½ tablespoon peppercorns	Yolks 3 eggs
1 onion, sliced	White 1 egg
	2 cups cream

Wipe veal, remove meat and cut in small pieces. Put meat and bone in soup kettle, add turnip, carrot, onion, salt, peppercorns, farina and cold water. Bring slowly to boiling point, and let simmer four hours; then strain and remove fat. Add egg white to egg yolks, beat slightly, and add cream; then add to soup. Heat nearly to boiling point and serve at once.

BREAD STICKS.

(See p. 141, under Easter Dinners, Menu No. I.)

COLD HALIBUT WITH SAUCE TYROLIENNE.

Clean a piece of halibut weighing two and one-half pounds. Steam or boil, remove outside skin and bones, chill and serve cold with

SAUCE TYROLIENNE.

¾ cup Mayonnaise Dressing	1 tablespoon parsley,
1 tablespoon capers, finely	finely chopped
chopped	1 gherkin, finely chopped
	2 tablespoons tomato purée

Mix ingredients in order given.

To obtain tomato purée, cook one-half can tomatoes until reduced to three tablespoons; then rub through a sieve. Chill before adding to Mayonnaise Dressing.

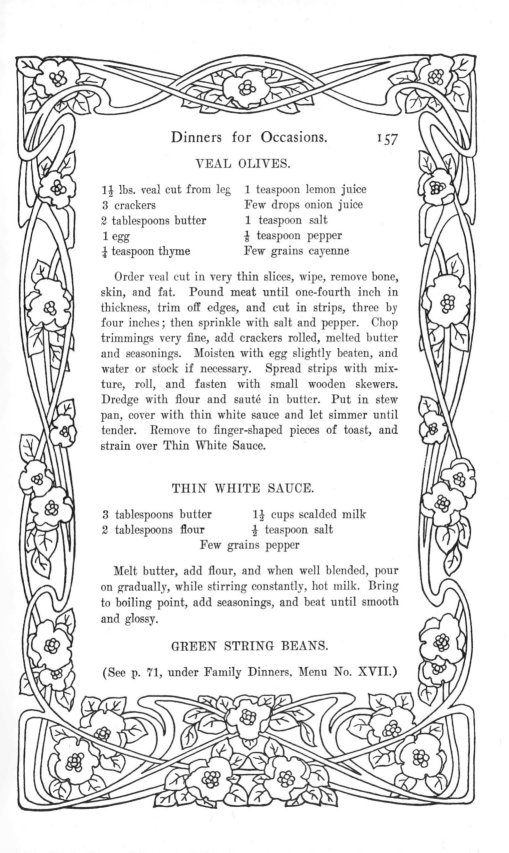

VEAL OLIVES.

1½ lbs. veal cut from leg	1 teaspoon lemon juice
3 crackers	Few drops onion juice
2 tablespoons butter	1 teaspoon salt
1 egg	⅛ teaspoon pepper
¼ teaspoon thyme	Few grains cayenne

Order veal cut in very thin slices, wipe, remove bone, skin, and fat. Pound meat until one-fourth inch in thickness, trim off edges, and cut in strips, three by four inches; then sprinkle with salt and pepper. Chop trimmings very fine, add crackers rolled, melted butter and seasonings. Moisten with egg slightly beaten, and water or stock if necessary. Spread strips with mixture, roll, and fasten with small wooden skewers. Dredge with flour and sauté in butter. Put in stew pan, cover with thin white sauce and let simmer until tender. Remove to finger-shaped pieces of toast, and strain over Thin White Sauce.

THIN WHITE SAUCE.

3 tablespoons butter	1½ cups scalded milk
2 tablespoons flour	½ teaspoon salt
Few grains pepper	

Melt butter, add flour, and when well blended, pour on gradually, while stirring constantly, hot milk. Bring to boiling point, add seasonings, and beat until smooth and glossy.

GREEN STRING BEANS.

(See p. 71, under Family Dinners, Menu No. XVII.)

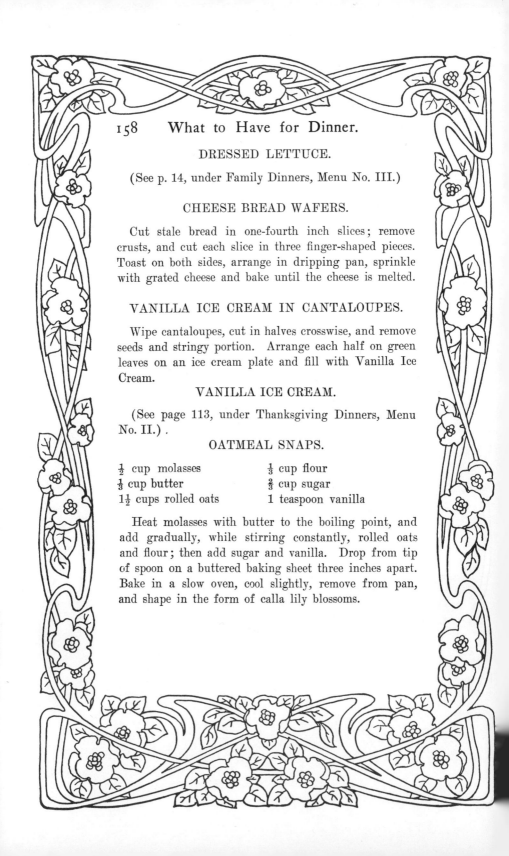

DRESSED LETTUCE.

(See p. 14, under Family Dinners, Menu No. III.)

CHEESE BREAD WAFERS.

Cut stale bread in one-fourth inch slices; remove crusts, and cut each slice in three finger-shaped pieces. Toast on both sides, arrange in dripping pan, sprinkle with grated cheese and bake until the cheese is melted.

VANILLA ICE CREAM IN CANTALOUPES.

Wipe cantaloupes, cut in halves crosswise, and remove seeds and stringy portion. Arrange each half on green leaves on an ice cream plate and fill with Vanilla Ice Cream.

VANILLA ICE CREAM.

(See page 113, under Thanksgiving Dinners, Menu No. II.) .

OATMEAL SNAPS.

$\frac{1}{2}$ cup molasses $\qquad$ $\frac{1}{3}$ cup flour
$\frac{1}{3}$ cup butter $\qquad$ $\frac{2}{3}$ cup sugar
$1\frac{1}{2}$ cups rolled oats $\qquad$ 1 teaspoon vanilla

Heat molasses with butter to the boiling point, and add gradually, while stirring constantly, rolled oats and flour; then add sugar and vanilla. Drop from tip of spoon on a buttered baking sheet three inches apart. Bake in a slow oven, cool slightly, remove from pan, and shape in the form of calla lily blossoms.

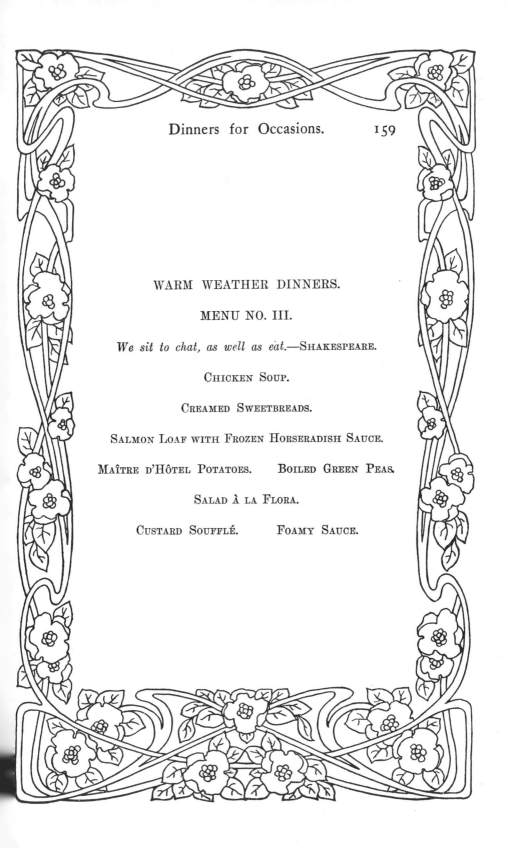

WARM WEATHER DINNERS.

MENU NO. III.

We sit to chat, as well as eat.—SHAKESPEARE.

CHICKEN SOUP.

CREAMED SWEETBREADS.

SALMON LOAF WITH FROZEN HORSERADISH SAUCE.

MAÎTRE D'HÔTEL POTATOES.   BOILED GREEN PEAS,

SALAD À LA FLORA.

CUSTARD SOUFFLÉ.   FOAMY SAUCE.

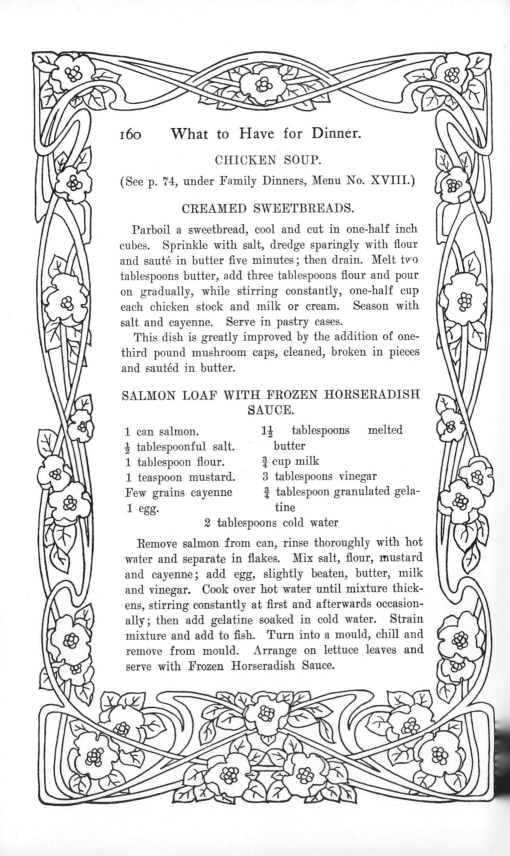

CHICKEN SOUP.

(See p. 74, under Family Dinners, Menu No. XVIII.)

CREAMED SWEETBREADS.

Parboil a sweetbread, cool and cut in one-half inch cubes. Sprinkle with salt, dredge sparingly with flour and sauté in butter five minutes; then drain. Melt two tablespoons butter, add three tablespoons flour and pour on gradually, while stirring constantly, one-half cup each chicken stock and milk or cream. Season with salt and cayenne. Serve in pastry cases.

This dish is greatly improved by the addition of one-third pound mushroom caps, cleaned, broken in pieces and sautéd in butter.

SALMON LOAF WITH FROZEN HORSERADISH SAUCE.

1 can salmon.	$1\frac{1}{2}$ tablespoons melted
$\frac{1}{2}$ tablespoonful salt.	butter
1 tablespoon flour.	$\frac{3}{4}$ cup milk
1 teaspoon mustard.	3 tablespoons vinegar
Few grains cayenne	$\frac{3}{4}$ tablespoon granulated gela-
1 egg.	tine
2 tablespoons cold water	

Remove salmon from can, rinse thoroughly with hot water and separate in flakes. Mix salt, flour, mustard and cayenne; add egg, slightly beaten, butter, milk and vinegar. Cook over hot water until mixture thickens, stirring constantly at first and afterwards occasionally; then add gelatine soaked in cold water. Strain mixture and add to fish. Turn into a mould, chill and remove from mould. Arrange on lettuce leaves and serve with Frozen Horseradish Sauce.

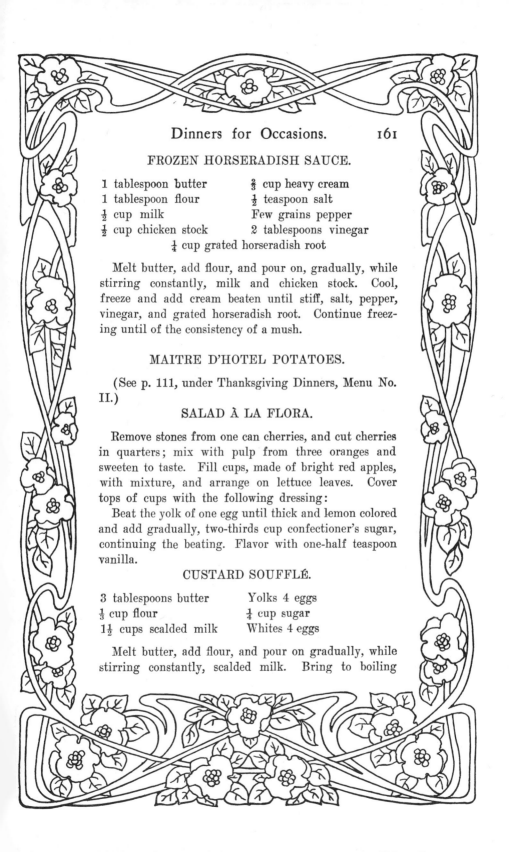

FROZEN HORSERADISH SAUCE.

1 tablespoon butter	⅔ cup heavy cream
1 tablespoon flour	½ teaspoon salt
½ cup milk	Few grains pepper
½ cup chicken stock	2 tablespoons vinegar

¼ cup grated horseradish root

Melt butter, add flour, and pour on, gradually, while stirring constantly, milk and chicken stock. Cool, freeze and add cream beaten until stiff, salt, pepper, vinegar, and grated horseradish root. Continue freezing until of the consistency of a mush.

MAITRE D'HOTEL POTATOES.

(See p. 111, under Thanksgiving Dinners, Menu No. II.)

SALAD À LA FLORA.

Remove stones from one can cherries, and cut cherries in quarters; mix with pulp from three oranges and sweeten to taste. Fill cups, made of bright red apples, with mixture, and arrange on lettuce leaves. Cover tops of cups with the following dressing:

Beat the yolk of one egg until thick and lemon colored and add gradually, two-thirds cup confectioner's sugar, continuing the beating. Flavor with one-half teaspoon vanilla.

CUSTARD SOUFFLÉ.

3 tablespoons butter	Yolks 4 eggs
⅓ cup flour	¼ cup sugar
1½ cups scalded milk	Whites 4 eggs

Melt butter, add flour, and pour on gradually, while stirring constantly, scalded milk. Bring to boiling

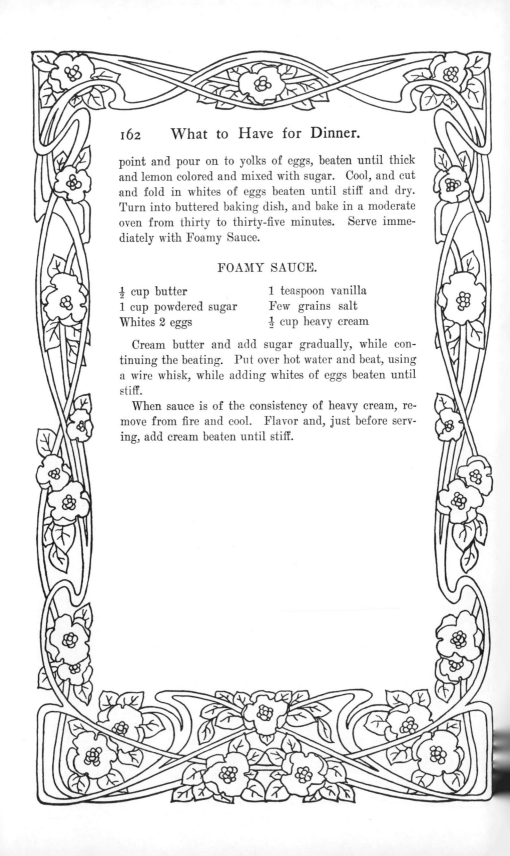

point and pour on to yolks of eggs, beaten until thick and lemon colored and mixed with sugar. Cool, and cut and fold in whites of eggs beaten until stiff and dry. Turn into buttered baking dish, and bake in a moderate oven from thirty to thirty-five minutes. Serve immediately with Foamy Sauce.

FOAMY SAUCE.

$\frac{1}{2}$ cup butter
1 cup powdered sugar
Whites 2 eggs

1 teaspoon vanilla
Few grains salt
$\frac{1}{2}$ cup heavy cream

Cream butter and add sugar gradually, while continuing the beating. Put over hot water and beat, using a wire whisk, while adding whites of eggs beaten until stiff.

When sauce is of the consistency of heavy cream, remove from fire and cool. Flavor and, just before serving, add cream beaten until stiff.

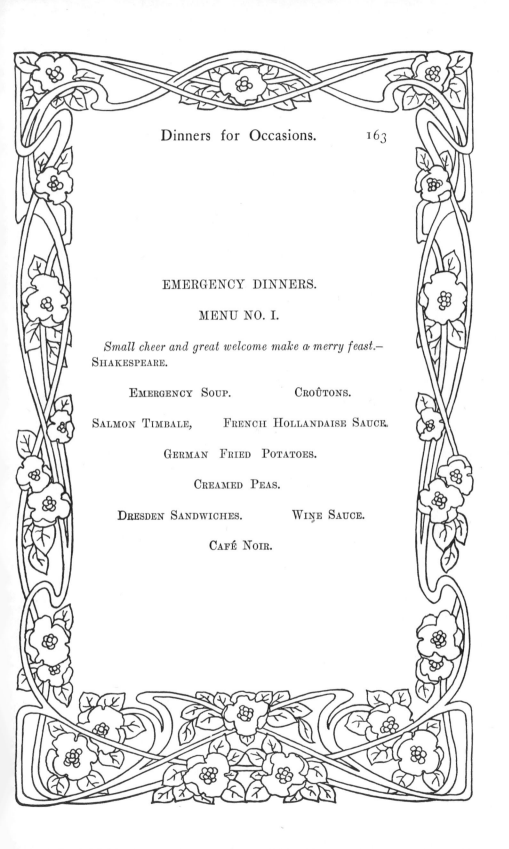

EMERGENCY DINNERS.

MENU NO. I.

Small cheer and great welcome make a merry feast.—
SHAKESPEARE.

EMERGENCY SOUP. CROÛTONS.

SALMON TIMBALE, FRENCH HOLLANDAISE SAUCE.

GERMAN FRIED POTATOES.

CREAMED PEAS.

DRESDEN SANDWICHES. WINE SAUCE.

CAFÉ NOIR.

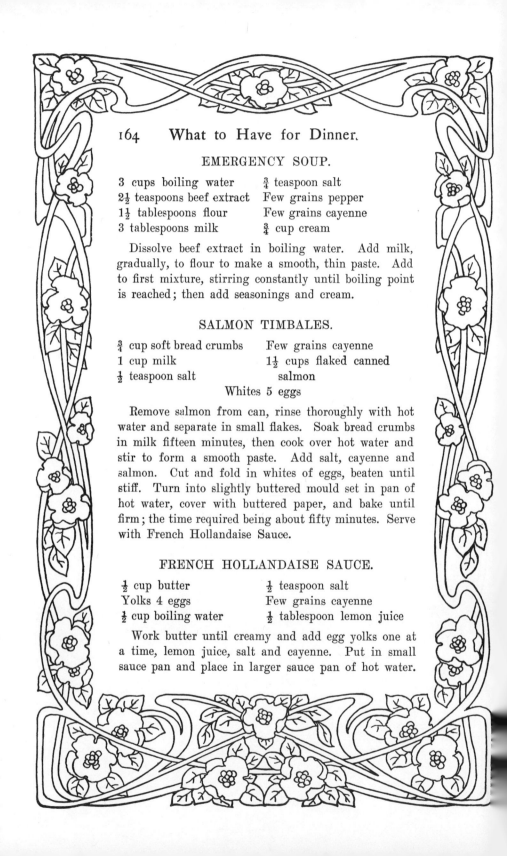

EMERGENCY SOUP.

3 cups boiling water	¾ teaspoon salt
2½ teaspoons beef extract	Few grains pepper
1½ tablespoons flour	Few grains cayenne
3 tablespoons milk	¾ cup cream

Dissolve beef extract in boiling water. Add milk, gradually, to flour to make a smooth, thin paste. Add to first mixture, stirring constantly until boiling point is reached; then add seasonings and cream.

SALMON TIMBALES.

¾ cup soft bread crumbs	Few grains cayenne
1 cup milk	1½ cups flaked canned
½ teaspoon salt	salmon

Whites 5 eggs

Remove salmon from can, rinse thoroughly with hot water and separate in small flakes. Soak bread crumbs in milk fifteen minutes, then cook over hot water and stir to form a smooth paste. Add salt, cayenne and salmon. Cut and fold in whites of eggs, beaten until stiff. Turn into slightly buttered mould set in pan of hot water, cover with buttered paper, and bake until firm; the time required being about fifty minutes. Serve with French Hollandaise Sauce.

FRENCH HOLLANDAISE SAUCE.

½ cup butter	½ teaspoon salt
Yolks 4 eggs	Few grains cayenne
½ cup boiling water	½ tablespoon lemon juice

Work butter until creamy and add egg yolks one at a time, lemon juice, salt and cayenne. Put in small sauce pan and place in larger sauce pan of hot water.

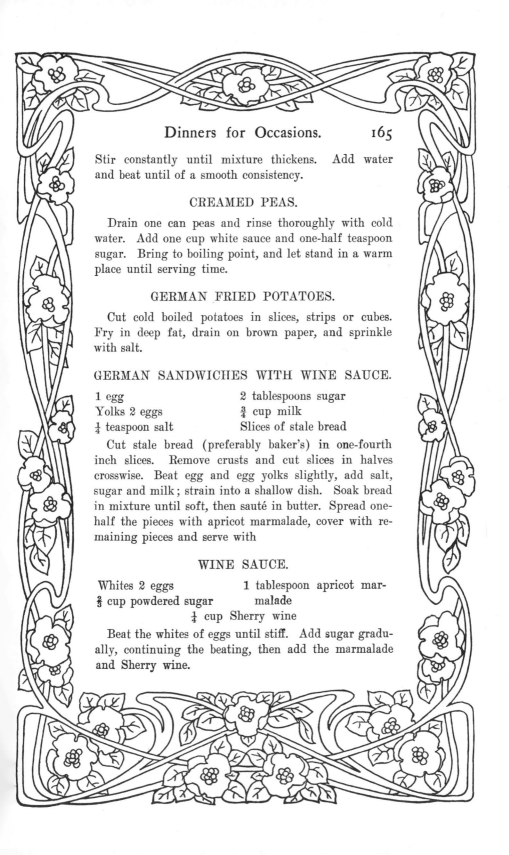

Stir constantly until mixture thickens.   Add water and beat until of a smooth consistency.

CREAMED PEAS.

Drain one can peas and rinse thoroughly with cold water. Add one cup white sauce and one-half teaspoon sugar. Bring to boiling point, and let stand in a warm place until serving time.

GERMAN FRIED POTATOES.

Cut cold boiled potatoes in slices, strips or cubes. Fry in deep fat, drain on brown paper, and sprinkle with salt.

GERMAN SANDWICHES WITH WINE SAUCE.

1 egg	2 tablespoons sugar
Yolks 2 eggs	¾ cup milk
¼ teaspoon salt	Slices of stale bread

Cut stale bread (preferably baker's) in one-fourth inch slices. Remove crusts and cut slices in halves crosswise. Beat egg and egg yolks slightly, add salt, sugar and milk; strain into a shallow dish. Soak bread in mixture until soft, then sauté in butter. Spread one-half the pieces with apricot marmalade, cover with remaining pieces and serve with

WINE SAUCE.

Whites 2 eggs	1 tablespoon apricot mar-
⅔ cup powdered sugar	malade
	¼ cup Sherry wine

Beat the whites of eggs until stiff. Add sugar gradually, continuing the beating, then add the marmalade and Sherry wine.

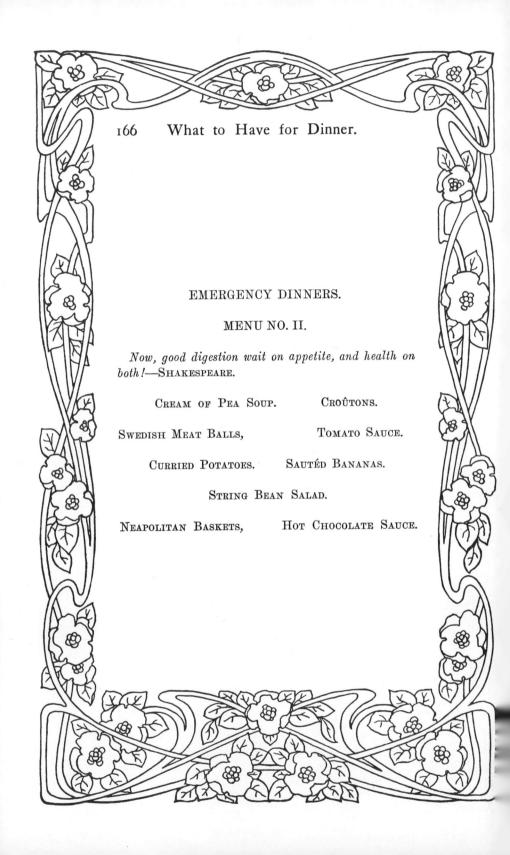

EMERGENCY DINNERS.

MENU NO. II.

Now, good digestion wait on appetite, and health on both!—SHAKESPEARE.

CREAM OF PEA SOUP.   CROÛTONS.

SWEDISH MEAT BALLS,   TOMATO SAUCE.

CURRIED POTATOES.   SAUTÉD BANANAS.

STRING BEAN SALAD.

NEAPOLITAN BASKETS,   HOT CHOCOLATE SAUCE.

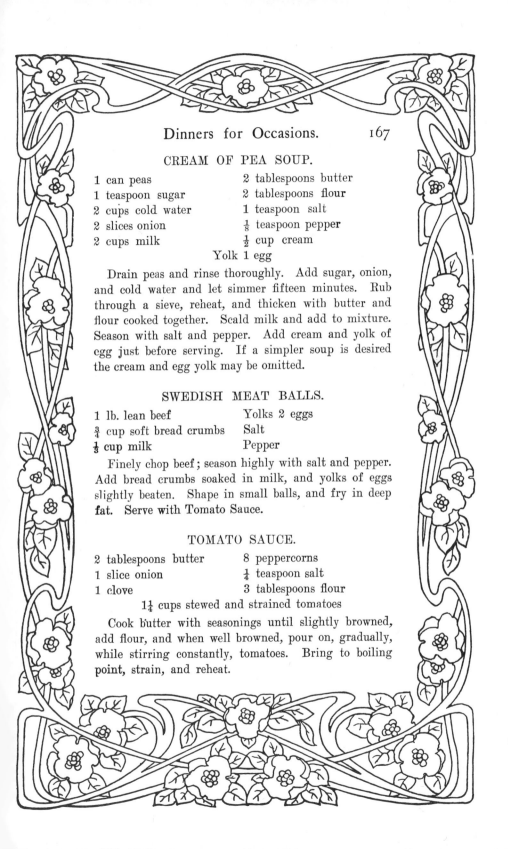

CREAM OF PEA SOUP.

1 can peas	2 tablespoons butter
1 teaspoon sugar	2 tablespoons flour
2 cups cold water	1 teaspoon salt
2 slices onion	$\frac{1}{8}$ teaspoon pepper
2 cups milk	$\frac{1}{2}$ cup cream

Yolk 1 egg

Drain peas and rinse thoroughly. Add sugar, onion, and cold water and let simmer fifteen minutes. Rub through a sieve, reheat, and thicken with butter and flour cooked together. Scald milk and add to mixture. Season with salt and pepper. Add cream and yolk of egg just before serving. If a simpler soup is desired the cream and egg yolk may be omitted.

SWEDISH MEAT BALLS.

1 lb. lean beef	Yolks 2 eggs
$\frac{3}{4}$ cup soft bread crumbs	Salt
$\frac{1}{3}$ cup milk	Pepper

Finely chop beef; season highly with salt and pepper. Add bread crumbs soaked in milk, and yolks of eggs slightly beaten. Shape in small balls, and fry in deep fat. Serve with Tomato Sauce.

TOMATO SAUCE.

2 tablespoons butter	8 peppercorns
1 slice onion	$\frac{1}{4}$ teaspoon salt
1 clove	3 tablespoons flour

$1\frac{1}{4}$ cups stewed and strained tomatoes

Cook butter with seasonings until slightly browned, add flour, and when well browned, pour on, gradually, while stirring constantly, tomatoes. Bring to boiling point, strain, and reheat.

CURRIED POTATOES.

Cook one-fourth cup butter with one small onion, finely chopped, until yellow. Add three cups cold boiled potato cubes and cook until potatoes have absorbed butter; then add one-half tablespoon curry powder, three-fourths teaspoon salt, few grains pepper, few drops lemon juice and one-half cup chicken stock. Cook until potatoes have absorbed stock.

SAUTÉD BANANAS.

Remove skins from bananas, and scrape to remove indigestible fibre. Cut in slices, dip in flour, sauté in butter, and drain on brown paper.

BEAN SALAD.

Remove string beans from can, put in strainer and pour over two quarts cold water. Drain and let stand exposed to the air fifteen minutes. Mix with French Dressing, arrange in salad bowl, sprinkle with finely chopped parsley and garnish with "hard boiled" eggs, cut in fancy shapes.

NEAPOLITAN BASKETS, HOT CHOCOLATE SAUCE.

Yolks 2 eggs	Flour
½ cup sugar	¾ teaspoon baking powder
1½ tablespoons cold water	Few grains salt
¾ tablespoon cornstarch	Whites 2 eggs
	½ teaspoon vanilla

Beat yolks of eggs until thick and lemon colored, and add sugar gradually, continuing the beating; then add

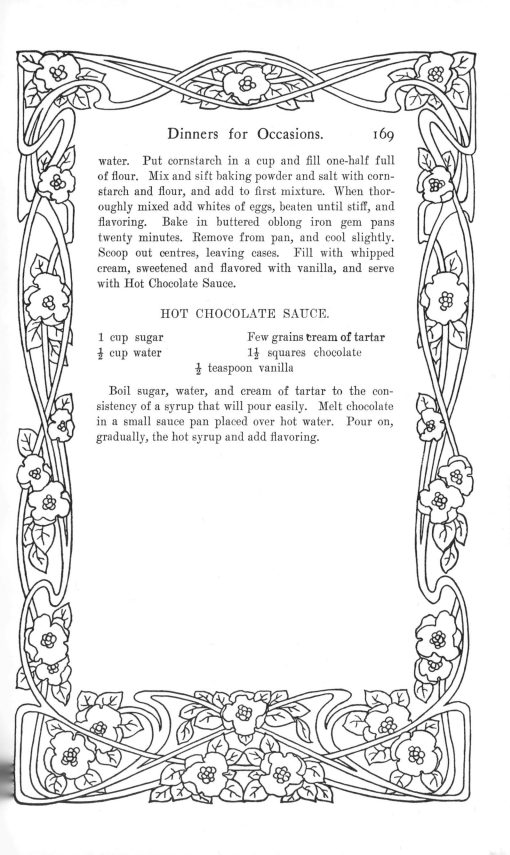

water. Put cornstarch in a cup and fill one-half full of flour. Mix and sift baking powder and salt with cornstarch and flour, and add to first mixture. When thoroughly mixed add whites of eggs, beaten until stiff, and flavoring. Bake in buttered oblong iron gem pans twenty minutes. Remove from pan, and cool slightly. Scoop out centres, leaving cases. Fill with whipped cream, sweetened and flavored with vanilla, and serve with Hot Chocolate Sauce.

HOT CHOCOLATE SAUCE.

1 cup sugar
½ cup water
Few grains cream of tartar
1½ squares chocolate
½ teaspoon vanilla

Boil sugar, water, and cream of tartar to the consistency of a syrup that will pour easily. Melt chocolate in a small sauce pan placed over hot water. Pour on, gradually, the hot syrup and add flavoring.

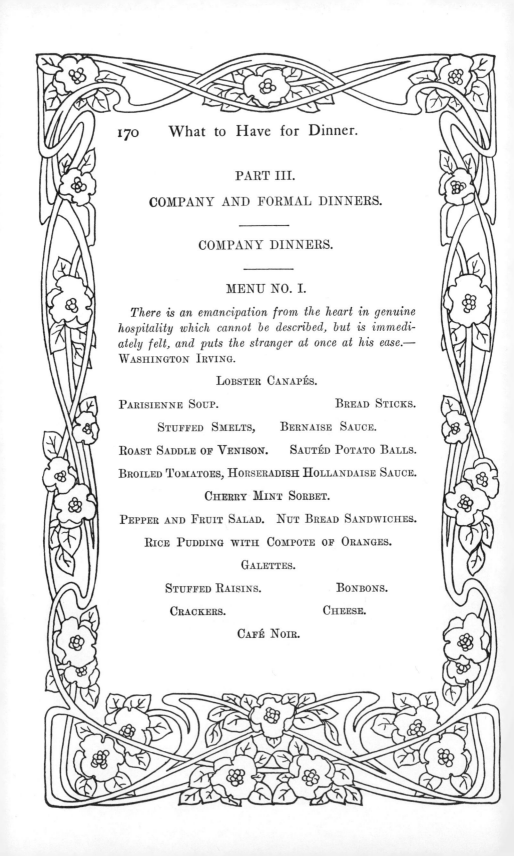

PART III.

COMPANY AND FORMAL DINNERS.

COMPANY DINNERS.

MENU NO. I.

There is an emancipation from the heart in genuine hospitality which cannot be described, but is immediately felt, and puts the stranger at once at his ease.—
WASHINGTON IRVING.

LOBSTER CANAPÉS.

PARISIENNE SOUP.   BREAD STICKS.

STUFFED SMELTS,   BERNAISE SAUCE.

ROAST SADDLE OF VENISON.   SAUTÉD POTATO BALLS.

BROILED TOMATOES, HORSERADISH HOLLANDAISE SAUCE.

CHERRY MINT SORBET.

PEPPER AND FRUIT SALAD.   NUT BREAD SANDWICHES.

RICE PUDDING WITH COMPOTE OF ORANGES.

GALETTES.

STUFFED RAISINS.   BONBONS.

CRACKERS.   CHEESE.

CAFÉ NOIR.

LOBSTER CANAPÉS.

Pound lobster meat in a mortar and add an equal quantity of the yolks of "hard boiled" eggs, mashed and moistened with melted butter. Season highly with salt, cayenne, and French mustard, and moisten with beef extract. Cut stale bread in slices and remove crusts. Cut slices in fancy shapes and sauté in butter until delicately browned. Cool, spread with lobster mixture and garnish with rings cut from whites of "hard boiled" eggs, and finely chopped olives.

PARISIENNE SOUP.

4 lbs. lean beef, cut from round
2 lbs. marrow bone
2 quarts cold water
1 can tomatoes
1 teaspoon peppercorns
1 tablespoon salt
2 tablespoons butter
1 tablespoon lean raw ham, finely chopped
$\frac{1}{3}$ cup, each, carrot, turnip, onion and celery, cut in small pieces.
2 sprigs parsley
$\frac{1}{2}$ bay leaf

Wipe meat and cut in inch cubes. Put one-half in kettle with marrow bone, water and tomatoes. Brown remaining half in hot frying pan with some of the marrow from marrow bone, then turn into kettle. Heat slowly to boiling point, and let simmer five hours. Cook ham and vegetables with butter five minutes, then add to soup with peppercorns, salt, parsley and bay leaf. Cook one and one-half hours, strain, cool quickly, remove fat and clear.

BREAD STICKS.

(See p. 141, under Easter Dinners, Menu No. I.)

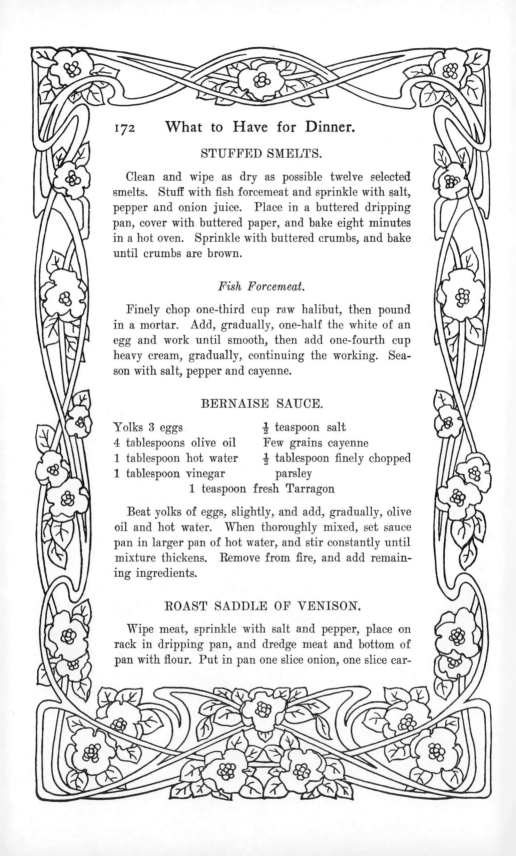

STUFFED SMELTS.

Clean and wipe as dry as possible twelve selected smelts. Stuff with fish forcemeat and sprinkle with salt, pepper and onion juice. Place in a buttered dripping pan, cover with buttered paper, and bake eight minutes in a hot oven. Sprinkle with buttered crumbs, and bake until crumbs are brown.

Fish Forcemeat.

Finely chop one-third cup raw halibut, then pound in a mortar. Add, gradually, one-half the white of an egg and work until smooth, then add one-fourth cup heavy cream, gradually, continuing the working. Season with salt, pepper and cayenne.

BERNAISE SAUCE.

Yolks 3 eggs
4 tablespoons olive oil
1 tablespoon hot water
1 tablespoon vinegar
$\frac{1}{2}$ teaspoon salt
Few grains cayenne
$\frac{1}{2}$ tablespoon finely chopped parsley
1 teaspoon fresh Tarragon

Beat yolks of eggs, slightly, and add, gradually, olive oil and hot water. When thoroughly mixed, set sauce pan in larger pan of hot water, and stir constantly until mixture thickens. Remove from fire, and add remaining ingredients.

ROAST SADDLE OF VENISON.

Wipe meat, sprinkle with salt and pepper, place on rack in dripping pan, and dredge meat and bottom of pan with flour. Put in pan one slice onion, one slice car-

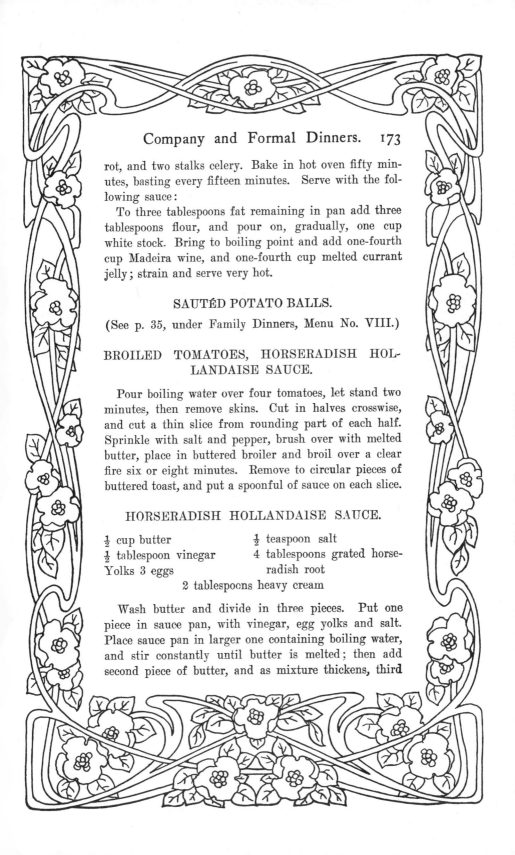

rot, and two stalks celery. Bake in hot oven fifty minutes, basting every fifteen minutes. Serve with the following sauce:

To three tablespoons fat remaining in pan add three tablespoons flour, and pour on, gradually, one cup white stock. Bring to boiling point and add one-fourth cup Madeira wine, and one-fourth cup melted currant jelly; strain and serve very hot.

SAUTÉD POTATO BALLS.

(See p. 35, under Family Dinners, Menu No. VIII.)

BROILED TOMATOES, HORSERADISH HOLLANDAISE SAUCE.

Pour boiling water over four tomatoes, let stand two minutes, then remove skins. Cut in halves crosswise, and cut a thin slice from rounding part of each half. Sprinkle with salt and pepper, brush over with melted butter, place in buttered broiler and broil over a clear fire six or eight minutes. Remove to circular pieces of buttered toast, and put a spoonful of sauce on each slice.

HORSERADISH HOLLANDAISE SAUCE.

½ cup butter	½ teaspoon salt
½ tablespoon vinegar	4 tablespoons grated horse-
Yolks 3 eggs	radish root
2 tablespoons heavy cream	

Wash butter and divide in three pieces. Put one piece in sauce pan, with vinegar, egg yolks and salt. Place sauce pan in larger one containing boiling water, and stir constantly until butter is melted; then add second piece of butter, and as mixture thickens, third piece. Remove from fire, add horseradish root, and cream beaten until stiff.

CHERRY MINT SORBET.

2 cups boiling water	⅔ cup grape fruit juice
⅓ cup mint leaves	¼ cup lemon juice
1 cup sugar	Few grains salt

Bruise mint leaves, pour over boiling water, and let stand ten minutes. Add sugar, and as soon as sugar is dissolved, strain mixture. Cool, add grape fruit juice, lemon juice, and freeze. Serve in champagne glasses and garnish with mint cherries, and a sprig of fresh mint.

PEPPER AND FRUIT SALAD.

Select an equal number of red and green peppers. If long, cut in halves crosswise; if short, cut a slice from stem ends. Remove seeds and arrange on a bed of water-cress, lettuce or chicory, having first a red and then a green pepper. Fill pepper cases with grape fruit pulp, Malaga grapes, skinned and seeded, and English walnut meats broken in pieces, allowing twice as much grape fruit as grapes and nut meats. Moisten with Mayonnaise Dressing. Mask top of each with Mayonnaise Dressing and sprinkle green peppers with chopped green pepper and red peppers with chopped red pepper, and garnish with halves of English walnut meats.

NUT BREAD SANDWICHES.

1 cup scalded milk	1 yeast cake, dissolved in
1 tablespoon butter	¼ cup lukewarm water
1 teaspoon salt	½ cup white flour
2 tablespoons molasses	Entire wheat flour
1 cup pecan nut meats, broken in pieces	

Put butter, salt, and molasses in a large bowl without a lip, and pour on the scalded milk; when lukewarm, add dissolved yeast cake, white flour, two cups entire wheat flour and nuts. Mix and turn on a floured board, leaving a clean bowl; knead, adding more flour until mixture is smooth, elastic to touch, and bubbles may be seen under the surface. Return to bowl, cover with a cloth and board or tin cover. Let rise until a little more than double its bulk, turn on a slightly floured board, and knead. Shape into a loaf, place in greased pan, having pan half full. Cover, let rise again to double its bulk, and bake in a moderate oven fifty to sixty minutes. Cut nut bread twenty-four hours old in very thin slices, and remove crusts. Spread one-half the slices sparingly with butter, cover the remaining pieces and cut in halves crosswise.

RICE PUDDING WITH COMPOTE OF ORANGES.

$\frac{1}{4}$ cup rice	Yolks 3 eggs
1 cup cold water	$\frac{3}{4}$ cup sugar
1$\frac{1}{4}$ cups milk	1 pint heavy cream
	Few grains salt

Wash and pick over rice, add cold water, and cook in double boiler thirty minutes. Drain, return to double boiler, add milk and cook until rice is tender; then rub through a sieve. Beat egg yolks, add sugar and salt and pour on, gradually, the hot rice. Cook until mixture thickens, cool and freeze. Fold in cream beaten until stiff, mould, pack in salt and ice, and let stand two hours.

Peel oranges, cut in slices crosswise, remove seeds, and cook in a thick syrup flavored with lemon juice;

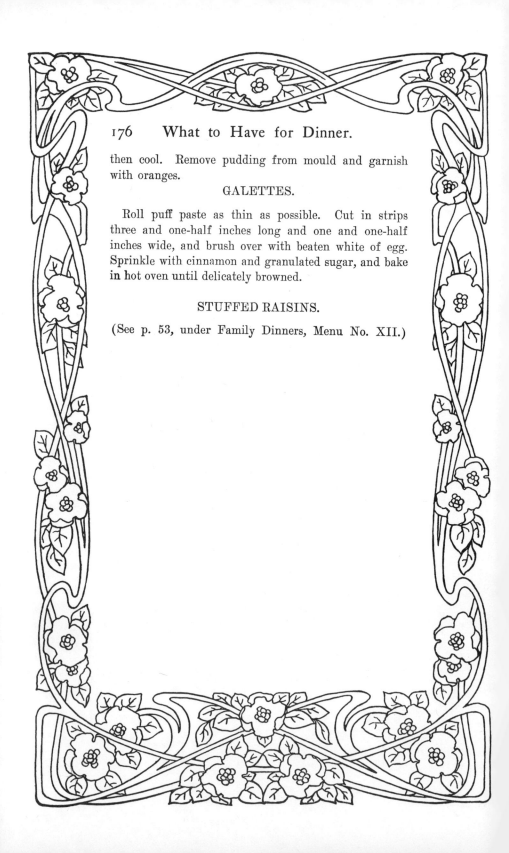

then cool. Remove pudding from mould and garnish with oranges.

GALETTES.

Roll puff paste as thin as possible. Cut in strips three and one-half inches long and one and one-half inches wide, and brush over with beaten white of egg. Sprinkle with cinnamon and granulated sugar, and bake in hot oven until delicately browned.

STUFFED RAISINS.

(See p. 53, under Family Dinners, Menu No. XII.)

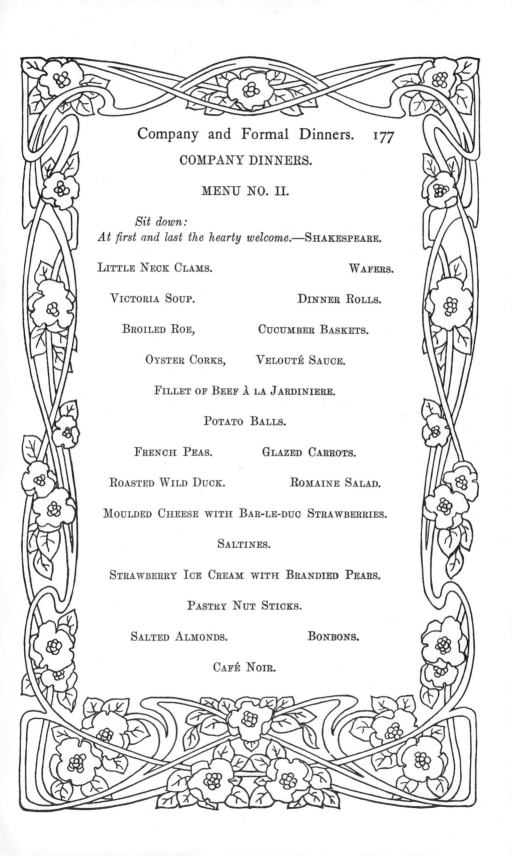

COMPANY DINNERS.

MENU NO. II.

Sit down:
At first and last the hearty welcome.—SHAKESPEARE.

LITTLE NECK CLAMS. WAFERS.

VICTORIA SOUP. DINNER ROLLS.

BROILED ROE, CUCUMBER BASKETS.

OYSTER CORKS, VELOUTÉ SAUCE.

FILLET OF BEEF À LA JARDINIERE.

POTATO BALLS.

FRENCH PEAS. GLAZED CARROTS.

ROASTED WILD DUCK. ROMAINE SALAD.

MOULDED CHEESE WITH BAR-LE-DUC STRAWBERRIES.

SALTINES.

STRAWBERRY ICE CREAM WITH BRANDIED PEARS.

PASTRY NUT STICKS.

SALTED ALMONDS. BONBONS.

CAFÉ NOIR.

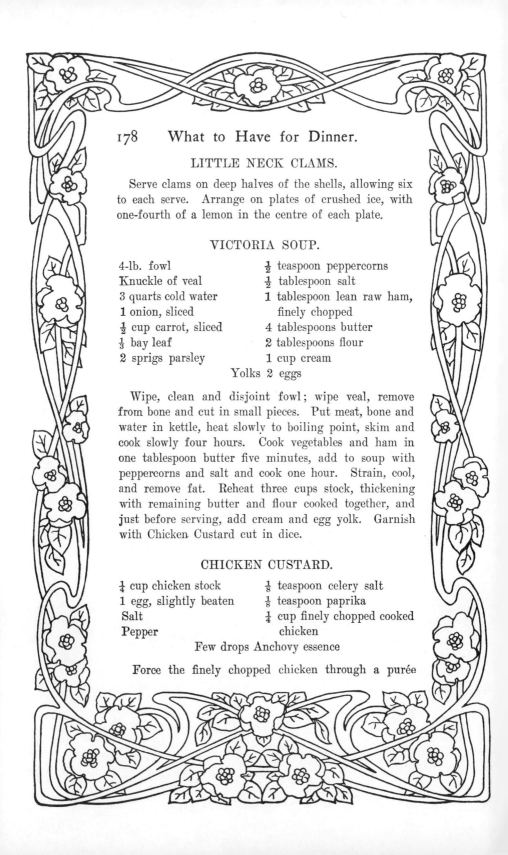

LITTLE NECK CLAMS.

Serve clams on deep halves of the shells, allowing six to each serve. Arrange on plates of crushed ice, with one-fourth of a lemon in the centre of each plate.

VICTORIA SOUP.

4-lb. fowl	$\frac{1}{2}$ teaspoon peppercorns
Knuckle of veal	$\frac{1}{2}$ tablespoon salt
3 quarts cold water	1 tablespoon lean raw ham,
1 onion, sliced	finely chopped
$\frac{1}{2}$ cup carrot, sliced	4 tablespoons butter
$\frac{1}{3}$ bay leaf	2 tablespoons flour
2 sprigs parsley	1 cup cream

Yolks 2 eggs

Wipe, clean and disjoint fowl; wipe veal, remove from bone and cut in small pieces. Put meat, bone and water in kettle, heat slowly to boiling point, skim and cook slowly four hours. Cook vegetables and ham in one tablespoon butter five minutes, add to soup with peppercorns and salt and cook one hour. Strain, cool, and remove fat. Reheat three cups stock, thickening with remaining butter and flour cooked together, and just before serving, add cream and egg yolk. Garnish with Chicken Custard cut in dice.

CHICKEN CUSTARD.

$\frac{1}{4}$ cup chicken stock	$\frac{1}{8}$ teaspoon celery salt
1 egg, slightly beaten	$\frac{1}{8}$ teaspoon paprika
Salt	$\frac{1}{4}$ cup finely chopped cooked
Pepper	chicken

Few drops Anchovy essence

Force the finely chopped chicken through a purée

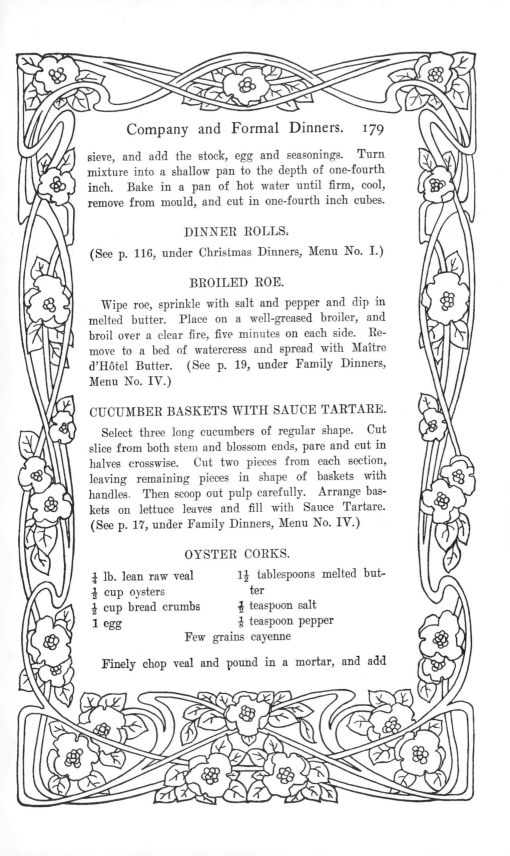

sieve, and add the stock, egg and seasonings. Turn mixture into a shallow pan to the depth of one-fourth inch. Bake in a pan of hot water until firm, cool, remove from mould, and cut in one-fourth inch cubes.

DINNER ROLLS.

(See p. 116, under Christmas Dinners, Menu No. I.)

BROILED ROE.

Wipe roe, sprinkle with salt and pepper and dip in melted butter. Place on a well-greased broiler, and broil over a clear fire, five minutes on each side. Remove to a bed of watercress and spread with Maître d'Hôtel Butter. (See p. 19, under Family Dinners, Menu No. IV.)

CUCUMBER BASKETS WITH SAUCE TARTARE.

Select three long cucumbers of regular shape. Cut slice from both stem and blossom ends, pare and cut in halves crosswise. Cut two pieces from each section, leaving remaining pieces in shape of baskets with handles. Then scoop out pulp carefully. Arrange baskets on lettuce leaves and fill with Sauce Tartare. (See p. 17, under Family Dinners, Menu No. IV.)

OYSTER CORKS.

¼ lb. lean raw veal
½ cup oysters
½ cup bread crumbs
1 egg

1½ tablespoons melted butter
½ teaspoon salt
⅛ teaspoon pepper
Few grains cayenne

Finely chop veal and pound in a mortar, and add

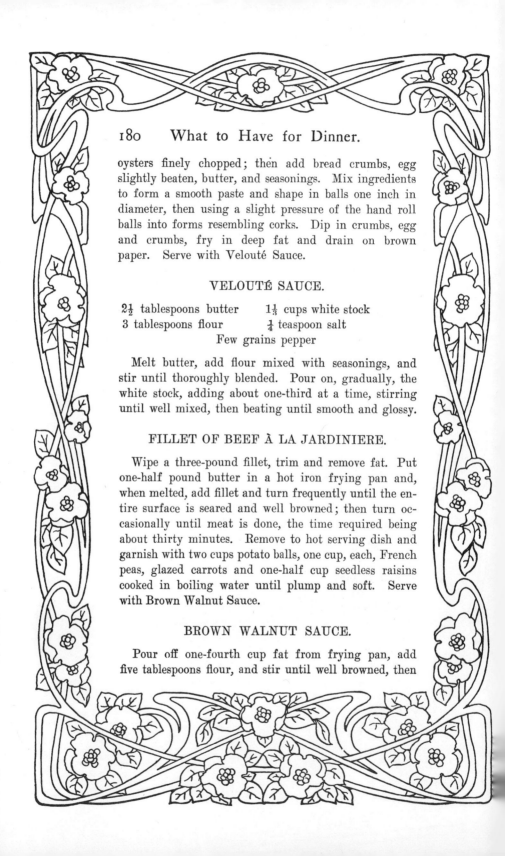

oysters finely chopped; then add bread crumbs, egg
slightly beaten, butter, and seasonings. Mix ingredients
to form a smooth paste and shape in balls one inch in
diameter, then using a slight pressure of the hand roll
balls into forms resembling corks. Dip in crumbs, egg
and crumbs, fry in deep fat and drain on brown
paper. Serve with Velouté Sauce.

VELOUTÉ SAUCE.

2½ tablespoons butter   1⅓ cups white stock
3 tablespoons flour   ¼ teaspoon salt
Few grains pepper

Melt butter, add flour mixed with seasonings, and
stir until thoroughly blended. Pour on, gradually, the
white stock, adding about one-third at a time, stirring
until well mixed, then beating until smooth and glossy.

FILLET OF BEEF À LA JARDINIERE.

Wipe a three-pound fillet, trim and remove fat. Put
one-half pound butter in a hot iron frying pan and,
when melted, add fillet and turn frequently until the entire surface is seared and well browned; then turn occasionally until meat is done, the time required being
about thirty minutes. Remove to hot serving dish and
garnish with two cups potato balls, one cup, each, French
peas, glazed carrots and one-half cup seedless raisins
cooked in boiling water until plump and soft. Serve
with Brown Walnut Sauce.

BROWN WALNUT SAUCE.

Pour off one-fourth cup fat from frying pan, add
five tablespoons flour, and stir until well browned, then

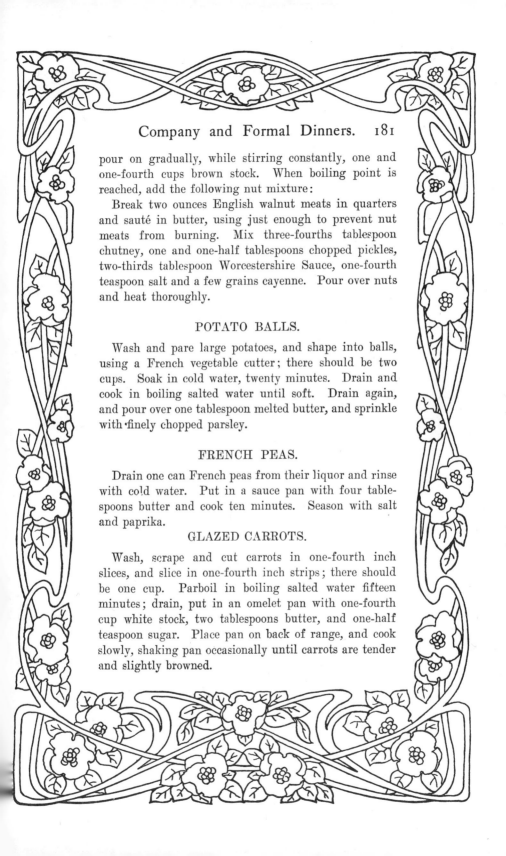

pour on gradually, while stirring constantly, one and one-fourth cups brown stock. When boiling point is reached, add the following nut mixture:

Break two ounces English walnut meats in quarters and sauté in butter, using just enough to prevent nut meats from burning. Mix three-fourths tablespoon chutney, one and one-half tablespoons chopped pickles, two-thirds tablespoon Worcestershire Sauce, one-fourth teaspoon salt and a few grains cayenne. Pour over nuts and heat thoroughly.

POTATO BALLS.

Wash and pare large potatoes, and shape into balls, using a French vegetable cutter; there should be two cups. Soak in cold water, twenty minutes. Drain and cook in boiling salted water until soft. Drain again, and pour over one tablespoon melted butter, and sprinkle with ·finely chopped parsley.

FRENCH PEAS.

Drain one can French peas from their liquor and rinse with cold water. Put in a sauce pan with four table-spoons butter and cook ten minutes. Season with salt and paprika.

GLAZED CARROTS.

Wash, scrape and cut carrots in one-fourth inch slices, and slice in one-fourth inch strips; there should be one cup. Parboil in boiling salted water fifteen minutes; drain, put in an omelet pan with one-fourth cup white stock, two tablespoons butter, and one-half teaspoon sugar. Place pan on back of range, and cook slowly, shaking pan occasionally until carrots are tender and slightly browned.

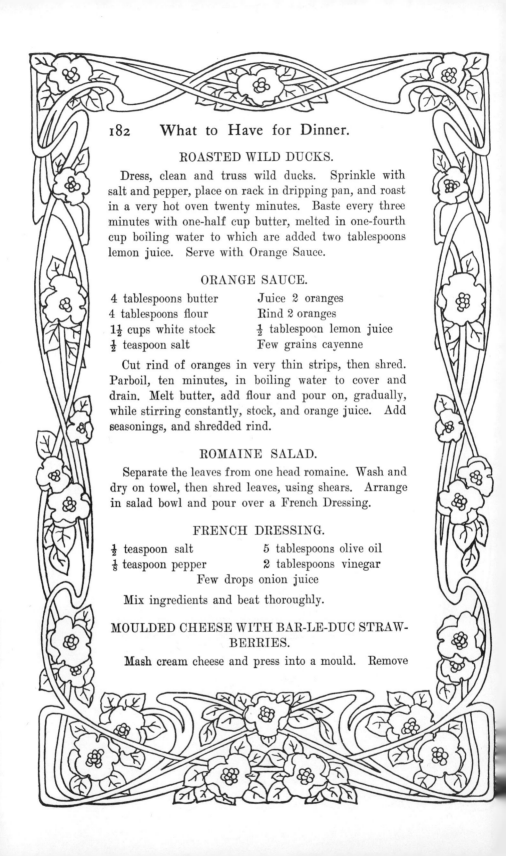

ROASTED WILD DUCKS.

Dress, clean and truss wild ducks. Sprinkle with salt and pepper, place on rack in dripping pan, and roast in a very hot oven twenty minutes. Baste every three minutes with one-half cup butter, melted in one-fourth cup boiling water to which are added two tablespoons lemon juice. Serve with Orange Sauce.

ORANGE SAUCE.

4 tablespoons butter	Juice 2 oranges
4 tablespoons flour	Rind 2 oranges
$1\frac{1}{2}$ cups white stock	$\frac{1}{2}$ tablespoon lemon juice
$\frac{1}{2}$ teaspoon salt	Few grains cayenne

Cut rind of oranges in very thin strips, then shred. Parboil, ten minutes, in boiling water to cover and drain. Melt butter, add flour and pour on, gradually, while stirring constantly, stock, and orange juice. Add seasonings, and shredded rind.

ROMAINE SALAD.

Separate the leaves from one head romaine. Wash and dry on towel, then shred leaves, using shears. Arrange in salad bowl and pour over a French Dressing.

FRENCH DRESSING.

$\frac{1}{2}$ teaspoon salt	5 tablespoons olive oil
$\frac{1}{8}$ teaspoon pepper	2 tablespoons vinegar
Few drops onion juice	

Mix ingredients and beat thoroughly.

MOULDED CHEESE WITH BAR-LE-DUC STRAW-BERRIES.

Mash cream cheese and press into a mould. Remove

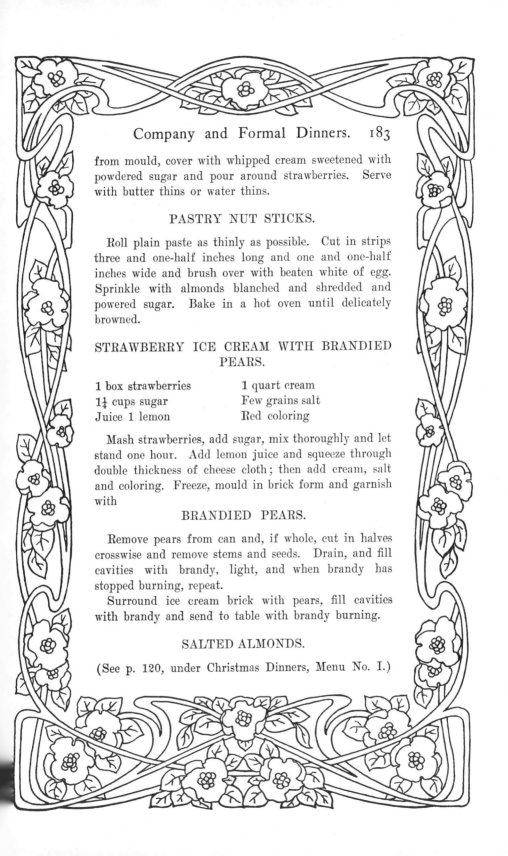

from mould, cover with whipped cream sweetened with powdered sugar and pour around strawberries. Serve with butter thins or water thins.

PASTRY NUT STICKS.

Roll plain paste as thinly as possible. Cut in strips three and one-half inches long and one and one-half inches wide and brush over with beaten white of egg. Sprinkle with almonds blanched and shredded and powered sugar. Bake in a hot oven until delicately browned.

STRAWBERRY ICE CREAM WITH BRANDIED PEARS.

1 box strawberries	1 quart cream
1¼ cups sugar	Few grains salt
Juice 1 lemon	Red coloring

Mash strawberries, add sugar, mix thoroughly and let stand one hour. Add lemon juice and squeeze through double thickness of cheese cloth; then add cream, salt and coloring. Freeze, mould in brick form and garnish with

BRANDIED PEARS.

Remove pears from can and, if whole, cut in halves crosswise and remove stems and seeds. Drain, and fill cavities with brandy, light, and when brandy has stopped burning, repeat.

Surround ice cream brick with pears, fill cavities with brandy and send to table with brandy burning.

SALTED ALMONDS.

(See p. 120, under Christmas Dinners, Menu No. I.)

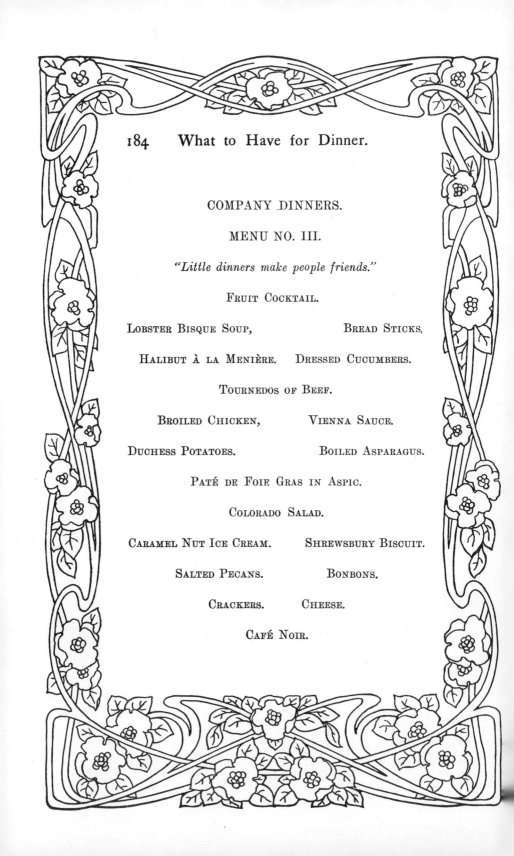

COMPANY DINNERS.

MENU NO. III.

"Little dinners make people friends."

FRUIT COCKTAIL.

LOBSTER BISQUE SOUP,   BREAD STICKS,

HALIBUT À LA MENIÈRE.   DRESSED CUCUMBERS.

TOURNEDOS OF BEEF.

BROILED CHICKEN,   VIENNA SAUCE.

DUCHESS POTATOES.   BOILED ASPARAGUS.

PATÉ DE FOIE GRAS IN ASPIC.

COLORADO SALAD.

CARAMEL NUT ICE CREAM.   SHREWSBURY BISCUIT.

SALTED PECANS.   BONBONS.

CRACKERS.   CHEESE.

CAFÉ NOIR.

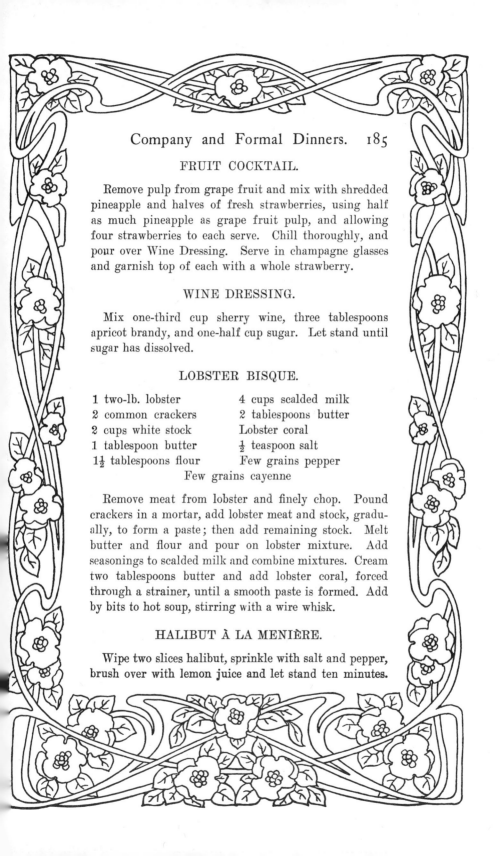

FRUIT COCKTAIL.

Remove pulp from grape fruit and mix with shredded pineapple and halves of fresh strawberries, using half as much pineapple as grape fruit pulp, and allowing four strawberries to each serve. Chill thoroughly, and pour over Wine Dressing. Serve in champagne glasses and garnish top of each with a whole strawberry.

WINE DRESSING.

Mix one-third cup sherry wine, three tablespoons apricot brandy, and one-half cup sugar. Let stand until sugar has dissolved.

LOBSTER BISQUE.

1 two-lb. lobster	4 cups scalded milk
2 common crackers	2 tablespoons butter
2 cups white stock	Lobster coral
1 tablespoon butter	$\frac{1}{2}$ teaspoon salt
1½ tablespoons flour	Few grains pepper
Few grains cayenne	

Remove meat from lobster and finely chop. Pound crackers in a mortar, add lobster meat and stock, gradually, to form a paste; then add remaining stock. Melt butter and flour and pour on lobster mixture. Add seasonings to scalded milk and combine mixtures. Cream two tablespoons butter and add lobster coral, forced through a strainer, until a smooth paste is formed. Add by bits to hot soup, stirring with a wire whisk.

HALIBUT À LA MENIÈRE.

Wipe two slices halibut, sprinkle with salt and pepper, brush over with lemon juice and let stand ten minutes.

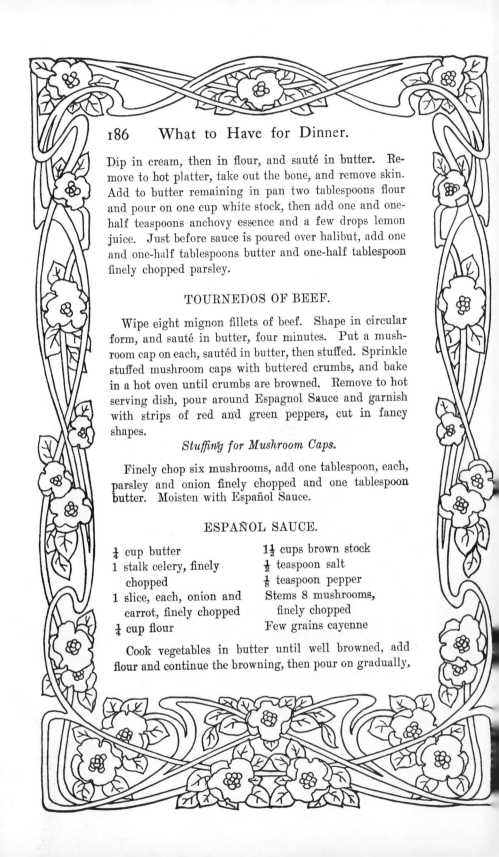

Dip in cream, then in flour, and sauté in butter. Remove to hot platter, take out the bone, and remove skin. Add to butter remaining in pan two tablespoons flour and pour on one cup white stock, then add one and one-half teaspoons anchovy essence and a few drops lemon juice. Just before sauce is poured over halibut, add one and one-half tablespoons butter and one-half tablespoon finely chopped parsley.

TOURNEDOS OF BEEF.

Wipe eight mignon fillets of beef. Shape in circular form, and sauté in butter, four minutes. Put a mushroom cap on each, sautéd in butter, then stuffed. Sprinkle stuffed mushroom caps with buttered crumbs, and bake in a hot oven until crumbs are browned. Remove to hot serving dish, pour around Espagnol Sauce and garnish with strips of red and green peppers, cut in fancy shapes.

Stuffing for Mushroom Caps.

Finely chop six mushrooms, add one tablespoon, each, parsley and onion finely chopped and one tablespoon butter. Moisten with Español Sauce.

ESPAÑOL SAUCE.

$\frac{1}{4}$ cup butter	$1\frac{1}{2}$ cups brown stock
1 stalk celery, finely chopped	$\frac{1}{2}$ teaspoon salt
	$\frac{1}{8}$ teaspoon pepper
1 slice, each, onion and carrot, finely chopped	Stems 8 mushrooms, finely chopped
$\frac{1}{4}$ cup flour	Few grains cayenne

Cook vegetables in butter until well browned, add flour and continue the browning, then pour on gradually,

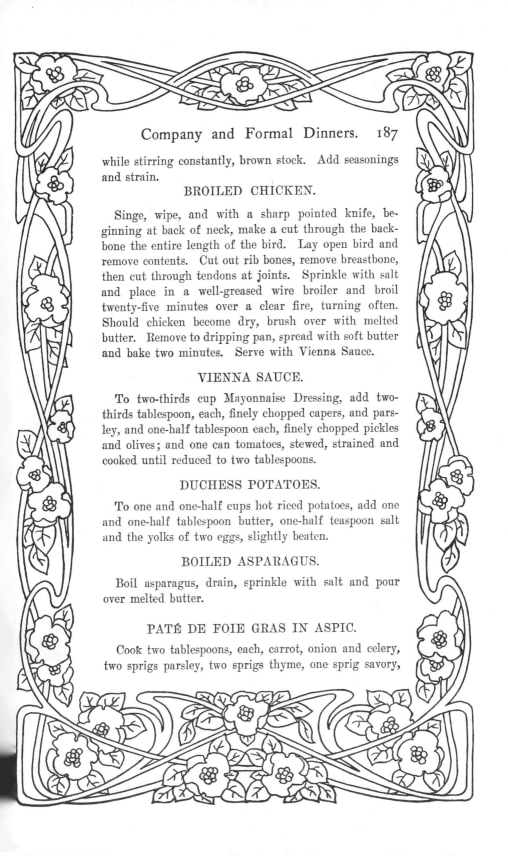

while stirring constantly, brown stock. Add seasonings
and strain.

BROILED CHICKEN.

Singe, wipe, and with a sharp pointed knife, beginning at back of neck, make a cut through the backbone the entire length of the bird. Lay open bird and
remove contents. Cut out rib bones, remove breastbone,
then cut through tendons at joints. Sprinkle with salt
and place in a well-greased wire broiler and broil
twenty-five minutes over a clear fire, turning often.
Should chicken become dry, brush over with melted
butter. Remove to dripping pan, spread with soft butter
and bake two minutes. Serve with Vienna Sauce.

VIENNA SAUCE.

To two-thirds cup Mayonnaise Dressing, add two-
thirds tablespoon, each, finely chopped capers, and parsley, and one-half tablespoon each, finely chopped pickles
and olives; and one can tomatoes, stewed, strained and
cooked until reduced to two tablespoons.

DUCHESS POTATOES.

To one and one-half cups hot riced potatoes, add one
and one-half tablespoon butter, one-half teaspoon salt
and the yolks of two eggs, slightly beaten.

BOILED ASPARAGUS.

Boil asparagus, drain, sprinkle with salt and pour
over melted butter.

PATÉ DE FOIE GRAS IN ASPIC.

Cook two tablespoons, each, carrot, onion and celery,
two sprigs parsley, two sprigs thyme, one sprig savory,

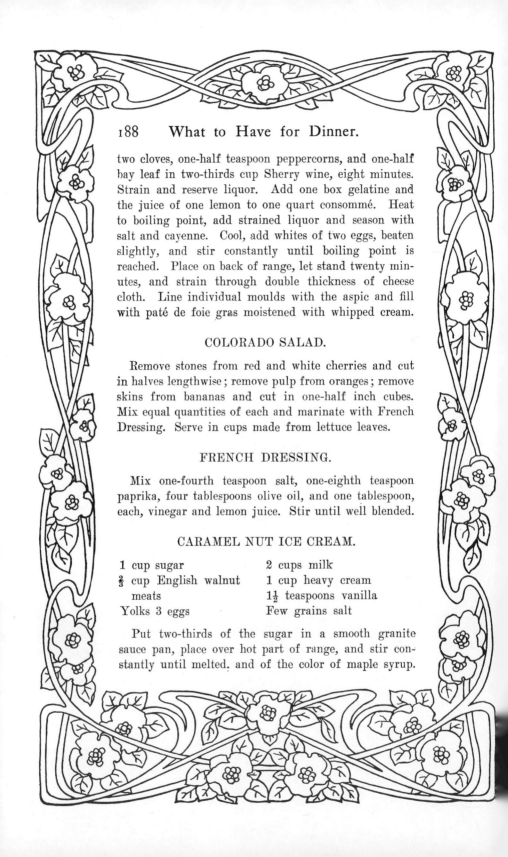

two cloves, one-half teaspoon peppercorns, and one-half bay leaf in two-thirds cup Sherry wine, eight minutes. Strain and reserve liquor. Add one box gelatine and the juice of one lemon to one quart consommé. Heat to boiling point, add strained liquor and season with salt and cayenne. Cool, add whites of two eggs, beaten slightly, and stir constantly until boiling point is reached. Place on back of range, let stand twenty minutes, and strain through double thickness of cheese cloth. Line individual moulds with the aspic and fill with paté de foie gras moistened with whipped cream.

COLORADO SALAD.

Remove stones from red and white cherries and cut in halves lengthwise; remove pulp from oranges; remove skins from bananas and cut in one-half inch cubes. Mix equal quantities of each and marinate with French Dressing. Serve in cups made from lettuce leaves.

FRENCH DRESSING.

Mix one-fourth teaspoon salt, one-eighth teaspoon paprika, four tablespoons olive oil, and one tablespoon, each, vinegar and lemon juice. Stir until well blended.

CARAMEL NUT ICE CREAM.

1 cup sugar	2 cups milk
⅔ cup English walnut meats	1 cup heavy cream
	1½ teaspoons vanilla
Yolks 3 eggs	Few grains salt

Put two-thirds of the sugar in a smooth granite sauce pan, place over hot part of range, and stir constantly until melted, and of the color of maple syrup.

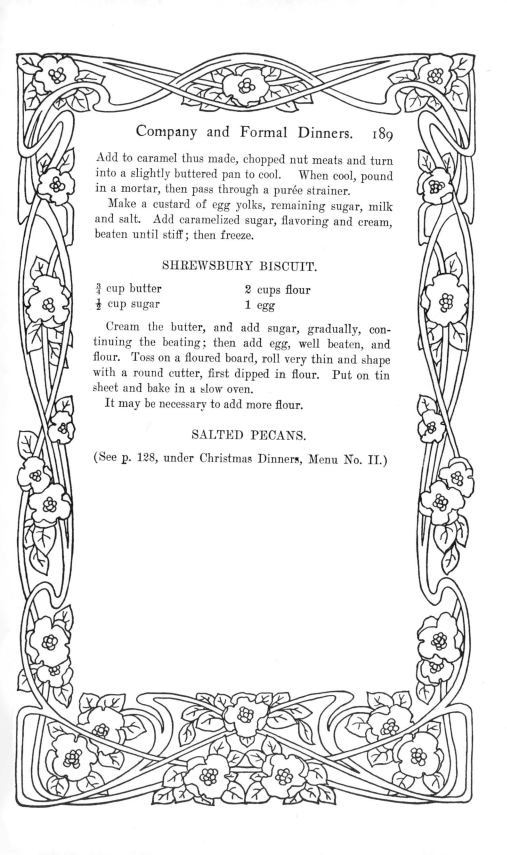

Add to caramel thus made, chopped nut meats and turn into a slightly buttered pan to cool. When cool, pound in a mortar, then pass through a purée strainer.

Make a custard of egg yolks, remaining sugar, milk and salt. Add caramelized sugar, flavoring and cream, beaten until stiff; then freeze.

SHREWSBURY BISCUIT.

¾ cup butter   2 cups flour
½ cup sugar   1 egg

Cream the butter, and add sugar, gradually, continuing the beating; then add egg, well beaten, and flour. Toss on a floured board, roll very thin and shape with a round cutter, first dipped in flour. Put on tin sheet and bake in a slow oven.

It may be necessary to add more flour.

SALTED PECANS.

(See p. 128, under Christmas Dinners, Menu No. II.)

COMPANY DINNERS.

MENU NO. IV.

"Without good company all dainties
Lose their true relish, and like painted grapes,
Are only seen, not tasted."

CAVIARE CANAPÉS.

CONSOMMÉ WITH EGG BALLS.

LOBSTER IN CASES.

SWEETBREADS À LA HUNTINGTON.

ROAST DUCK.   STUFFED APPLES.

FRIED HOMINY.   CREAMED CAULIFLOWER.

CHICORY SALAD.   CHEESE CROQUETTES.

MACAROON ICE CREAM.   SPONGE DROPS.

SALTED ALMONDS.   BONBONS.

CAFÉ NOIR.

CAVIARE CANAPÉS.

Cut stale bread in one-fourth inch slices; then shape
into crescents, using a round cutter. Sauté in butter
until delicately browned, and, when cold, spread with
caviare. Serve each canapé on a fancy plate and garnish with a sprig of watercress.

CONSOMMÉ WITH EGG BALLS.

For consommé, (see p. 122, under Christmas Dinners, Menu No. II.)

EGG BALLS.

2 "hard boiled" eggs	Few grains cayenne
⅓ teaspoon salt	1 teaspoon butter
½ teaspoon parsley, finely chopped	

Chop eggs and rub through a sieve, then add remaining ingredients. Moisten with raw egg yolk to
make of consistency to handle, shape in small balls,
and poach in boiling water or milk.

LOBSTER IN CASES.

1 two-lb. lobster	Few grains cayenne
3 tablespoons butter	2 tablespoons butter
3 tablespoons flour	2 tablespoons Sherry wine
1 cup milk	1 tablespoon brandy
1 teaspoon salt	Yolks 2 eggs
¼ teaspoon pepper	⅓ cup cream
Buttered bread crumbs	

Remove lobster meat from shell, and cut in small
cubes, reserving the coral. Make a white sauce of butter, flour, milk, salt, pepper and cayenne. Melt two

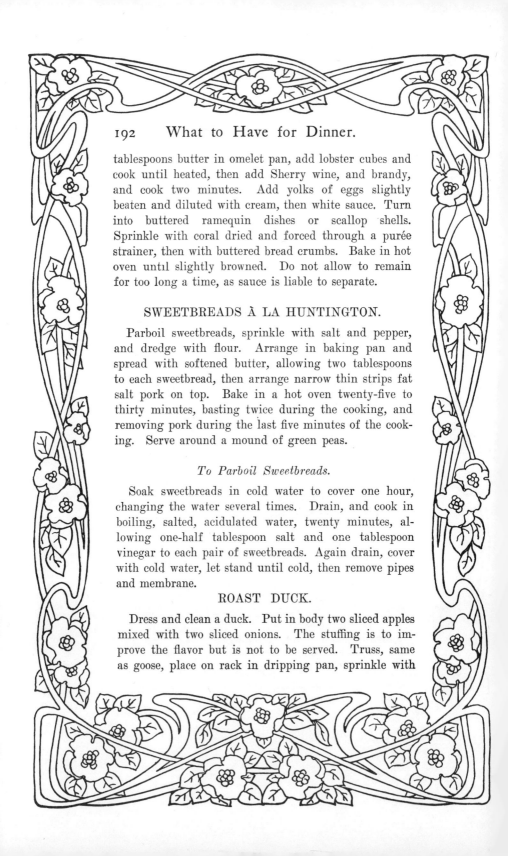

tablespoons butter in omelet pan, add lobster cubes and cook until heated, then add Sherry wine, and brandy, and cook two minutes. Add yolks of eggs slightly beaten and diluted with cream, then white sauce. Turn into buttered ramequin dishes or scallop shells. Sprinkle with coral dried and forced through a purée strainer, then with buttered bread crumbs. Bake in hot oven until slightly browned. Do not allow to remain for too long a time, as sauce is liable to separate.

SWEETBREADS À LA HUNTINGTON.

Parboil sweetbreads, sprinkle with salt and pepper, and dredge with flour. Arrange in baking pan and spread with softened butter, allowing two tablespoons to each sweetbread, then arrange narrow thin strips fat salt pork on top. Bake in a hot oven twenty-five to thirty minutes, basting twice during the cooking, and removing pork during the last five minutes of the cooking. Serve around a mound of green peas.

To Parboil Sweetbreads.

Soak sweetbreads in cold water to cover one hour, changing the water several times. Drain, and cook in boiling, salted, acidulated water, twenty minutes, allowing one-half tablespoon salt and one tablespoon vinegar to each pair of sweetbreads. Again drain, cover with cold water, let stand until cold, then remove pipes and membrane.

ROAST DUCK.

Dress and clean a duck. Put in body two sliced apples mixed with two sliced onions. The stuffing is to improve the flavor but is not to be served. Truss, same as goose, place on rack in dripping pan, sprinkle with

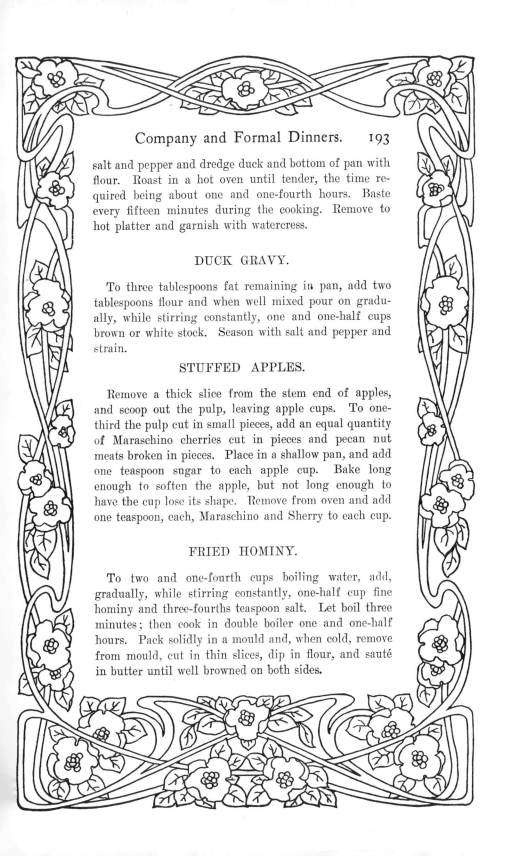

salt and pepper and dredge duck and bottom of pan with flour. Roast in a hot oven until tender, the time required being about one and one-fourth hours. Baste every fifteen minutes during the cooking. Remove to hot platter and garnish with watercress.

DUCK GRAVY.

To three tablespoons fat remaining in pan, add two tablespoons flour and when well mixed pour on gradually, while stirring constantly, one and one-half cups brown or white stock. Season with salt and pepper and strain.

STUFFED APPLES.

Remove a thick slice from the stem end of apples, and scoop out the pulp, leaving apple cups. To one-third the pulp cut in small pieces, add an equal quantity of Maraschino cherries cut in pieces and pecan nut meats broken in pieces. Place in a shallow pan, and add one teaspoon sugar to each apple cup. Bake long enough to soften the apple, but not long enough to have the cup lose its shape. Remove from oven and add one teaspoon, each, Maraschino and Sherry to each cup.

FRIED HOMINY.

To two and one-fourth cups boiling water, add, gradually, while stirring constantly, one-half cup fine hominy and three-fourths teaspoon salt. Let boil three minutes; then cook in double boiler one and one-half hours. Pack solidly in a mould and, when cold, remove from mould, cut in thin slices, dip in flour, and sauté in butter until well browned on both sides.

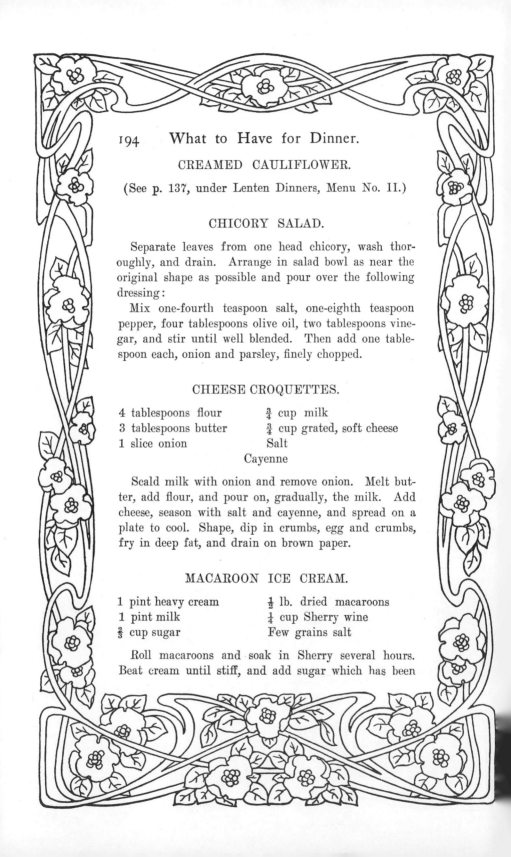

CREAMED CAULIFLOWER.

(See p. 137, under Lenten Dinners, Menu No. II.)

CHICORY SALAD.

Separate leaves from one head chicory, wash thoroughly, and drain. Arrange in salad bowl as near the original shape as possible and pour over the following dressing:

Mix one-fourth teaspoon salt, one-eighth teaspoon pepper, four tablespoons olive oil, two tablespoons vinegar, and stir until well blended. Then add one tablespoon each, onion and parsley, finely chopped.

CHEESE CROQUETTES.

4 tablespoons flour	$\frac{3}{4}$ cup milk
3 tablespoons butter	$\frac{3}{4}$ cup grated, soft cheese
1 slice onion	Salt
	Cayenne

Scald milk with onion and remove onion. Melt butter, add flour, and pour on, gradually, the milk. Add cheese, season with salt and cayenne, and spread on a plate to cool. Shape, dip in crumbs, egg and crumbs, fry in deep fat, and drain on brown paper.

MACAROON ICE CREAM.

1 pint heavy cream	$\frac{1}{2}$ lb. dried macaroons
1 pint milk	$\frac{1}{4}$ cup Sherry wine
$\frac{2}{3}$ cup sugar	Few grains salt

Roll macaroons and soak in Sherry several hours. Beat cream until stiff, and add sugar which has been

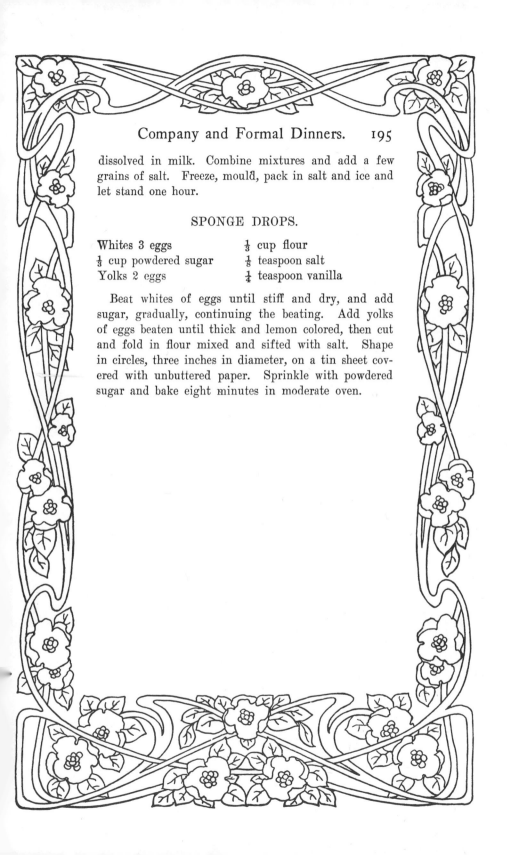

dissolved in milk. Combine mixtures and add a few grains of salt. Freeze, mould, pack in salt and ice and let stand one hour.

SPONGE DROPS.

Whites 3 eggs	⅓ cup flour
⅓ cup powdered sugar	⅛ teaspoon salt
Yolks 2 eggs	¼ teaspoon vanilla

Beat whites of eggs until stiff and dry, and add sugar, gradually, continuing the beating. Add yolks of eggs beaten until thick and lemon colored, then cut and fold in flour mixed and sifted with salt. Shape in circles, three inches in diameter, on a tin sheet covered with unbuttered paper. Sprinkle with powdered sugar and bake eight minutes in moderate oven.

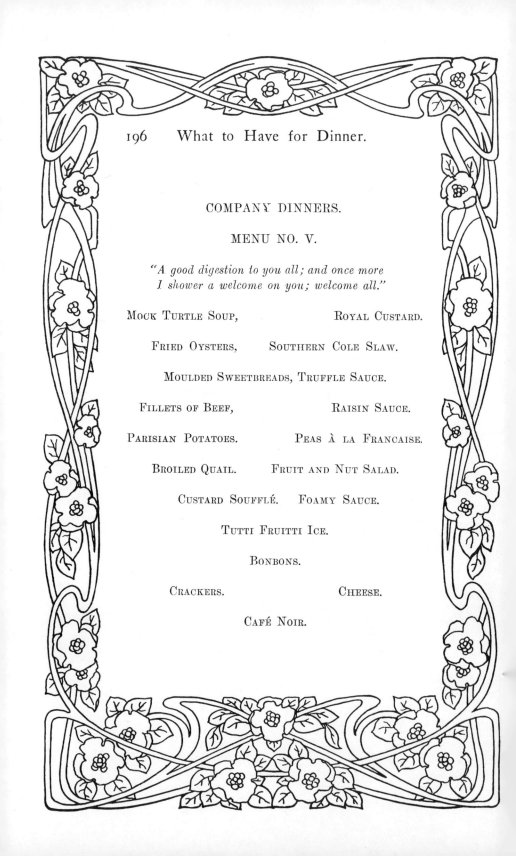

COMPANY DINNERS.

MENU NO. V.

*"A good digestion to you all; and once more
I shower a welcome on you; welcome all."*

MOCK TURTLE SOUP,   ROYAL CUSTARD.

FRIED OYSTERS,   SOUTHERN COLE SLAW.

MOULDED SWEETBREADS, TRUFFLE SAUCE.

FILLETS OF BEEF,   RAISIN SAUCE.

PARISIAN POTATOES.   PEAS À LA FRANCAISE.

BROILED QUAIL.   FRUIT AND NUT SALAD.

CUSTARD SOUFFLÉ. FOAMY SAUCE.

TUTTI FRUITTI ICE.

BONBONS.

CRACKERS.   CHEESE.

CAFÉ NOIR.

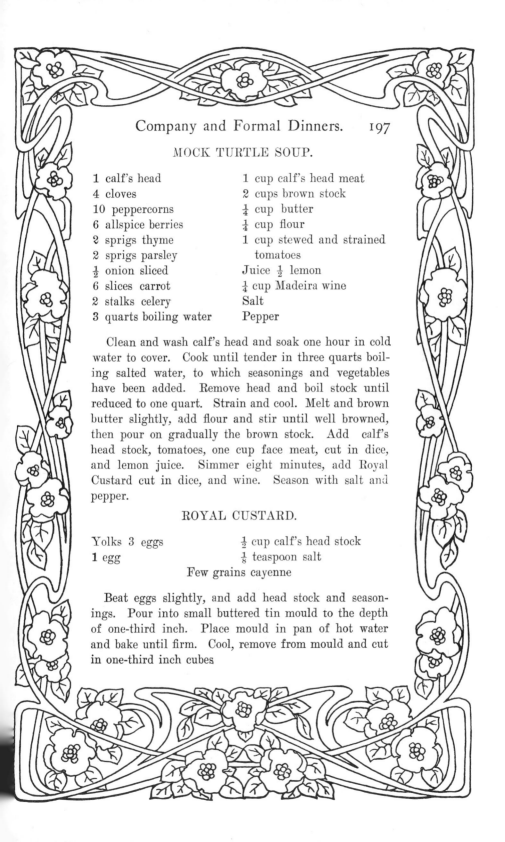

MOCK TURTLE SOUP.

1 calf's head	1 cup calf's head meat
4 cloves	2 cups brown stock
10 peppercorns	$\frac{1}{4}$ cup butter
6 allspice berries	$\frac{1}{4}$ cup flour
2 sprigs thyme	1 cup stewed and strained
2 sprigs parsley	tomatoes
$\frac{1}{2}$ onion sliced	Juice $\frac{1}{2}$ lemon
6 slices carrot	$\frac{1}{4}$ cup Madeira wine
2 stalks celery	Salt
3 quarts boiling water	Pepper

Clean and wash calf's head and soak one hour in cold water to cover. Cook until tender in three quarts boiling salted water, to which seasonings and vegetables have been added. Remove head and boil stock until reduced to one quart. Strain and cool. Melt and brown butter slightly, add flour and stir until well browned, then pour on gradually the brown stock. Add calf's head stock, tomatoes, one cup face meat, cut in dice, and lemon juice. Simmer eight minutes, add Royal Custard cut in dice, and wine. Season with salt and pepper.

ROYAL CUSTARD.

Yolks 3 eggs	$\frac{1}{2}$ cup calf's head stock
1 egg	$\frac{1}{8}$ teaspoon salt
Few grains cayenne	

Beat eggs slightly, and add head stock and seasonings. Pour into small buttered tin mould to the depth of one-third inch. Place mould in pan of hot water and bake until firm. Cool, remove from mould and cut in one-third inch cubes

FRIED OYSTERS.

Wash oysters, parboil in their own liquor; and dry between towels. Dip in fine bread crumbs, seasoned with salt and pepper, egg slightly beaten and diluted with one tablespoon milk, then in crumbs again. Fry in deep fat until well browned, and drain on brown paper. Serve with Southern Cole Slaw.

SOUTHERN COLE SLAW.

1 cup cabbage, finely shredded	1 green pepper, finely chopped
1 cup celery, finely cut	1 teaspoon celery seed
1 red pepper, finely chopped	$\frac{1}{2}$ teaspoon salt
	2 teaspoons sugar

$\frac{1}{4}$ cup vinegar

Mix ingredients in the order given, and serve without cooking.

MOULDED SWEETBREADS.

Parboil a pair of sweetbreads and cut in small cubes. Fold into a chicken forcemeat and turn into a border mould, first decorated with truffles. Set in pan of hot water, cover with buttered paper, and bake until firm. Remove from mould and pour around Truffle Sauce.

Chicken Forcemeat.

Finely chop the breast of an uncooked chicken, pound in a mortar, then rub through a sieve. Add, gradually, the whites of two eggs, and work until smooth. Season highly with salt and paprika; and add heavy cream until of right consistency, which can only be determined by cooking a small ball in boiling salted water. When mix-

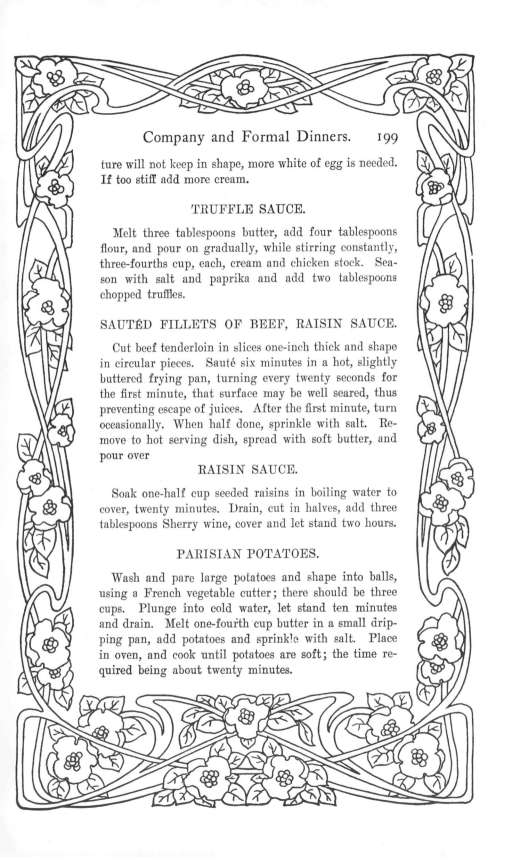

ture will not keep in shape, more white of egg is needed. If too stiff add more cream.

TRUFFLE SAUCE.

Melt three tablespoons butter, add four tablespoons flour, and pour on gradually, while stirring constantly, three-fourths cup, each, cream and chicken stock. Season with salt and paprika and add two tablespoons chopped truffles.

SAUTÉD FILLETS OF BEEF, RAISIN SAUCE.

Cut beef tenderloin in slices one-inch thick and shape in circular pieces. Sauté six minutes in a hot, slightly buttered frying pan, turning every twenty seconds for the first minute, that surface may be well seared, thus preventing escape of juices. After the first minute, turn occasionally. When half done, sprinkle with salt. Remove to hot serving dish, spread with soft butter, and pour over

RAISIN SAUCE.

Soak one-half cup seeded raisins in boiling water to cover, twenty minutes. Drain, cut in halves, add three tablespoons Sherry wine, cover and let stand two hours.

PARISIAN POTATOES.

Wash and pare large potatoes and shape into balls, using a French vegetable cutter; there should be three cups. Plunge into cold water, let stand ten minutes and drain. Melt one-fourth cup butter in a small dripping pan, add potatoes and sprinkle with salt. Place in oven, and cook until potatoes are soft; the time required being about twenty minutes.

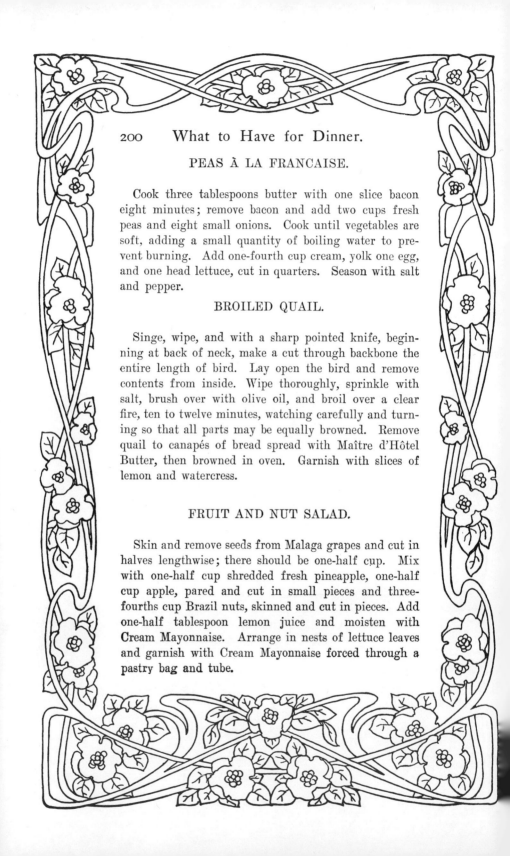

PEAS À LA FRANCAISE.

Cook three tablespoons butter with one slice bacon eight minutes; remove bacon and add two cups fresh peas and eight small onions. Cook until vegetables are soft, adding a small quantity of boiling water to prevent burning. Add one-fourth cup cream, yolk one egg, and one head lettuce, cut in quarters. Season with salt and pepper.

BROILED QUAIL.

Singe, wipe, and with a sharp pointed knife, beginning at back of neck, make a cut through backbone the entire length of bird. Lay open the bird and remove contents from inside. Wipe thoroughly, sprinkle with salt, brush over with olive oil, and broil over a clear fire, ten to twelve minutes, watching carefully and turning so that all parts may be equally browned. Remove quail to canapés of bread spread with Maître d'Hôtel Butter, then browned in oven. Garnish with slices of lemon and watercress.

FRUIT AND NUT SALAD.

Skin and remove seeds from Malaga grapes and cut in halves lengthwise; there should be one-half cup. Mix with one-half cup shredded fresh pineapple, one-half cup apple, pared and cut in small pieces and three-fourths cup Brazil nuts, skinned and cut in pieces. Add one-half tablespoon lemon juice and moisten with Cream Mayonnaise. Arrange in nests of lettuce leaves and garnish with Cream Mayonnaise forced through a pastry bag and tube.

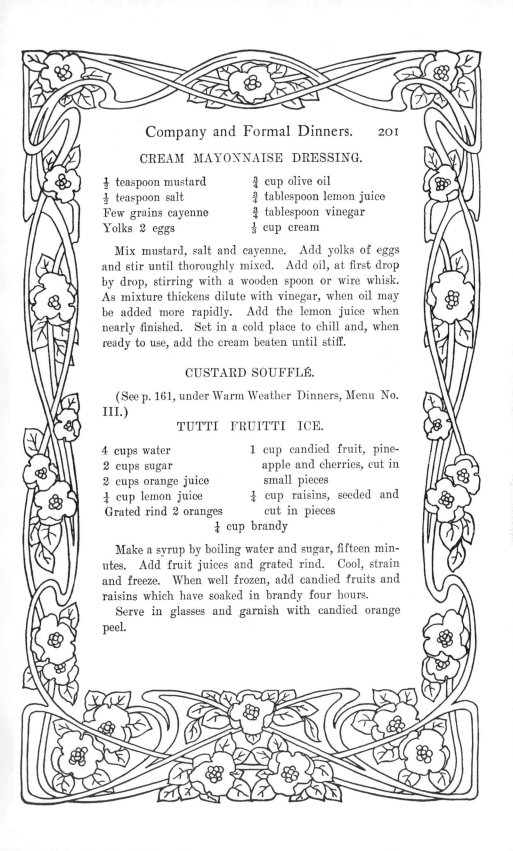

CREAM MAYONNAISE DRESSING.

½ teaspoon mustard
½ teaspoon salt
Few grains cayenne
Yolks 2 eggs

¾ cup olive oil
¾ tablespoon lemon juice
¾ tablespoon vinegar
⅓ cup cream

Mix mustard, salt and cayenne. Add yolks of eggs and stir until thoroughly mixed. Add oil, at first drop by drop, stirring with a wooden spoon or wire whisk. As mixture thickens dilute with vinegar, when oil may be added more rapidly. Add the lemon juice when nearly finished. Set in a cold place to chill and, when ready to use, add the cream beaten until stiff.

CUSTARD SOUFFLÉ.

(See p. 161, under Warm Weather Dinners, Menu No. III.)

TUTTI FRUITTI ICE.

4 cups water
2 cups sugar
2 cups orange juice
¼ cup lemon juice
Grated rind 2 oranges

1 cup candied fruit, pineapple and cherries, cut in
small pieces
¼ cup raisins, seeded and
cut in pieces

¼ cup brandy

Make a syrup by boiling water and sugar, fifteen minutes. Add fruit juices and grated rind. Cool, strain and freeze. When well frozen, add candied fruits and raisins which have soaked in brandy four hours.

Serve in glasses and garnish with candied orange peel.

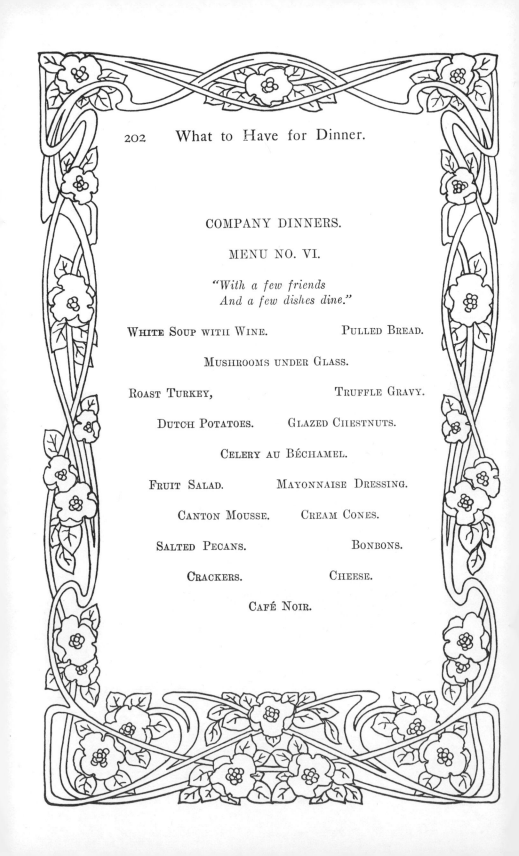

COMPANY DINNERS.

MENU NO. VI.

*"With a few friends
And a few dishes dine."*

WHITE SOUP WITH WINE.   PULLED BREAD.

MUSHROOMS UNDER GLASS.

ROAST TURKEY,   TRUFFLE GRAVY.

DUTCH POTATOES.   GLAZED CHESTNUTS.

CELERY AU BÉCHAMEL.

FRUIT SALAD.   MAYONNAISE DRESSING.

CANTON MOUSSE.   CREAM CONES.

SALTED PECANS.   BONBONS.

CRACKERS.   CHEESE.

CAFÉ NOIR.

WHITE SOUP WITH WINE.

4 lbs. knuckle of veal	1 tablespoon salt
2 quarts cold water	Few grains cayenne
3 slices carrot	$\frac{1}{2}$ teaspoon peppercorns
1 sliced onion	2 tablespoons Sauterne
4 stalks celery	wine
2 sprigs parsley	1 teaspoon beef extract
Bit of bay leaf	1 cup cream

Wipe meat, remove from bone and cut in small pieces. Put meat and bone in soup kettle, cover with water and add carrot, onion, celery, parsley, bay leaf, salt, cayenne, and peppercorns. Bring quickly to boiling point, simmer five hours and strain. Chill, remove fat, reheat, add wine, beef extract and cream. Season with salt and cayenne.

PULLED BREAD.

Cut crusts from a loaf of bread just from the oven. With a fork pull the bread apart into strips five inches long and quite thin. Dry in a slow oven until crisp, taking care bread is only a delicate brown when finished. Serve as an accompaniment to soups.

MUSHROOMS UNDER GLASS.

Cream two tablespoons butter, and add one-half tablespoon lemon juice, one-fourth teaspoon salt, a few grains pepper, and one-half tablespoon finely chopped parsley. Toast a circular piece of bread one-half inch in thickness and five inches in diameter. Spread one-half the mixture on toast, and put buttered side down in baking dish. Pile mushroom caps on toast in conical shape. Dot remaining sauce over mushrooms, and pour over

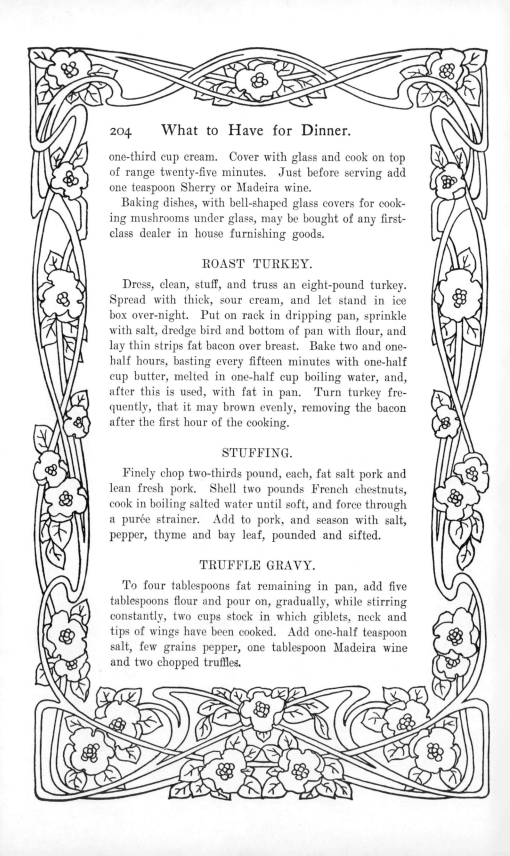

one-third cup cream. Cover with glass and cook on top
of range twenty-five minutes. Just before serving add
one teaspoon Sherry or Madeira wine.

Baking dishes, with bell-shaped glass covers for cooking mushrooms under glass, may be bought of any first-
class dealer in house furnishing goods.

ROAST TURKEY.

Dress, clean, stuff, and truss an eight-pound turkey.
Spread with thick, sour cream, and let stand in ice
box over-night. Put on rack in dripping pan, sprinkle
with salt, dredge bird and bottom of pan with flour, and
lay thin strips fat bacon over breast. Bake two and one-
half hours, basting every fifteen minutes with one-half
cup butter, melted in one-half cup boiling water, and,
after this is used, with fat in pan. Turn turkey frequently, that it may brown evenly, removing the bacon
after the first hour of the cooking.

STUFFING.

Finely chop two-thirds pound, each, fat salt pork and
lean fresh pork. Shell two pounds French chestnuts,
cook in boiling salted water until soft, and force through
a purée strainer. Add to pork, and season with salt,
pepper, thyme and bay leaf, pounded and sifted.

TRUFFLE GRAVY.

To four tablespoons fat remaining in pan, add five
tablespoons flour and pour on, gradually, while stirring
constantly, two cups stock in which giblets, neck and
tips of wings have been cooked. Add one-half teaspoon
salt, few grains pepper, one tablespoon Madeira wine
and two chopped truffles.

DUTCH POTATOES.

Wash and pare eight small potatoes, and soak in cold water, to cover, one-half hour. Drain, put in sauce pan and cover with one quart boiling water to which has been added two tablespoons butter, and one-half tablespoon salt. Cook until soft, and drain. Return to sauce pan, add three tablespoons butter, one tablespoon lemon juice, one-third teaspoon salt and a few grains cayenne. Cook three minutes, shaking pan frequently. Remove to hot serving dish, and sprinkle with one tablespoon finely chopped parsley.

GLAZED CHESTNUTS.

Remove shells from one pint French chestnuts. Put in sauce pan, cover with boiling water, and let boil five minutes. Drain, plunge into cold water, and rub off the dark skins. Return to sauce pan, add one-half cup brown stock, and let simmer gently. Shake sauce pan frequently, allowing chestnuts to cook until soft, when stock will be evaporated.

CELERY AU BÉCHAMEL.

3 cups celery	2 tablespoons flour
1½ cups white stock	½ teaspoon salt
2 tablespoons butter	⅛ teaspoon pepper

Wash, scrape and cut celery in one-inch pieces; there should be three cups. Plunge into boiling water and let boil five minutes. Drain, add white stock, and let simmer thirty minutes or until soft. Melt butter, add flour; and pour on, gradually, the cooked celery. Season with salt and pepper.

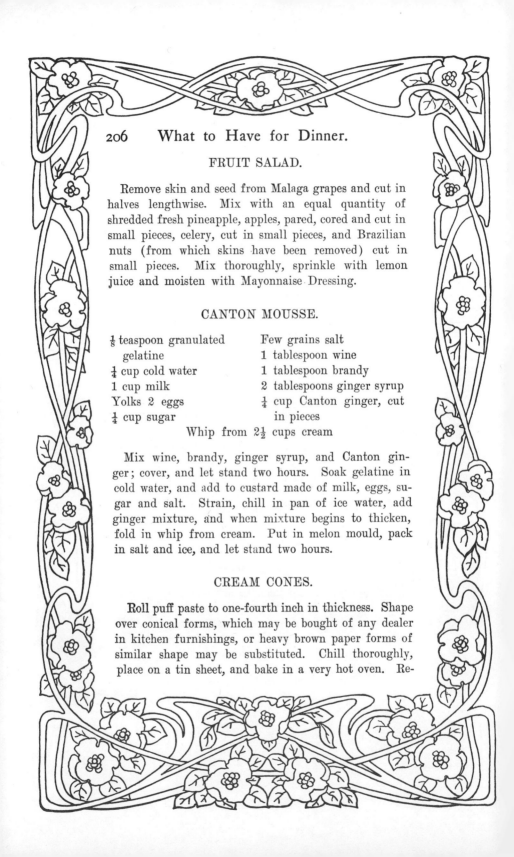

FRUIT SALAD.

Remove skin and seed from Malaga grapes and cut in halves lengthwise. Mix with an equal quantity of shredded fresh pineapple, apples, pared, cored and cut in small pieces, celery, cut in small pieces, and Brazilian nuts (from which skins have been removed) cut in small pieces. Mix thoroughly, sprinkle with lemon juice and moisten with Mayonnaise Dressing.

CANTON MOUSSE.

$\frac{1}{8}$ teaspoon granulated gelatine	Few grains salt
$\frac{1}{4}$ cup cold water	1 tablespoon wine
1 cup milk	1 tablespoon brandy
Yolks 2 eggs	2 tablespoons ginger syrup
$\frac{1}{4}$ cup sugar	$\frac{1}{4}$ cup Canton ginger, cut in pieces

Whip from $2\frac{1}{2}$ cups cream

Mix wine, brandy, ginger syrup, and Canton ginger; cover, and let stand two hours. Soak gelatine in cold water, and add to custard made of milk, eggs, sugar and salt. Strain, chill in pan of ice water, add ginger mixture, and when mixture begins to thicken, fold in whip from cream. Put in melon mould, pack in salt and ice, and let stand two hours.

CREAM CONES.

Roll puff paste to one-fourth inch in thickness. Shape over conical forms, which may be bought of any dealer in kitchen furnishings, or heavy brown paper forms of similar shape may be substituted. Chill thoroughly, place on a tin sheet, and bake in a very hot oven. Re-

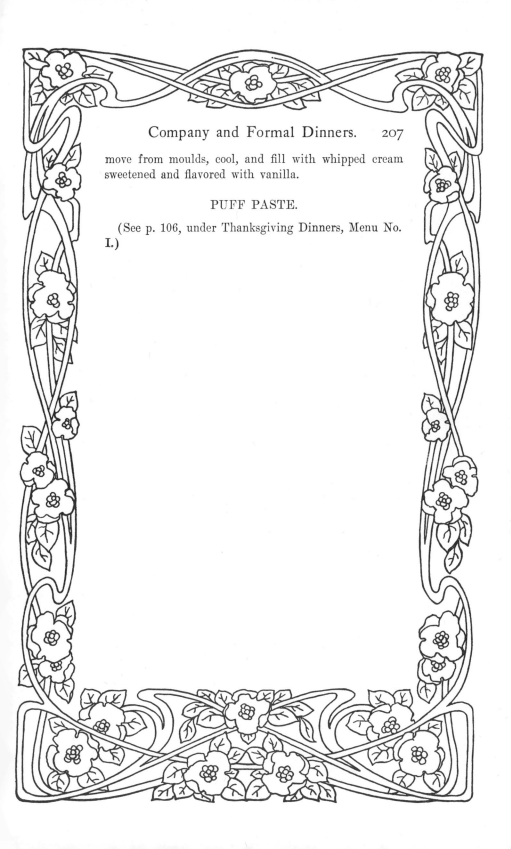

move from moulds, cool, and fill with whipped cream sweetened and flavored with vanilla.

PUFF PASTE.

(See p. 106, under Thanksgiving Dinners, Menu No. I.)

COMPANY DINNERS.

MENU NO. VII.

A well cooked and well served dinner implies on the part of the entertainer a sense of the respect he owes to his guests, whose comfort and happiness he controls while they are under his roof.—DIDSBURY.

ITALIAN SOUP.   IMPERIAL CRUSTS.

OYSTERS AND MUSHROOM PATTIES.

ROAST HAM WITH CIDER SAUCE.

BOILED POTATOES.   SPINACH.

BROWNED SWEETBREADS.

TOMATO AND CUCUMBER BASKETS.

ORANGE CREAM SHERBET.   CHOCOLATE PETITS FOURS.

CRACKERS.   CHEESE.

CAFÉ NOIR.

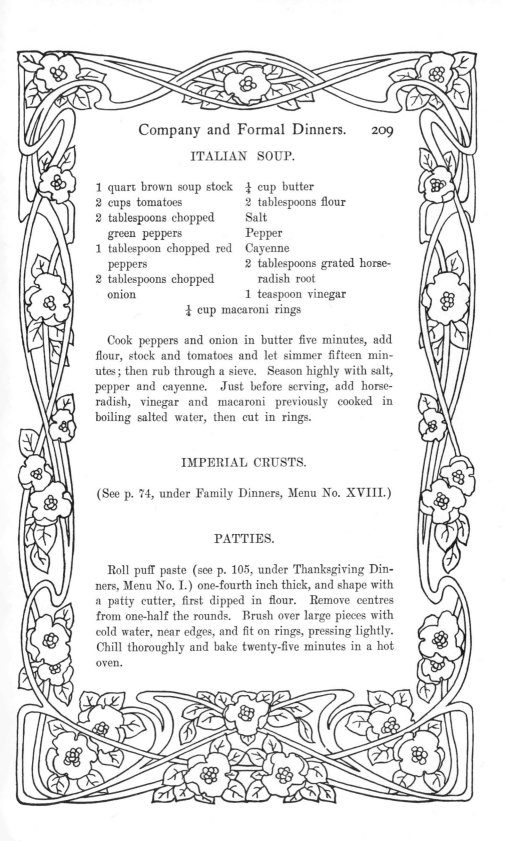

ITALIAN SOUP.

1 quart brown soup stock	¼ cup butter
2 cups tomatoes	2 tablespoons flour
2 tablespoons chopped green peppers	Salt
	Pepper
1 tablespoon chopped red peppers	Cayenne
	2 tablespoons grated horse-radish root
2 tablespoons chopped onion	1 teaspoon vinegar

¼ cup macaroni rings

Cook peppers and onion in butter five minutes, add flour, stock and tomatoes and let simmer fifteen minutes; then rub through a sieve. Season highly with salt, pepper and cayenne. Just before serving, add horse-radish, vinegar and macaroni previously cooked in boiling salted water, then cut in rings.

IMPERIAL CRUSTS.

(See p. 74, under Family Dinners, Menu No. XVIII.)

PATTIES.

Roll puff paste (see p. 105, under Thanksgiving Dinners, Menu No. I.) one-fourth inch thick, and shape with a patty cutter, first dipped in flour. Remove centres from one-half the rounds. Brush over large pieces with cold water, near edges, and fit on rings, pressing lightly. Chill thoroughly and bake twenty-five minutes in a hot oven.

OYSTERS AND MUSHROOMS

(For Patty Fillings).

1 pint oysters	1 cup oyster liquor
1 cup mushroom caps, broken in pieces	½ cup brown stock
¼ cup butter	½ teaspoon salt
¼ cup flour	⅛ teaspoon pepper
	Few grains cayenne

1 tablespoon Sherry wine

Parboil oysters, drain, reserve liquor and strain; there should be one cup. Brown, butter, add flour and cook until well browned; then pour on, gradually, oyster liquor and stock. Add oysters, mushroom caps and seasonings.

ROAST HAM WITH CIDER SAUCE.

Soak a twelve-pound ham several hours, or over-night, in cold water to cover. Wash thoroughly, scrape and trim off hard skin near end of bone. Put in a kettle with one-half cup each, sliced onion and carrot, two sprigs parsley, one-half bay leaf, four cloves, and five peppercorns. Cover with cold water, bring slowly to boiling point, and let simmer until tender, the time required being about four hours. After two hours of the cooking, add one quart cider. Allow ham to cool in liquor. Remove from liquor, take off skin, sprinkle with sugar and fine bread crumbs. Put dashes of paprika over ham, about every two inches, and insert a clove in centre of each dash. Bake one hour in a slow oven. Serve hot with

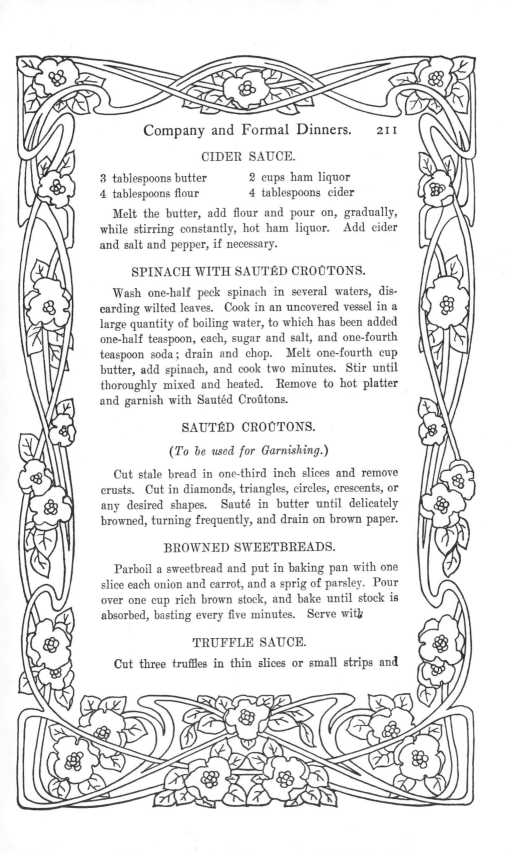

CIDER SAUCE.

3 tablespoons butter	2 cups ham liquor
4 tablespoons flour	4 tablespoons cider

Melt the butter, add flour and pour on, gradually, while stirring constantly, hot ham liquor. Add cider and salt and pepper, if necessary.

SPINACH WITH SAUTÉD CROÛTONS.

Wash one-half peck spinach in several waters, discarding wilted leaves. Cook in an uncovered vessel in a large quantity of boiling water, to which has been added one-half teaspoon, each, sugar and salt, and one-fourth teaspoon soda; drain and chop. Melt one-fourth cup butter, add spinach, and cook two minutes. Stir until thoroughly mixed and heated. Remove to hot platter and garnish with Sautéd Croûtons.

SAUTÉD CROÛTONS.

(*To be used for Garnishing.*)

Cut stale bread in one-third inch slices and remove crusts. Cut in diamonds, triangles, circles, crescents, or any desired shapes. Sauté in butter until delicately browned, turning frequently, and drain on brown paper.

BROWNED SWEETBREADS.

Parboil a sweetbread and put in baking pan with one slice each onion and carrot, and a sprig of parsley. Pour over one cup rich brown stock, and bake until stock is absorbed, basting every five minutes. Serve with

TRUFFLE SAUCE.

Cut three truffles in thin slices or small strips and

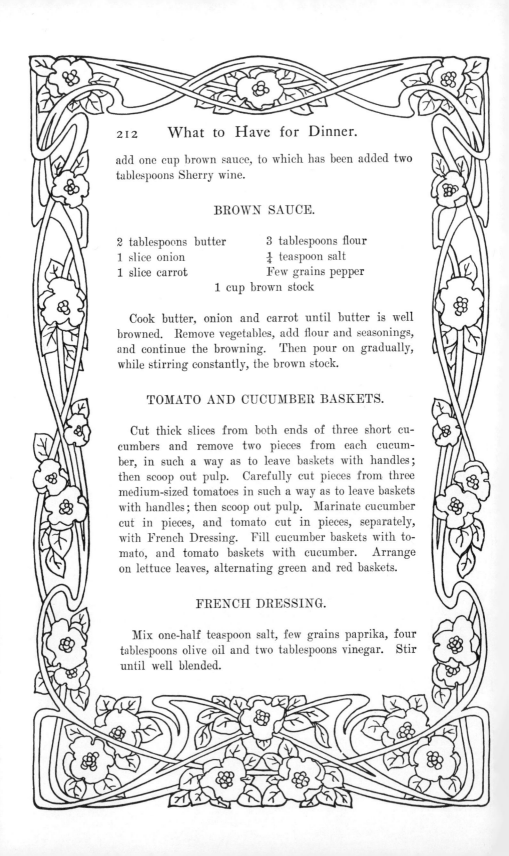

add one cup brown sauce, to which has been added two tablespoons Sherry wine.

BROWN SAUCE.

2 tablespoons butter	3 tablespoons flour
1 slice onion	$\frac{1}{4}$ teaspoon salt
1 slice carrot	Few grains pepper

1 cup brown stock

Cook butter, onion and carrot until butter is well browned. Remove vegetables, add flour and seasonings, and continue the browning. Then pour on gradually, while stirring constantly, the brown stock.

TOMATO AND CUCUMBER BASKETS.

Cut thick slices from both ends of three short cucumbers and remove two pieces from each cucumber, in such a way as to leave baskets with handles; then scoop out pulp. Carefully cut pieces from three medium-sized tomatoes in such a way as to leave baskets with handles; then scoop out pulp. Marinate cucumber cut in pieces, and tomato cut in pieces, separately, with French Dressing. Fill cucumber baskets with tomato, and tomato baskets with cucumber. Arrange on lettuce leaves, alternating green and red baskets.

FRENCH DRESSING.

Mix one-half teaspoon salt, few grains paprika, four tablespoons olive oil and two tablespoons vinegar. Stir until well blended.

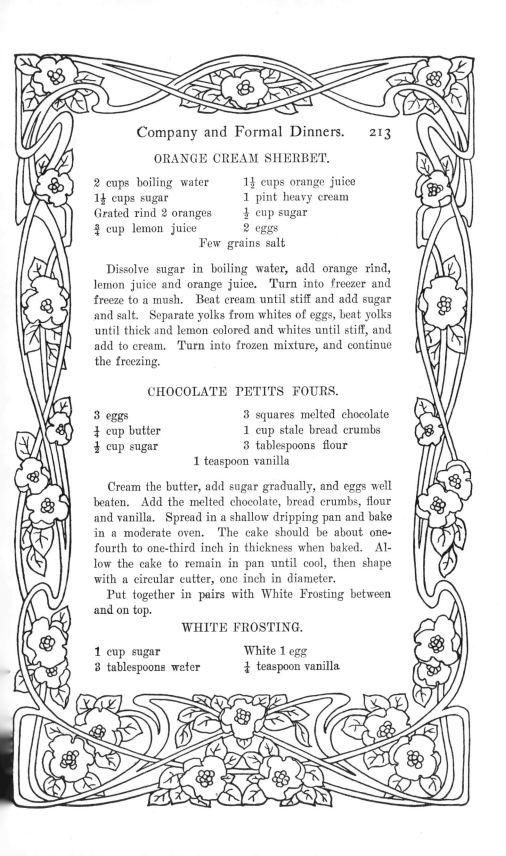

ORANGE CREAM SHERBET.

2 cups boiling water
1½ cups sugar
Grated rind 2 oranges
¾ cup lemon juice

1½ cups orange juice
1 pint heavy cream
½ cup sugar
2 eggs

Few grains salt

Dissolve sugar in boiling water, add orange rind, lemon juice and orange juice. Turn into freezer and freeze to a mush. Beat cream until stiff and add sugar and salt. Separate yolks from whites of eggs, beat yolks until thick and lemon colored and whites until stiff, and add to cream. Turn into frozen mixture, and continue the freezing.

CHOCOLATE PETITS FOURS.

3 eggs
¼ cup butter
½ cup sugar

3 squares melted chocolate
1 cup stale bread crumbs
3 tablespoons flour

1 teaspoon vanilla

Cream the butter, add sugar gradually, and eggs well beaten. Add the melted chocolate, bread crumbs, flour and vanilla. Spread in a shallow dripping pan and bake in a moderate oven. The cake should be about one-fourth to one-third inch in thickness when baked. Allow the cake to remain in pan until cool, then shape with a circular cutter, one inch in diameter.

Put together in pairs with White Frosting between and on top.

WHITE FROSTING.

1 cup sugar
3 tablespoons water

White 1 egg
¼ teaspoon vanilla

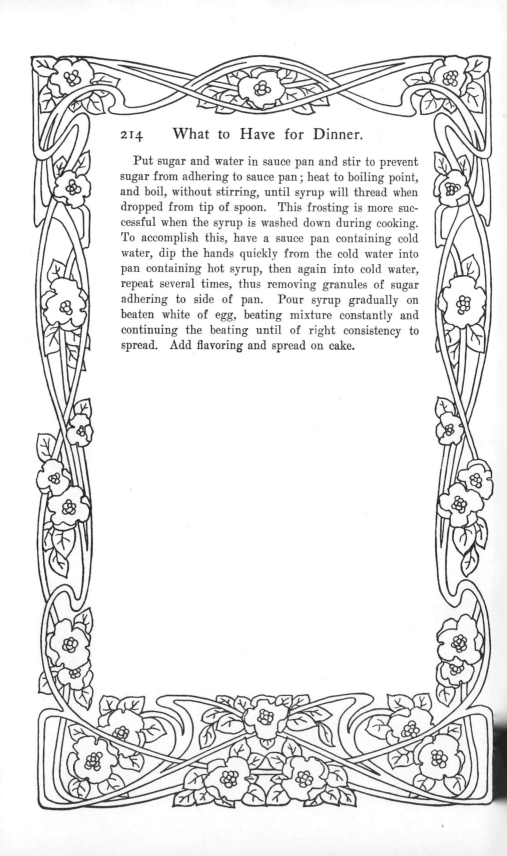

Put sugar and water in sauce pan and stir to prevent sugar from adhering to sauce pan; heat to boiling point, and boil, without stirring, until syrup will thread when dropped from tip of spoon. This frosting is more successful when the syrup is washed down during cooking. To accomplish this, have a sauce pan containing cold water, dip the hands quickly from the cold water into pan containing hot syrup, then again into cold water, repeat several times, thus removing granules of sugar adhering to side of pan. Pour syrup gradually on beaten white of egg, beating mixture constantly and continuing the beating until of right consistency to spread. Add flavoring and spread on cake.

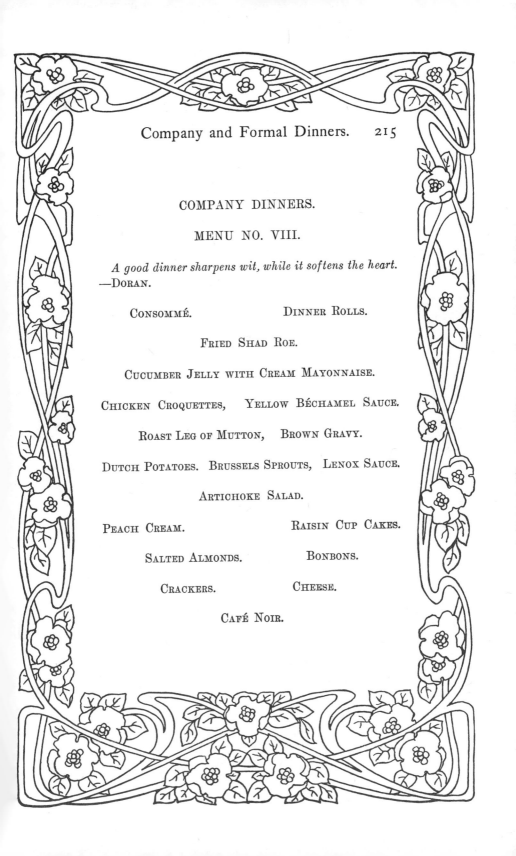

COMPANY DINNERS.

MENU NO. VIII.

A good dinner sharpens wit, while it softens the heart.
—DORAN.

CONSOMMÉ.   DINNER ROLLS.

FRIED SHAD ROE.

CUCUMBER JELLY WITH CREAM MAYONNAISE.

CHICKEN CROQUETTES,   YELLOW BÉCHAMEL SAUCE.

ROAST LEG OF MUTTON,   BROWN GRAVY.

DUTCH POTATOES. BRUSSELS SPROUTS, LENOX SAUCE.

ARTICHOKE SALAD.

PEACH CREAM.   RAISIN CUP CAKES.

SALTED ALMONDS.   BONBONS.

CRACKERS.   CHEESE.

CAFÉ NOIR.

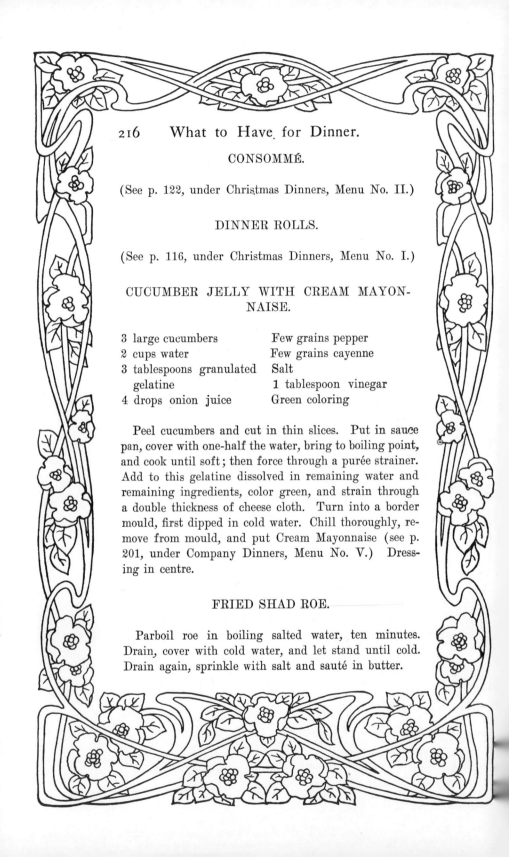

CONSOMMÉ.

(See p. 122, under Christmas Dinners, Menu No. II.)

DINNER ROLLS.

(See p. 116, under Christmas Dinners, Menu No. I.)

CUCUMBER JELLY WITH CREAM MAYON-NAISE.

3 large cucumbers	Few grains pepper
2 cups water	Few grains cayenne
3 tablespoons granulated gelatine	Salt
4 drops onion juice	1 tablespoon vinegar
	Green coloring

Peel cucumbers and cut in thin slices. Put in sauce pan, cover with one-half the water, bring to boiling point, and cook until soft; then force through a purée strainer. Add to this gelatine dissolved in remaining water and remaining ingredients, color green, and strain through a double thickness of cheese cloth. Turn into a border mould, first dipped in cold water. Chill thoroughly, remove from mould, and put Cream Mayonnaise (see p. 201, under Company Dinners, Menu No. V.) Dressing in centre.

FRIED SHAD ROE.

Parboil roe in boiling salted water, ten minutes. Drain, cover with cold water, and let stand until cold. Drain again, sprinkle with salt and sauté in butter.

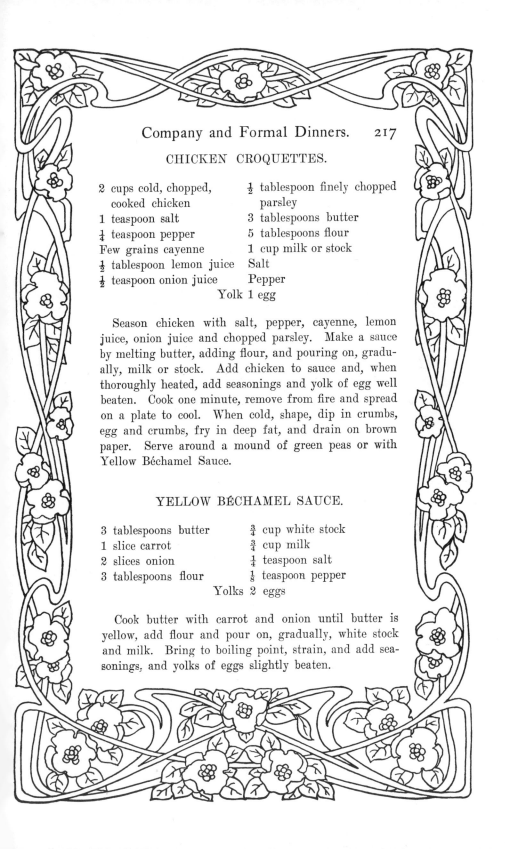

CHICKEN CROQUETTES.

2 cups cold, chopped, cooked chicken
1 teaspoon salt
¼ teaspoon pepper
Few grains cayenne
½ tablespoon lemon juice
½ teaspoon onion juice

¼ tablespoon finely chopped parsley
3 tablespoons butter
5 tablespoons flour
1 cup milk or stock
Salt
Pepper
Yolk 1 egg

Season chicken with salt, pepper, cayenne, lemon juice, onion juice and chopped parsley. Make a sauce by melting butter, adding flour, and pouring on, gradually, milk or stock. Add chicken to sauce and, when thoroughly heated, add seasonings and yolk of egg well beaten. Cook one minute, remove from fire and spread on a plate to cool. When cold, shape, dip in crumbs, egg and crumbs, fry in deep fat, and drain on brown paper. Serve around a mound of green peas or with Yellow Béchamel Sauce.

YELLOW BÉCHAMEL SAUCE.

3 tablespoons butter
1 slice carrot
2 slices onion
3 tablespoons flour

¾ cup white stock
¾ cup milk
¼ teaspoon salt
⅛ teaspoon pepper
Yolks 2 eggs

Cook butter with carrot and onion until butter is yellow, add flour and pour on, gradually, white stock and milk. Bring to boiling point, strain, and add seasonings, and yolks of eggs slightly beaten.

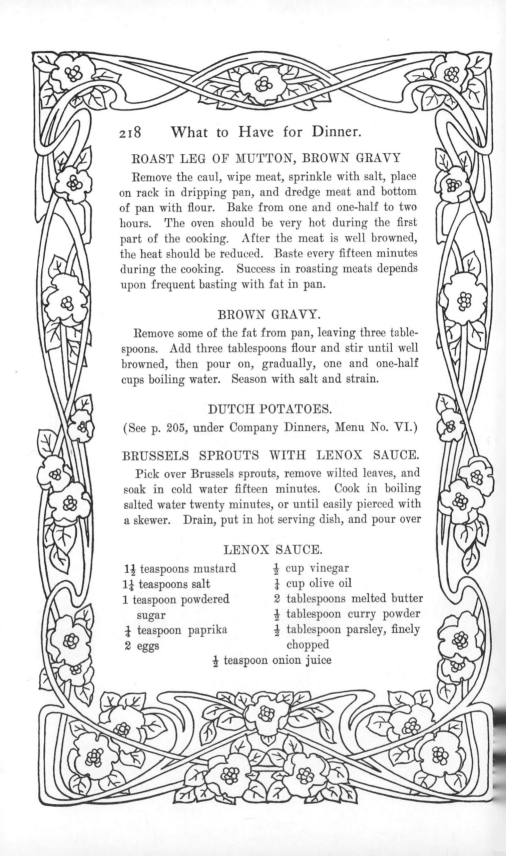

ROAST LEG OF MUTTON, BROWN GRAVY

Remove the caul, wipe meat, sprinkle with salt, place on rack in dripping pan, and dredge meat and bottom of pan with flour. Bake from one and one-half to two hours. The oven should be very hot during the first part of the cooking. After the meat is well browned, the heat should be reduced. Baste every fifteen minutes during the cooking. Success in roasting meats depends upon frequent basting with fat in pan.

BROWN GRAVY.

Remove some of the fat from pan, leaving three tablespoons. Add three tablespoons flour and stir until well browned, then pour on, gradually, one and one-half cups boiling water. Season with salt and strain.

DUTCH POTATOES.

(See p. 205, under Company Dinners, Menu No. VI.)

BRUSSELS SPROUTS WITH LENOX SAUCE.

Pick over Brussels sprouts, remove wilted leaves, and soak in cold water fifteen minutes. Cook in boiling salted water twenty minutes, or until easily pierced with a skewer. Drain, put in hot serving dish, and pour over

LENOX SAUCE.

1½ teaspoons mustard	½ cup vinegar
1¼ teaspoons salt	¼ cup olive oil
1 teaspoon powdered	2 tablespoons melted butter
sugar	½ tablespoon curry powder
¼ teaspoon paprika	½ tablespoon parsley, finely
2 eggs	chopped
½ teaspoon onion juice	

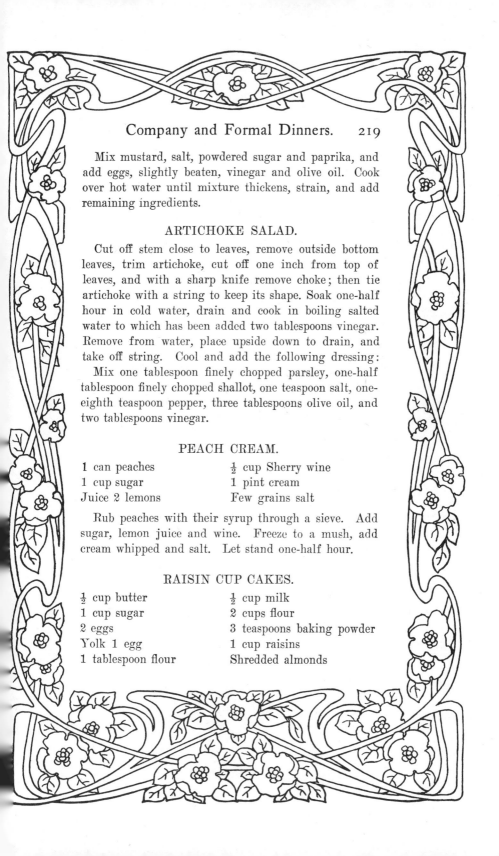

Mix mustard, salt, powdered sugar and paprika, and add eggs, slightly beaten, vinegar and olive oil. Cook over hot water until mixture thickens, strain, and add remaining ingredients.

ARTICHOKE SALAD.

Cut off stem close to leaves, remove outside bottom leaves, trim artichoke, cut off one inch from top of leaves, and with a sharp knife remove choke; then tie artichoke with a string to keep its shape. Soak one-half hour in cold water, drain and cook in boiling salted water to which has been added two tablespoons vinegar. Remove from water, place upside down to drain, and take off string.   Cool and add the following dressing:

Mix one tablespoon finely chopped parsley, one-half tablespoon finely chopped shallot, one teaspoon salt, one-eighth teaspoon pepper, three tablespoons olive oil, and two tablespoons vinegar.

PEACH CREAM.

1 can peaches	$\frac{1}{2}$ cup Sherry wine
1 cup sugar	1 pint cream
Juice 2 lemons	Few grains salt

Rub peaches with their syrup through a sieve.   Add sugar, lemon juice and wine.   Freeze to a mush, add cream whipped and salt.   Let stand one-half hour.

RAISIN CUP CAKES.

$\frac{1}{2}$ cup butter	$\frac{1}{2}$ cup milk
1 cup sugar	2 cups flour
2 eggs	3 teaspoons baking powder
Yolk 1 egg	1 cup raisins
1 tablespoon flour	Shredded almonds

Cream the butter, add sugar gradually, and eggs and egg yolks well beaten. Then add milk, flour mixed and sifted with baking powder, and raisins seeded and cut in pieces and dredged with one tablespoon flour. Beat vigorously and turn into buttered individual tins. Sprinkle tops with shredded almonds and powdered sugar and bake in a moderate oven.

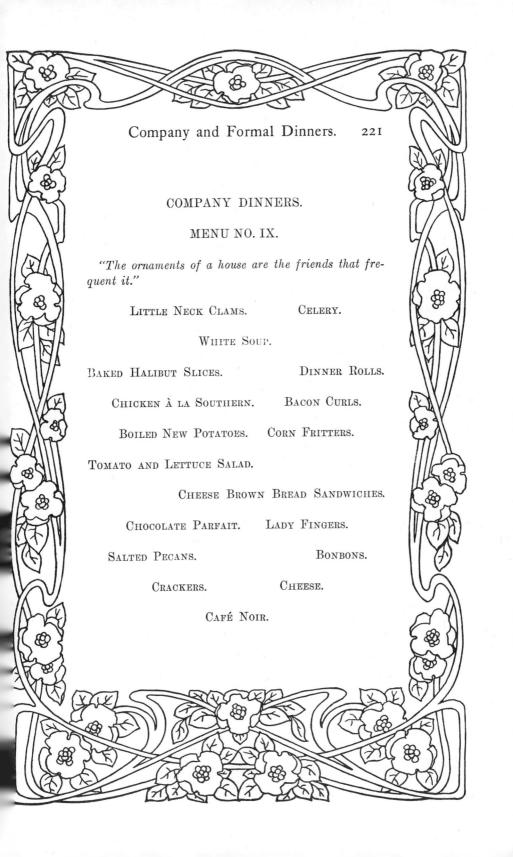

COMPANY DINNERS.

MENU NO. IX.

"The ornaments of a house are the friends that frequent it."

LITTLE NECK CLAMS.   CELERY.

WHITE SOUP.

BAKED HALIBUT SLICES.   DINNER ROLLS.

CHICKEN À LA SOUTHERN.   BACON CURLS.

BOILED NEW POTATOES.   CORN FRITTERS.

TOMATO AND LETTUCE SALAD.

CHEESE BROWN BREAD SANDWICHES.

CHOCOLATE PARFAIT.   LADY FINGERS.

SALTED PECANS.   BONBONS.

CRACKERS.   CHEESE.

CAFÉ NOIR.

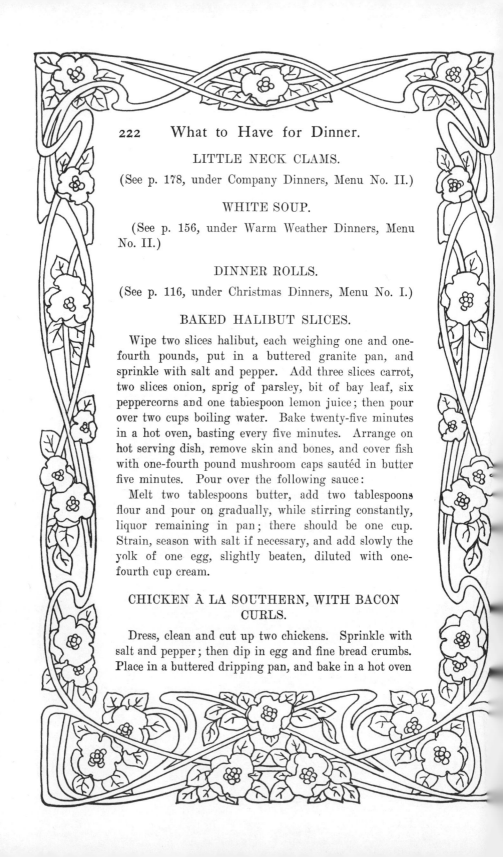

LITTLE NECK CLAMS.

(See p. 178, under Company Dinners, Menu No. II.)

WHITE SOUP.

(See p. 156, under Warm Weather Dinners, Menu No. II.)

DINNER ROLLS.

(See p. 116, under Christmas Dinners, Menu No. I.)

BAKED HALIBUT SLICES.

Wipe two slices halibut, each weighing one and one-fourth pounds, put in a buttered granite pan, and sprinkle with salt and pepper. Add three slices carrot, two slices onion, sprig of parsley, bit of bay leaf, six peppercorns and one tablespoon lemon juice; then pour over two cups boiling water. Bake twenty-five minutes in a hot oven, basting every five minutes. Arrange on hot serving dish, remove skin and bones, and cover fish with one-fourth pound mushroom caps sautéd in butter five minutes. Pour over the following sauce:

Melt two tablespoons butter, add two tablespoons flour and pour on gradually, while stirring constantly, liquor remaining in pan; there should be one cup. Strain, season with salt if necessary, and add slowly the yolk of one egg, slightly beaten, diluted with one-fourth cup cream.

CHICKEN À LA SOUTHERN, WITH BACON CURLS.

Dress, clean and cut up two chickens. Sprinkle with salt and pepper; then dip in egg and fine bread crumbs. Place in a buttered dripping pan, and bake in a hot oven

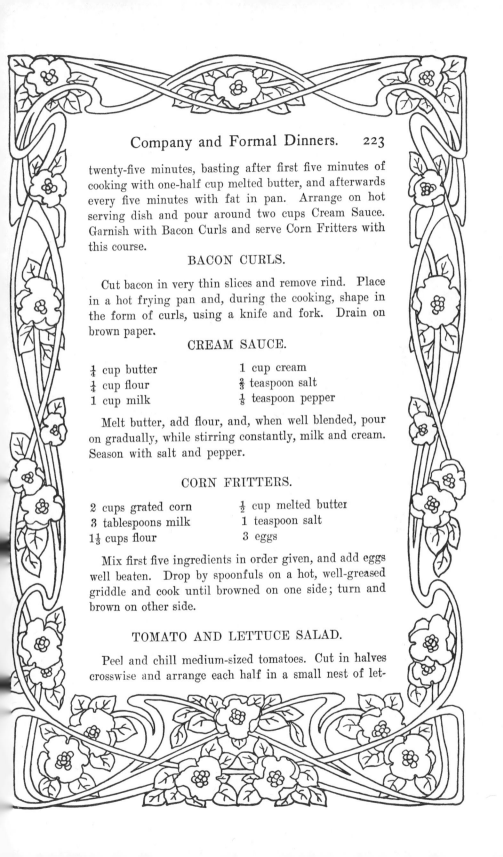

twenty-five minutes, basting after first five minutes of cooking with one-half cup melted butter, and afterwards every five minutes with fat in pan. Arrange on hot serving dish and pour around two cups Cream Sauce. Garnish with Bacon Curls and serve Corn Fritters with this course.

BACON CURLS.

Cut bacon in very thin slices and remove rind. Place in a hot frying pan and, during the cooking, shape in the form of curls, using a knife and fork. Drain on brown paper.

CREAM SAUCE.

$\frac{1}{4}$ cup butter   1 cup cream
$\frac{1}{4}$ cup flour $\frac{2}{3}$ teaspoon salt
1 cup milk $\frac{1}{8}$ teaspoon pepper

Melt butter, add flour, and, when well blended, pour on gradually, while stirring constantly, milk and cream. Season with salt and pepper.

CORN FRITTERS.

2 cups grated corn $\frac{1}{2}$ cup melted butter
3 tablespoons milk   1 teaspoon salt
1$\frac{1}{3}$ cups flour   3 eggs

Mix first five ingredients in order given, and add eggs well beaten. Drop by spoonfuls on a hot, well-greased griddle and cook until browned on one side; turn and brown on other side.

TOMATO AND LETTUCE SALAD.

Peel and chill medium-sized tomatoes. Cut in halves crosswise and arrange each half in a small nest of let-

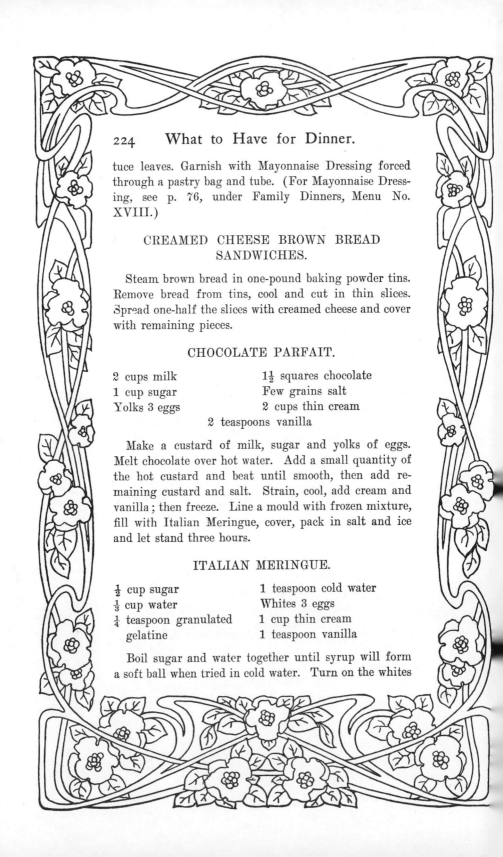

tuce leaves. Garnish with Mayonnaise Dressing forced through a pastry bag and tube. (For Mayonnaise Dressing, see p. 76, under Family Dinners, Menu No. XVIII.)

CREAMED CHEESE BROWN BREAD SANDWICHES.

Steam brown bread in one-pound baking powder tins. Remove bread from tins, cool and cut in thin slices. Spread one-half the slices with creamed cheese and cover with remaining pieces.

CHOCOLATE PARFAIT.

2 cups milk	$1\frac{1}{2}$ squares chocolate
1 cup sugar	Few grains salt
Yolks 3 eggs	2 cups thin cream
	2 teaspoons vanilla

Make a custard of milk, sugar and yolks of eggs. Melt chocolate over hot water. Add a small quantity of the hot custard and beat until smooth, then add remaining custard and salt. Strain, cool, add cream and vanilla; then freeze. Line a mould with frozen mixture, fill with Italian Meringue, cover, pack in salt and ice and let stand three hours.

ITALIAN MERINGUE.

$\frac{1}{2}$ cup sugar	1 teaspoon cold water
$\frac{1}{3}$ cup water	Whites 3 eggs
$\frac{1}{4}$ teaspoon granulated gelatine	1 cup thin cream
	1 teaspoon vanilla

Boil sugar and water together until syrup will form a soft ball when tried in cold water. Turn on the whites

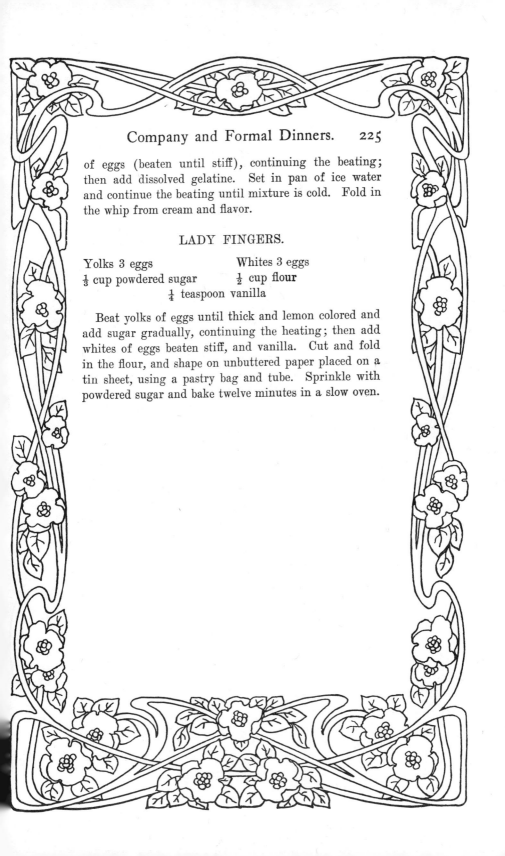

of eggs (beaten until stiff), continuing the beating; then add dissolved gelatine. Set in pan of ice water and continue the beating until mixture is cold. Fold in the whip from cream and flavor.

LADY FINGERS.

Yolks 3 eggs   Whites 3 eggs
⅓ cup powdered sugar   ½ cup flour
            ¼ teaspoon vanilla

Beat yolks of eggs until thick and lemon colored and add sugar gradually, continuing the heating; then add whites of eggs beaten stiff, and vanilla. Cut and fold in the flour, and shape on unbuttered paper placed on a tin sheet, using a pastry bag and tube. Sprinkle with powdered sugar and bake twelve minutes in a slow oven.

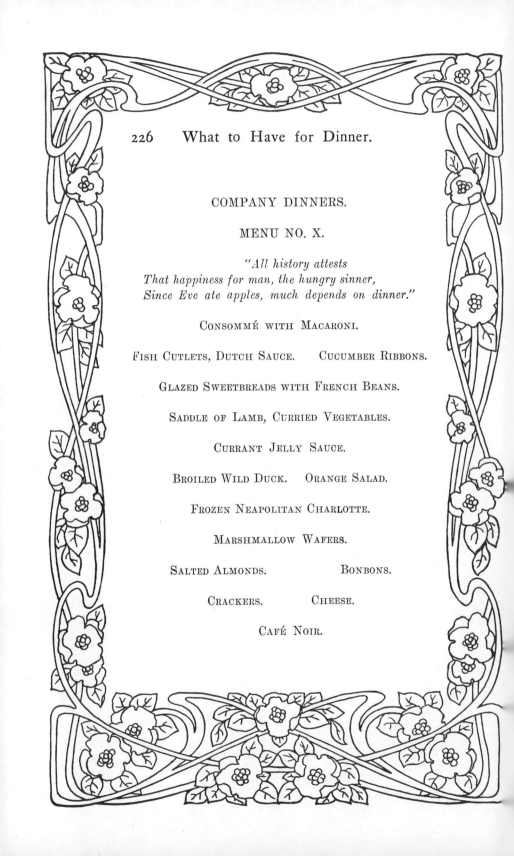

COMPANY DINNERS.

MENU NO. X.

"All history attests
That happiness for man, the hungry sinner,
Since Eve ate apples, much depends on dinner."

CONSOMMÉ WITH MACARONI.

FISH CUTLETS, DUTCH SAUCE.   CUCUMBER RIBBONS.

GLAZED SWEETBREADS WITH FRENCH BEANS.

SADDLE OF LAMB, CURRIED VEGETABLES.

CURRANT JELLY SAUCE.

BROILED WILD DUCK.   ORANGE SALAD.

FROZEN NEAPOLITAN CHARLOTTE.

MARSHMALLOW WAFERS.

SALTED ALMONDS.   BONBONS.

CRACKERS.   CHEESE.

CAFÉ NOIR.

CONSOMMÉ WITH MACARONI.

Serve consommé with rings of macaroni cooked in boiling salted water until soft.

FISH CUTLETS.

Remove skin and bones from a thick piece of halibut, finely chop fish and force through a sieve; there should be one and one-third cups. Pound in a mortar, adding gradually whites of two eggs. Add one and one-third cups heavy cream and season with salt, pepper and cayenne. Turn into buttered cutlet moulds, set in pan of hot water, cover with buttered paper and bake until fish is firm. Turn on a serving dish and pour around Dutch Sauce.

DUTCH SAUCE.

Yolks 3 eggs	¼ teaspoon salt
3 tablespoons olive oil	1 tablespoon chopped pars-
⅓ cup vinegar	ley
Few grains pepper	

Mix first four ingredients in a small sauce pan, place in a larger sauce pan containing hot water and cook over the fire, stirring constantly, until mixture thickens; then add parsley.

CUCUMBER RIBBONS.

(See p. 147, under Easter Dinners, Menu No. II.)

GLAZED SWEETBREADS.

Parboil a sweetbread cut in two lengthwise, sprinkle with salt, dredge with flour and sauté in butter until delicately browned. Add one-half cup white stock and cook until reduced to a glaze. Remove sweetbread to

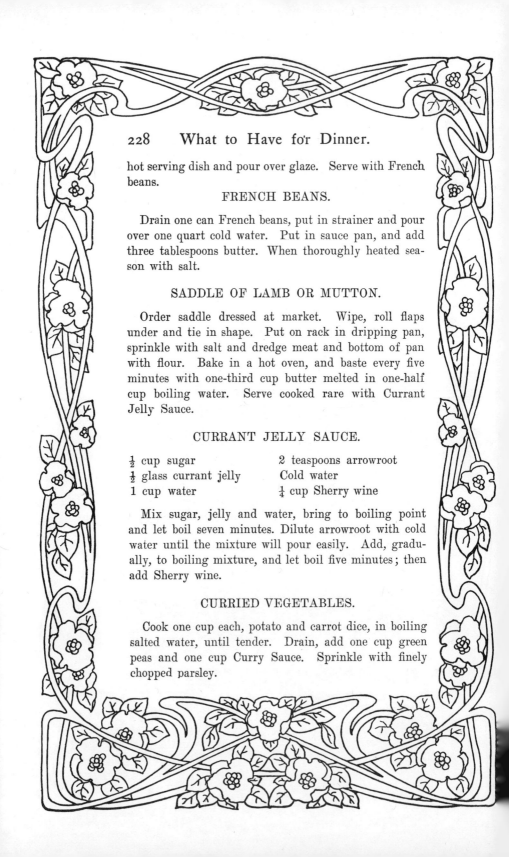

hot serving dish and pour over glaze. Serve with French beans.

FRENCH BEANS.

Drain one can French beans, put in strainer and pour over one quart cold water. Put in sauce pan, and add three tablespoons butter. When thoroughly heated season with salt.

SADDLE OF LAMB OR MUTTON.

Order saddle dressed at market. Wipe, roll flaps under and tie in shape. Put on rack in dripping pan, sprinkle with salt and dredge meat and bottom of pan with flour. Bake in a hot oven, and baste every five minutes with one-third cup butter melted in one-half cup boiling water. Serve cooked rare with Currant Jelly Sauce.

CURRANT JELLY SAUCE.

$\frac{1}{2}$ cup sugar   2 teaspoons arrowroot
$\frac{1}{2}$ glass currant jelly   Cold water
1 cup water $\frac{1}{4}$ cup Sherry wine

Mix sugar, jelly and water, bring to boiling point and let boil seven minutes. Dilute arrowroot with cold water until the mixture will pour easily. Add, gradually, to boiling mixture, and let boil five minutes; then add Sherry wine.

CURRIED VEGETABLES.

Cook one cup each, potato and carrot dice, in boiling salted water, until tender. Drain, add one cup green peas and one cup Curry Sauce. Sprinkle with finely chopped parsley.

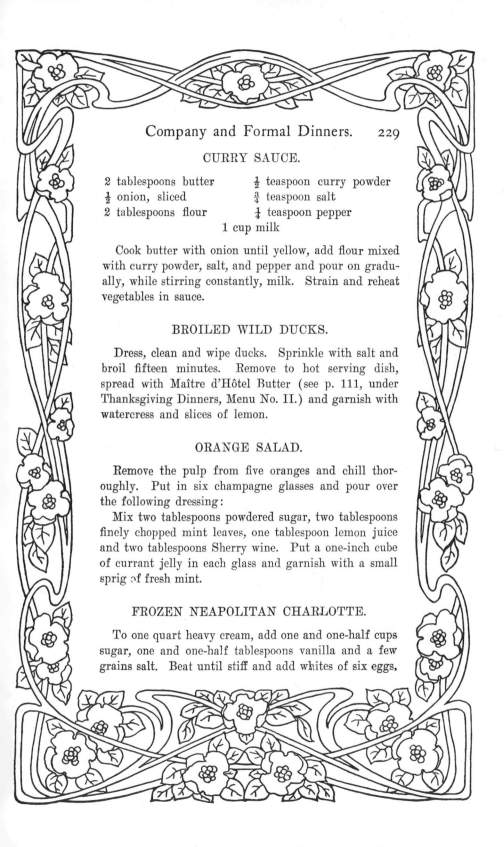

CURRY SAUCE.

2 tablespoons butter   ½ teaspoon curry powder
½ onion, sliced   ¾ teaspoon salt
2 tablespoons flour   ¼ teaspoon pepper
1 cup milk

Cook butter with onion until yellow, add flour mixed with curry powder, salt, and pepper and pour on gradually, while stirring constantly, milk. Strain and reheat vegetables in sauce.

BROILED WILD DUCKS.

Dress, clean and wipe ducks. Sprinkle with salt and broil fifteen minutes. Remove to hot serving dish, spread with Maître d'Hôtel Butter (see p. 111, under Thanksgiving Dinners, Menu No. II.) and garnish with watercress and slices of lemon.

ORANGE SALAD.

Remove the pulp from five oranges and chill thoroughly. Put in six champagne glasses and pour over the following dressing:

Mix two tablespoons powdered sugar, two tablespoons finely chopped mint leaves, one tablespoon lemon juice and two tablespoons Sherry wine. Put a one-inch cube of currant jelly in each glass and garnish with a small sprig of fresh mint.

FROZEN NEAPOLITAN CHARLOTTE.

To one quart heavy cream, add one and one-half cups sugar, one and one-half tablespoons vanilla and a few grains salt. Beat until stiff and add whites of six eggs,

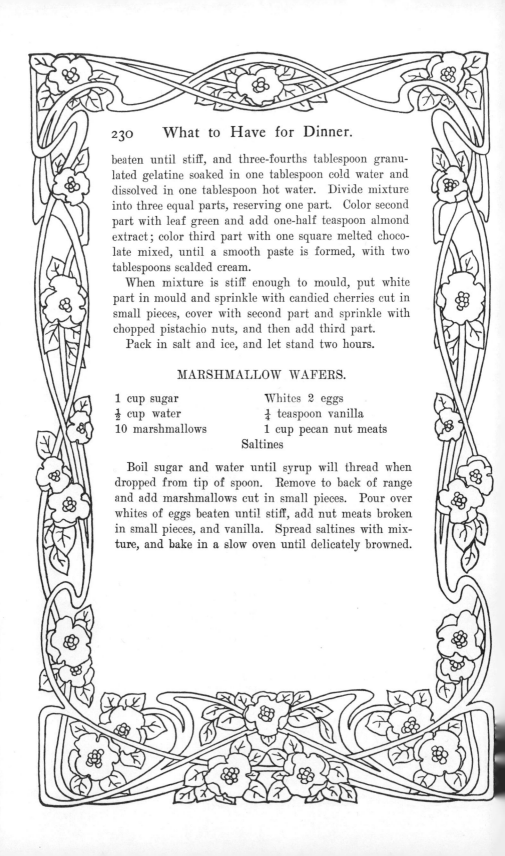

beaten until stiff, and three-fourths tablespoon granulated gelatine soaked in one tablespoon cold water and dissolved in one tablespoon hot water. Divide mixture into three equal parts, reserving one part. Color second part with leaf green and add one-half teaspoon almond extract; color third part with one square melted chocolate mixed, until a smooth paste is formed, with two tablespoons scalded cream.

When mixture is stiff enough to mould, put white part in mould and sprinkle with candied cherries cut in small pieces, cover with second part and sprinkle with chopped pistachio nuts, and then add third part.

Pack in salt and ice, and let stand two hours.

MARSHMALLOW WAFERS.

1 cup sugar	Whites 2 eggs
$\frac{1}{2}$ cup water	$\frac{1}{4}$ teaspoon vanilla
10 marshmallows	1 cup pecan nut meats
	Saltines

Boil sugar and water until syrup will thread when dropped from tip of spoon. Remove to back of range and add marshmallows cut in small pieces. Pour over whites of eggs beaten until stiff, add nut meats broken in small pieces, and vanilla. Spread saltines with mixture, and bake in a slow oven until delicately browned.

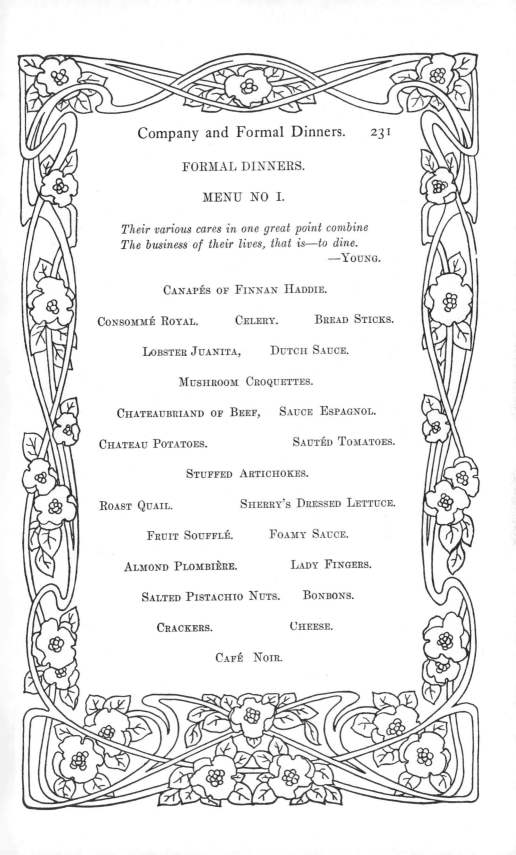

FORMAL DINNERS.

MENU NO I.

Their various cares in one great point combine
The business of their lives, that is—to dine.
                    —YOUNG.

CANAPÉS OF FINNAN HADDIE.

CONSOMMÉ ROYAL.   CELERY.   BREAD STICKS.

LOBSTER JUANITA,   DUTCH SAUCE.

MUSHROOM CROQUETTES.

CHATEAUBRIAND OF BEEF,   SAUCE ESPAGNOL.

CHATEAU POTATOES.   SAUTÉD TOMATOES.

STUFFED ARTICHOKES.

ROAST QUAIL.   SHERRY'S DRESSED LETTUCE.

FRUIT SOUFFLÉ.   FOAMY SAUCE.

ALMOND PLOMBIÈRE.   LADY FINGERS.

SALTED PISTACHIO NUTS.   BONBONS.

CRACKERS.   CHEESE.

CAFÉ NOIR.

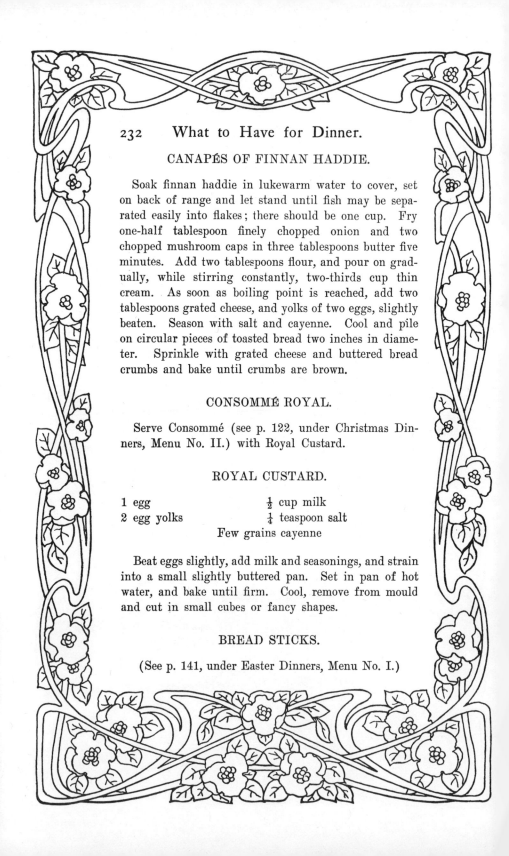

CANAPÉS OF FINNAN HADDIE.

Soak finnan haddie in lukewarm water to cover, set on back of range and let stand until fish may be separated easily into flakes; there should be one cup. Fry one-half tablespoon finely chopped onion and two chopped mushroom caps in three tablespoons butter five minutes. Add two tablespoons flour, and pour on gradually, while stirring constantly, two-thirds cup thin cream. As soon as boiling point is reached, add two tablespoons grated cheese, and yolks of two eggs, slightly beaten. Season with salt and cayenne. Cool and pile on circular pieces of toasted bread two inches in diameter. Sprinkle with grated cheese and buttered bread crumbs and bake until crumbs are brown.

CONSOMMÉ ROYAL.

Serve Consommé (see p. 122, under Christmas Dinners, Menu No. II.) with Royal Custard.

ROYAL CUSTARD.

1 egg	½ cup milk
2 egg yolks	¼ teaspoon salt
Few grains cayenne	

Beat eggs slightly, add milk and seasonings, and strain into a small slightly buttered pan. Set in pan of hot water, and bake until firm. Cool, remove from mould and cut in small cubes or fancy shapes.

BREAD STICKS.

(See p. 141, under Easter Dinners, Menu No. I.)

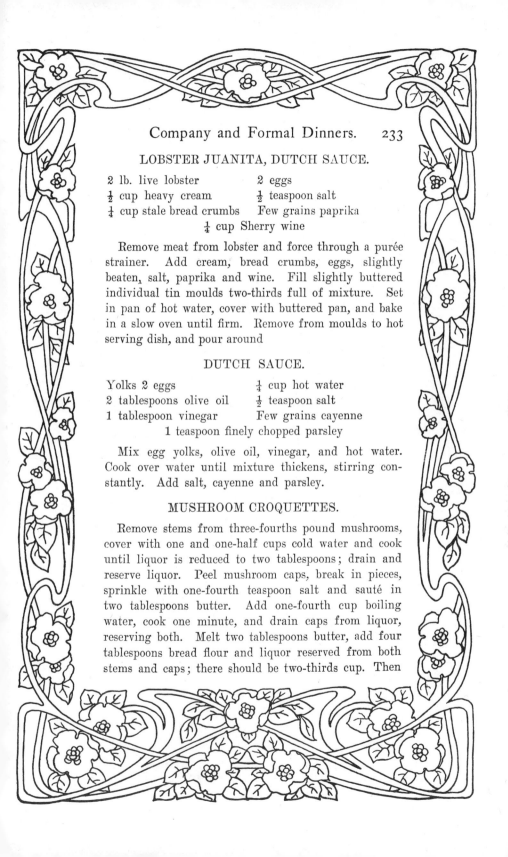

LOBSTER JUANITA, DUTCH SAUCE.

2 lb. live lobster	2 eggs
½ cup heavy cream	½ teaspoon salt
¼ cup stale bread crumbs	Few grains paprika

¼ cup Sherry wine

Remove meat from lobster and force through a purée strainer. Add cream, bread crumbs, eggs, slightly beaten, salt, paprika and wine. Fill slightly buttered individual tin moulds two-thirds full of mixture. Set in pan of hot water, cover with buttered pan, and bake in a slow oven until firm. Remove from moulds to hot serving dish, and pour around

DUTCH SAUCE.

Yolks 2 eggs	¼ cup hot water
2 tablespoons olive oil	½ teaspoon salt
1 tablespoon vinegar	Few grains cayenne

1 teaspoon finely chopped parsley

Mix egg yolks, olive oil, vinegar, and hot water. Cook over water until mixture thickens, stirring constantly. Add salt, cayenne and parsley.

MUSHROOM CROQUETTES.

Remove stems from three-fourths pound mushrooms, cover with one and one-half cups cold water and cook until liquor is reduced to two tablespoons; drain and reserve liquor. Peel mushroom caps, break in pieces, sprinkle with one-fourth teaspoon salt and sauté in two tablespoons butter. Add one-fourth cup boiling water, cook one minute, and drain caps from liquor, reserving both. Melt two tablespoons butter, add four tablespoons bread flour and liquor reserved from both stems and caps; there should be two-thirds cup. Then

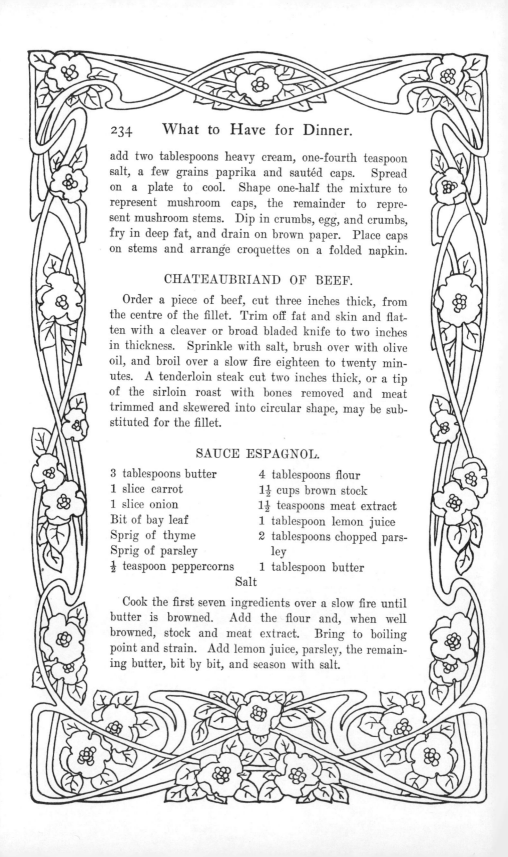

add two tablespoons heavy cream, one-fourth teaspoon salt, a few grains paprika and sautéd caps. Spread on a plate to cool. Shape one-half the mixture to represent mushroom caps, the remainder to represent mushroom stems. Dip in crumbs, egg, and crumbs, fry in deep fat, and drain on brown paper. Place caps on stems and arrange croquettes on a folded napkin.

CHATEAUBRIAND OF BEEF.

Order a piece of beef, cut three inches thick, from the centre of the fillet. Trim off fat and skin and flatten with a cleaver or broad bladed knife to two inches in thickness. Sprinkle with salt, brush over with olive oil, and broil over a slow fire eighteen to twenty minutes. A tenderloin steak cut two inches thick, or a tip of the sirloin roast with bones removed and meat trimmed and skewered into circular shape, may be substituted for the fillet.

SAUCE ESPAGNOL.

3 tablespoons butter
1 slice carrot
1 slice onion
Bit of bay leaf
Sprig of thyme
Sprig of parsley
½ teaspoon peppercorns

4 tablespoons flour
1½ cups brown stock
1½ teaspoons meat extract
1 tablespoon lemon juice
2 tablespoons chopped parsley
1 tablespoon butter
Salt

Cook the first seven ingredients over a slow fire until butter is browned. Add the flour and, when well browned, stock and meat extract. Bring to boiling point and strain. Add lemon juice, parsley, the remaining butter, bit by bit, and season with salt.

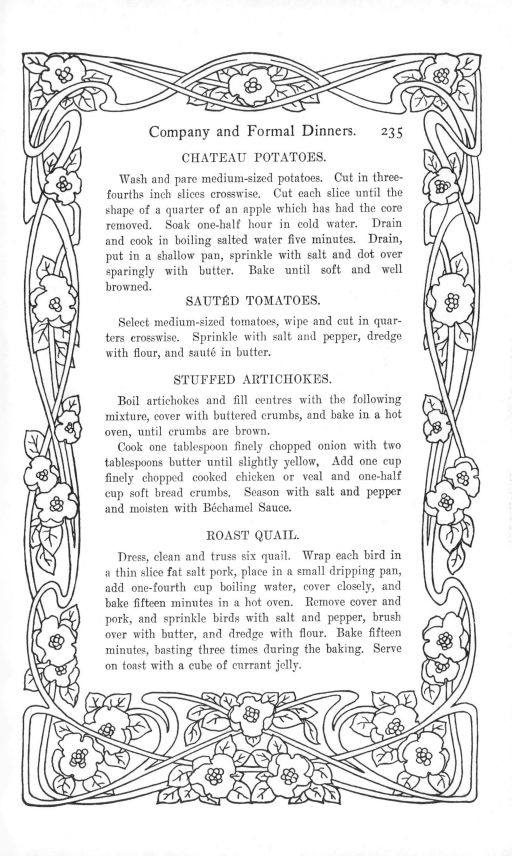

CHATEAU POTATOES.

Wash and pare medium-sized potatoes. Cut in three-fourths inch slices crosswise. Cut each slice until the shape of a quarter of an apple which has had the core removed. Soak one-half hour in cold water. Drain and cook in boiling salted water five minutes. Drain, put in a shallow pan, sprinkle with salt and dot over sparingly with butter. Bake until soft and well browned.

SAUTÉD TOMATOES.

Select medium-sized tomatoes, wipe and cut in quarters crosswise. Sprinkle with salt and pepper, dredge with flour, and sauté in butter.

STUFFED ARTICHOKES.

Boil artichokes and fill centres with the following mixture, cover with buttered crumbs, and bake in a hot oven, until crumbs are brown.

Cook one tablespoon finely chopped onion with two tablespoons butter until slightly yellow, Add one cup finely chopped cooked chicken or veal and one-half cup soft bread crumbs. Season with salt and pepper and moisten with Béchamel Sauce.

ROAST QUAIL.

Dress, clean and truss six quail. Wrap each bird in a thin slice fat salt pork, place in a small dripping pan, add one-fourth cup boiling water, cover closely, and bake fifteen minutes in a hot oven. Remove cover and pork, and sprinkle birds with salt and pepper, brush over with butter, and dredge with flour. Bake fifteen minutes, basting three times during the baking. Serve on toast with a cube of currant jelly.

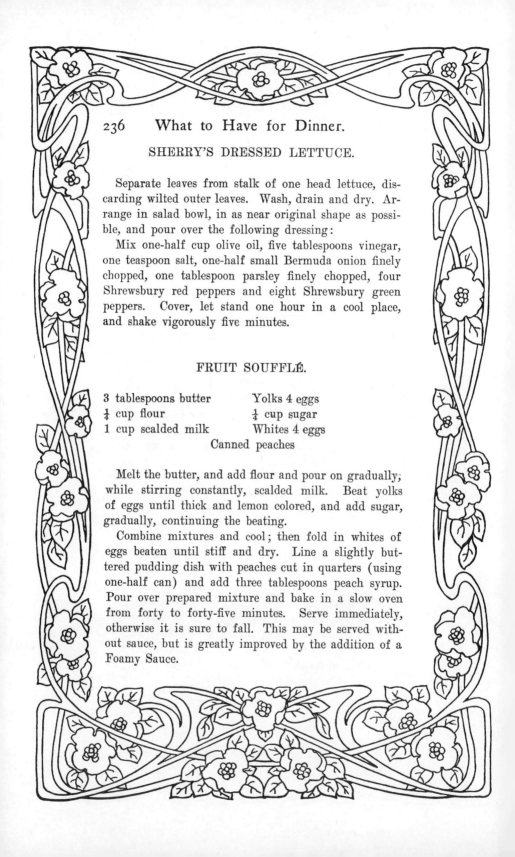

SHERRY'S DRESSED LETTUCE.

Separate leaves from stalk of one head lettuce, discarding wilted outer leaves. Wash, drain and dry. Arrange in salad bowl, in as near original shape as possible, and pour over the following dressing:

Mix one-half cup olive oil, five tablespoons vinegar, one teaspoon salt, one-half small Bermuda onion finely chopped, one tablespoon parsley finely chopped, four Shrewsbury red peppers and eight Shrewsbury green peppers. Cover, let stand one hour in a cool place, and shake vigorously five minutes.

FRUIT SOUFFLÉ.

3 tablespoons butter	Yolks 4 eggs
$\frac{1}{4}$ cup flour	$\frac{1}{4}$ cup sugar
1 cup scalded milk	Whites 4 eggs

Canned peaches

Melt the butter, and add flour and pour on gradually; while stirring constantly, scalded milk. Beat yolks of eggs until thick and lemon colored, and add sugar, gradually, continuing the beating.

Combine mixtures and cool; then fold in whites of eggs beaten until stiff and dry. Line a slightly buttered pudding dish with peaches cut in quarters (using one-half can) and add three tablespoons peach syrup. Pour over prepared mixture and bake in a slow oven from forty to forty-five minutes. Serve immediately, otherwise it is sure to fall. This may be served without sauce, but is greatly improved by the addition of a Foamy Sauce.

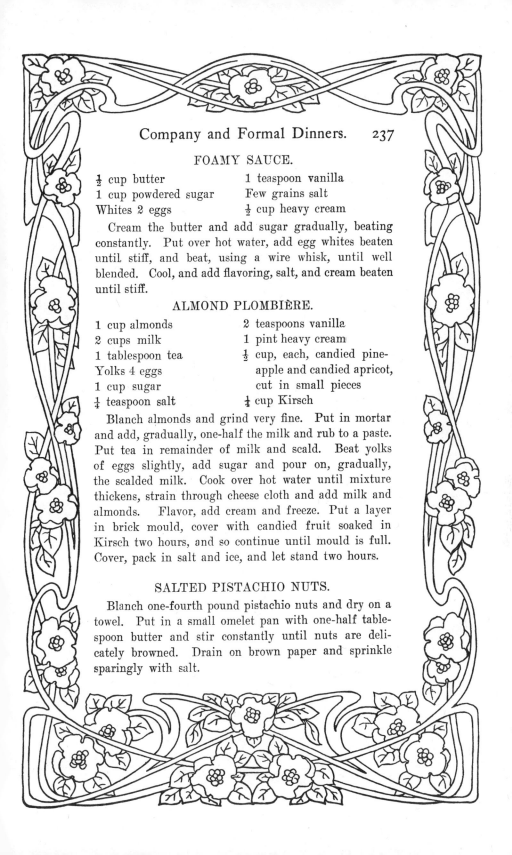

FOAMY SAUCE.

½ cup butter   1 teaspoon vanilla
1 cup powdered sugar   Few grains salt
Whites 2 eggs   ½ cup heavy cream

Cream the butter and add sugar gradually, beating constantly. Put over hot water, add egg whites beaten until stiff, and beat, using a wire whisk, until well blended. Cool, and add flavoring, salt, and cream beaten until stiff.

ALMOND PLOMBIÈRE.

1 cup almonds   2 teaspoons vanilla
2 cups milk   1 pint heavy cream
1 tablespoon tea   ½ cup, each, candied pine-
Yolks 4 eggs   apple and candied apricot,
1 cup sugar   cut in small pieces
¼ teaspoon salt   ¼ cup Kirsch

Blanch almonds and grind very fine. Put in mortar and add, gradually, one-half the milk and rub to a paste. Put tea in remainder of milk and scald. Beat yolks of eggs slightly, add sugar and pour on, gradually, the scalded milk. Cook over hot water until mixture thickens, strain through cheese cloth and add milk and almonds. Flavor, add cream and freeze. Put a layer in brick mould, cover with candied fruit soaked in Kirsch two hours, and so continue until mould is full. Cover, pack in salt and ice, and let stand two hours.

SALTED PISTACHIO NUTS.

Blanch one-fourth pound pistachio nuts and dry on a towel. Put in a small omelet pan with one-half tablespoon butter and stir constantly until nuts are delicately browned. Drain on brown paper and sprinkle sparingly with salt.

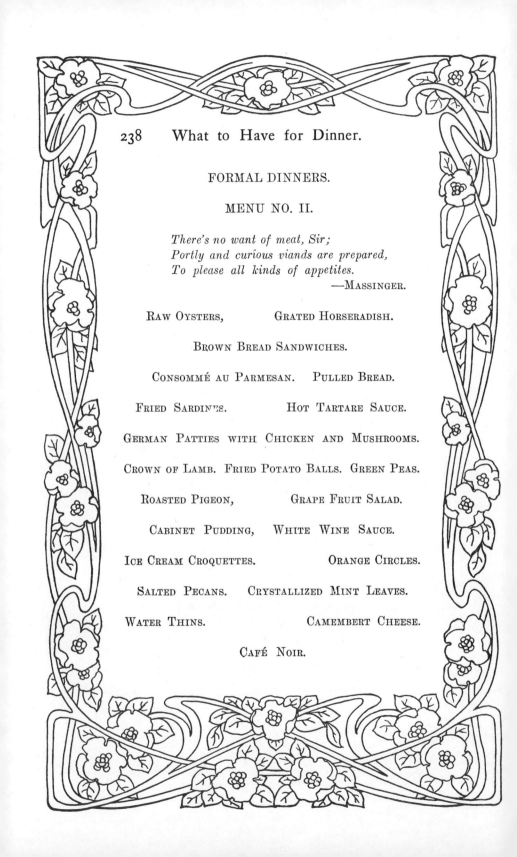

FORMAL DINNERS.

MENU NO. II.

There's no want of meat, Sir;
Portly and curious viands are prepared,
To please all kinds of appetites.
              —MASSINGER.

RAW OYSTERS,   GRATED HORSERADISH.

BROWN BREAD SANDWICHES.

CONSOMMÉ AU PARMESAN.   PULLED BREAD.

FRIED SARDINES.   HOT TARTARE SAUCE.

GERMAN PATTIES WITH CHICKEN AND MUSHROOMS.

CROWN OF LAMB. FRIED POTATO BALLS. GREEN PEAS.

ROASTED PIGEON,   GRAPE FRUIT SALAD.

CABINET PUDDING,   WHITE WINE SAUCE.

ICE CREAM CROQUETTES.   ORANGE CIRCLES.

SALTED PECANS.   CRYSTALLIZED MINT LEAVES.

WATER THINS.   CAMEMBERT CHEESE.

CAFÉ NOIR.

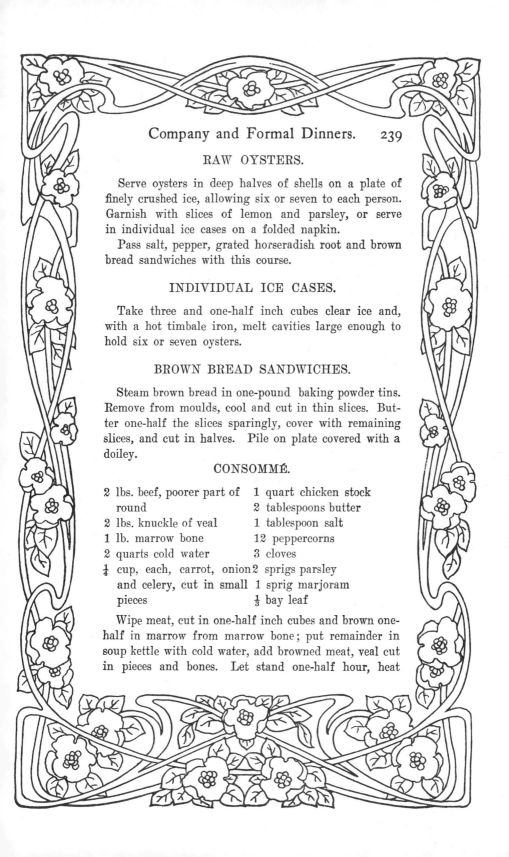

RAW OYSTERS.

Serve oysters in deep halves of shells on a plate of finely crushed ice, allowing six or seven to each person. Garnish with slices of lemon and parsley, or serve in individual ice cases on a folded napkin.

Pass salt, pepper, grated horseradish root and brown bread sandwiches with this course.

INDIVIDUAL ICE CASES.

Take three and one-half inch cubes clear ice and, with a hot timbale iron, melt cavities large enough to hold six or seven oysters.

BROWN BREAD SANDWICHES.

Steam brown bread in one-pound baking powder tins. Remove from moulds, cool and cut in thin slices. Butter one-half the slices sparingly, cover with remaining slices, and cut in halves. Pile on plate covered with a doiley.

CONSOMMÉ.

2 lbs. beef, poorer part of round	1 quart chicken stock
	2 tablespoons butter
2 lbs. knuckle of veal	1 tablespoon salt
1 lb. marrow bone	12 peppercorns
2 quarts cold water	3 cloves
$\frac{1}{4}$ cup, each, carrot, onion and celery, cut in small pieces	2 sprigs parsley
	1 sprig marjoram
	$\frac{1}{3}$ bay leaf

Wipe meat, cut in one-half inch cubes and brown one-half in marrow from marrow bone; put remainder in soup kettle with cold water, add browned meat, veal cut in pieces and bones. Let stand one-half hour, heat

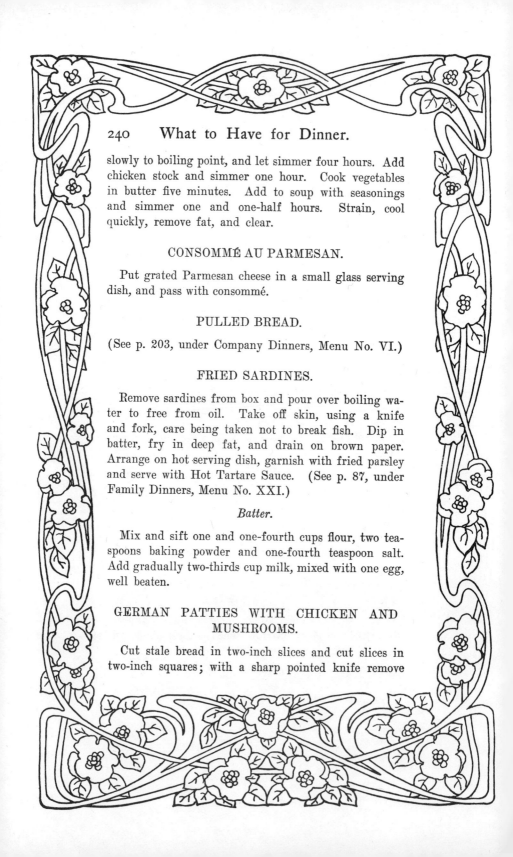

slowly to boiling point, and let simmer four hours. Add chicken stock and simmer one hour. Cook vegetables in butter five minutes. Add to soup with seasonings and simmer one and one-half hours. Strain, cool quickly, remove fat, and clear.

CONSOMMÉ AU PARMESAN.

Put grated Parmesan cheese in a small glass serving dish, and pass with consommé.

PULLED BREAD.

(See p. 203, under Company Dinners, Menu No. VI.)

FRIED SARDINES.

Remove sardines from box and pour over boiling water to free from oil. Take off skin, using a knife and fork, care being taken not to break fish. Dip in batter, fry in deep fat, and drain on brown paper. Arrange on hot serving dish, garnish with fried parsley and serve with Hot Tartare Sauce. (See p. 87, under Family Dinners, Menu No. XXI.)

Batter.

Mix and sift one and one-fourth cups flour, two teaspoons baking powder and one-fourth teaspoon salt. Add gradually two-thirds cup milk, mixed with one egg, well beaten.

GERMAN PATTIES WITH CHICKEN AND MUSHROOMS.

Cut stale bread in two-inch slices and cut slices in two-inch squares; with a sharp pointed knife remove

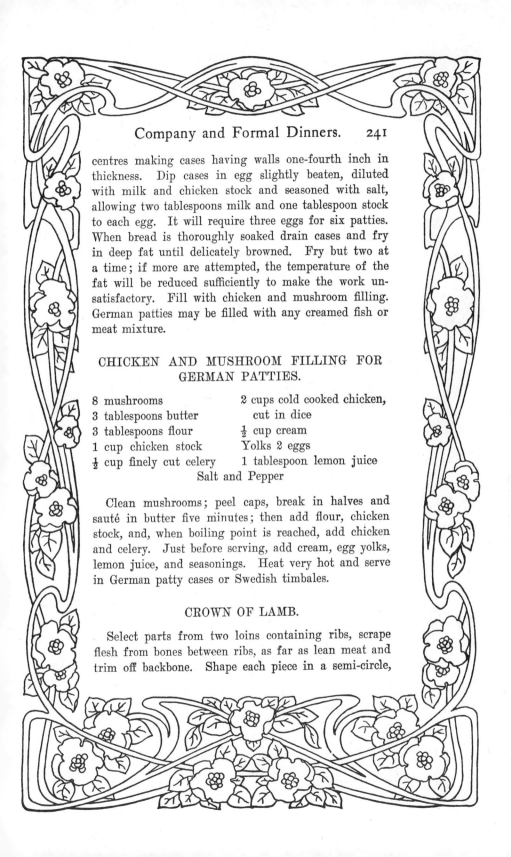

centres making cases having walls one-fourth inch in thickness. Dip cases in egg slightly beaten, diluted with milk and chicken stock and seasoned with salt, allowing two tablespoons milk and one tablespoon stock to each egg. It will require three eggs for six patties. When bread is thoroughly soaked drain cases and fry in deep fat until delicately browned. Fry but two at a time; if more are attempted, the temperature of the fat will be reduced sufficiently to make the work unsatisfactory. Fill with chicken and mushroom filling. German patties may be filled with any creamed fish or meat mixture.

CHICKEN AND MUSHROOM FILLING FOR GERMAN PATTIES.

8 mushrooms	2 cups cold cooked chicken,
3 tablespoons butter	cut in dice
3 tablespoons flour	$\frac{1}{2}$ cup cream
1 cup chicken stock	Yolks 2 eggs
$\frac{1}{2}$ cup finely cut celery	1 tablespoon lemon juice

Salt and Pepper

Clean mushrooms; peel caps, break in halves and sauté in butter five minutes; then add flour, chicken stock, and, when boiling point is reached, add chicken and celery. Just before serving, add cream, egg yolks, lemon juice, and seasonings. Heat very hot and serve in German patty cases or Swedish timbales.

CROWN OF LAMB.

Select parts from two loins containing ribs, scrape flesh from bones between ribs, as far as lean meat and trim off backbone. Shape each piece in a semi-circle,

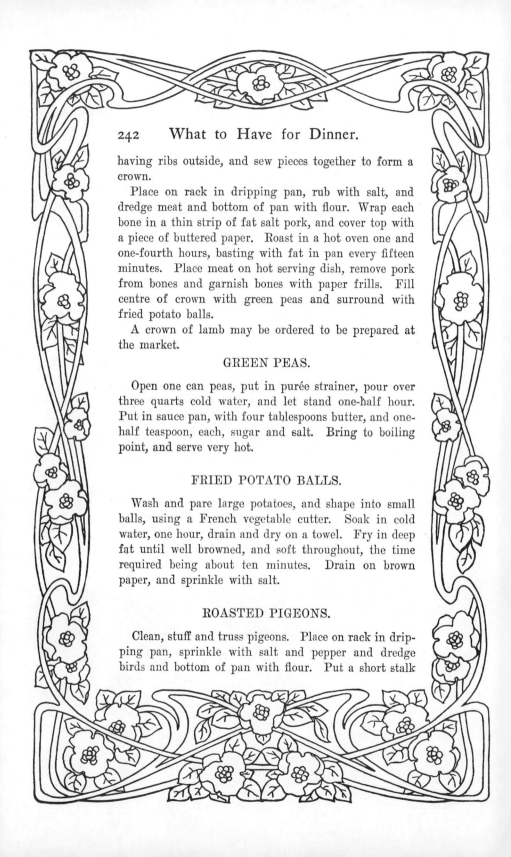

having ribs outside, and sew pieces together to form a crown.

Place on rack in dripping pan, rub with salt, and dredge meat and bottom of pan with flour. Wrap each bone in a thin strip of fat salt pork, and cover top with a piece of buttered paper. Roast in a hot oven one and one-fourth hours, basting with fat in pan every fifteen minutes. Place meat on hot serving dish, remove pork from bones and garnish bones with paper frills. Fill centre of crown with green peas and surround with fried potato balls.

A crown of lamb may be ordered to be prepared at the market.

GREEN PEAS.

Open one can peas, put in purée strainer, pour over three quarts cold water, and let stand one-half hour. Put in sauce pan, with four tablespoons butter, and one-half teaspoon, each, sugar and salt. Bring to boiling point, and serve very hot.

FRIED POTATO BALLS.

Wash and pare large potatoes, and shape into small balls, using a French vegetable cutter. Soak in cold water, one hour, drain and dry on a towel. Fry in deep fat until well browned, and soft throughout, the time required being about ten minutes. Drain on brown paper, and sprinkle with salt.

ROASTED PIGEONS.

Clean, stuff and truss pigeons. Place on rack in dripping pan, sprinkle with salt and pepper and dredge birds and bottom of pan with flour. Put a short stalk

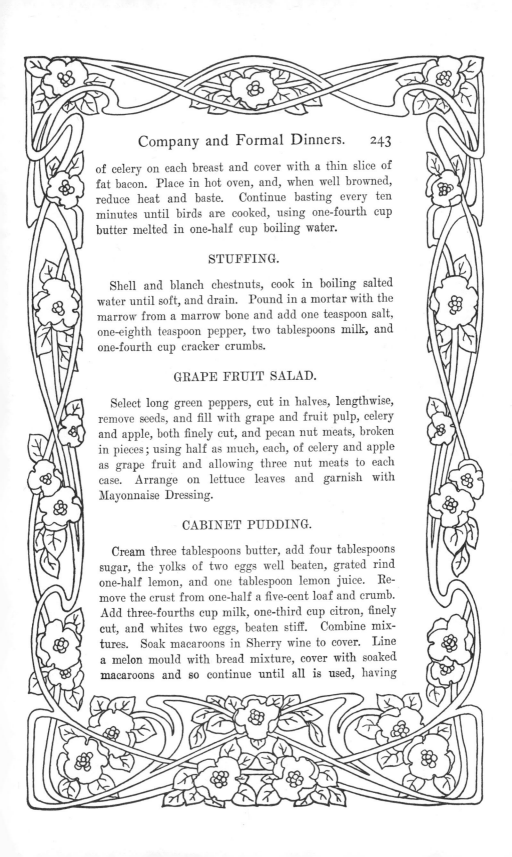

of celery on each breast and cover with a thin slice of
fat bacon. Place in hot oven, and, when well browned,
reduce heat and baste. Continue basting every ten
minutes until birds are cooked, using one-fourth cup
butter melted in one-half cup boiling water.

STUFFING.

Shell and blanch chestnuts, cook in boiling salted
water until soft, and drain. Pound in a mortar with the
marrow from a marrow bone and add one teaspoon salt,
one-eighth teaspoon pepper, two tablespoons milk, and
one-fourth cup cracker crumbs.

GRAPE FRUIT SALAD.

Select long green peppers, cut in halves, lengthwise,
remove seeds, and fill with grape and fruit pulp, celery
and apple, both finely cut, and pecan nut meats, broken
in pieces; using half as much, each, of celery and apple
as grape fruit and allowing three nut meats to each
case. Arrange on lettuce leaves and garnish with
Mayonnaise Dressing.

CABINET PUDDING.

Cream three tablespoons butter, add four tablespoons
sugar, the yolks of two eggs well beaten, grated rind
one-half lemon, and one tablespoon lemon juice. Remove the crust from one-half a five-cent loaf and crumb.
Add three-fourths cup milk, one-third cup citron, finely
cut, and whites two eggs, beaten stiff. Combine mixtures. Soak macaroons in Sherry wine to cover. Line
a melon mould with bread mixture, cover with soaked
macaroons and so continue until all is used, having

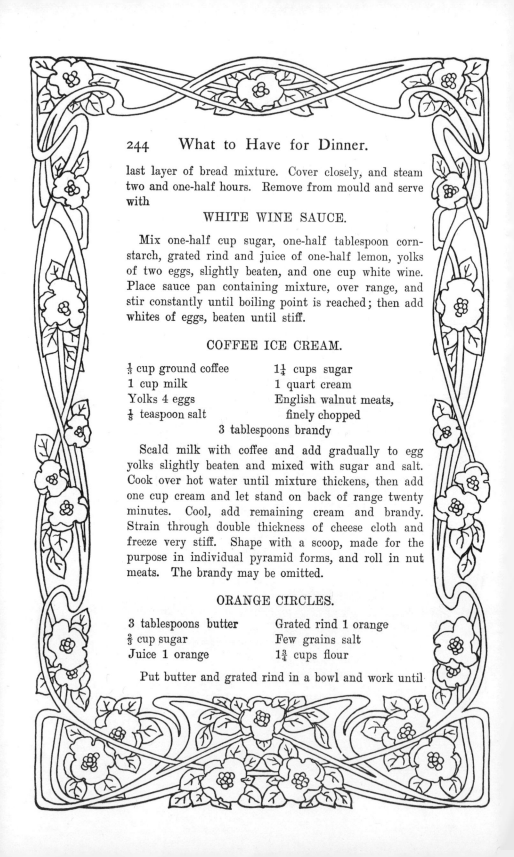

last layer of bread mixture. Cover closely, and steam two and one-half hours. Remove from mould and serve with

WHITE WINE SAUCE.

Mix one-half cup sugar, one-half tablespoon cornstarch, grated rind and juice of one-half lemon, yolks of two eggs, slightly beaten, and one cup white wine. Place sauce pan containing mixture, over range, and stir constantly until boiling point is reached; then add whites of eggs, beaten until stiff.

COFFEE ICE CREAM.

$\frac{1}{3}$ cup ground coffee
1 cup milk
Yolks 4 eggs
$\frac{1}{8}$ teaspoon salt

$1\frac{1}{4}$ cups sugar
1 quart cream
English walnut meats,
　　finely chopped

3 tablespoons brandy

Scald milk with coffee and add gradually to egg yolks slightly beaten and mixed with sugar and salt. Cook over hot water until mixture thickens, then add one cup cream and let stand on back of range twenty minutes. Cool, add remaining cream and brandy. Strain through double thickness of cheese cloth and freeze very stiff. Shape with a scoop, made for the purpose in individual pyramid forms, and roll in nut meats. The brandy may be omitted.

ORANGE CIRCLES.

3 tablespoons butter
$\frac{2}{3}$ cup sugar
Juice 1 orange

Grated rind 1 orange
Few grains salt
$1\frac{3}{4}$ cups flour

Put butter and grated rind in a bowl and work until

creamy, using a wooden spoon. Add sugar, gradually, continuing the beating; then add salt and orange juice and flour, a little at a time. Toss on a floured board, pat and roll to one-eighth inch in thickness. Shape with a circular cutter, first dipped in flour, put on a sheet covered with a buttered paper, and bake in a moderate oven.

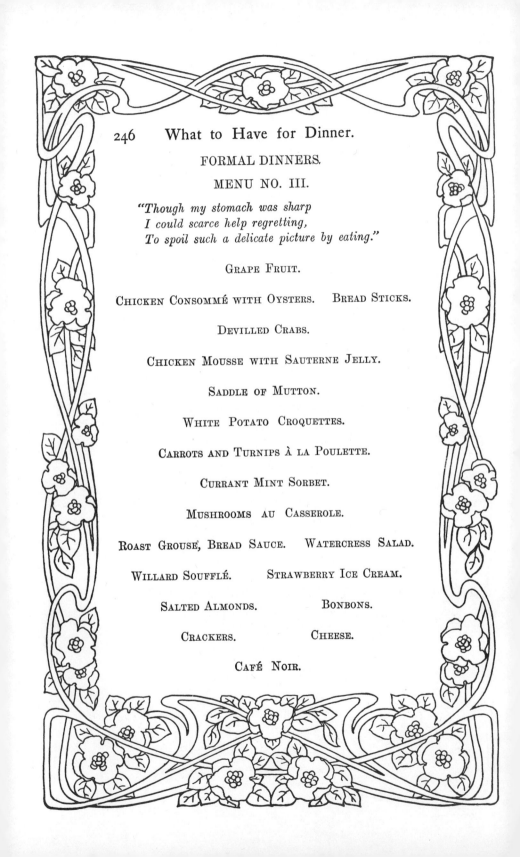

FORMAL DINNERS.

MENU NO. III.

"Though my stomach was sharp
I could scarce help regretting,
To spoil such a delicate picture by eating."

GRAPE FRUIT.

CHICKEN CONSOMMÉ WITH OYSTERS.　　BREAD STICKS.

DEVILLED CRABS.

CHICKEN MOUSSE WITH SAUTERNE JELLY.

SADDLE OF MUTTON.

WHITE POTATO CROQUETTES.

CARROTS AND TURNIPS À LA POULETTE.

CURRANT MINT SORBET.

MUSHROOMS AU CASSEROLE.

ROAST GROUSE, BREAD SAUCE.　　WATERCRESS SALAD.

WILLARD SOUFFLÉ.　　STRAWBERRY ICE CREAM.

SALTED ALMONDS.　　BONBONS.

CRACKERS.　　CHEESE.

CAFÉ NOIR.

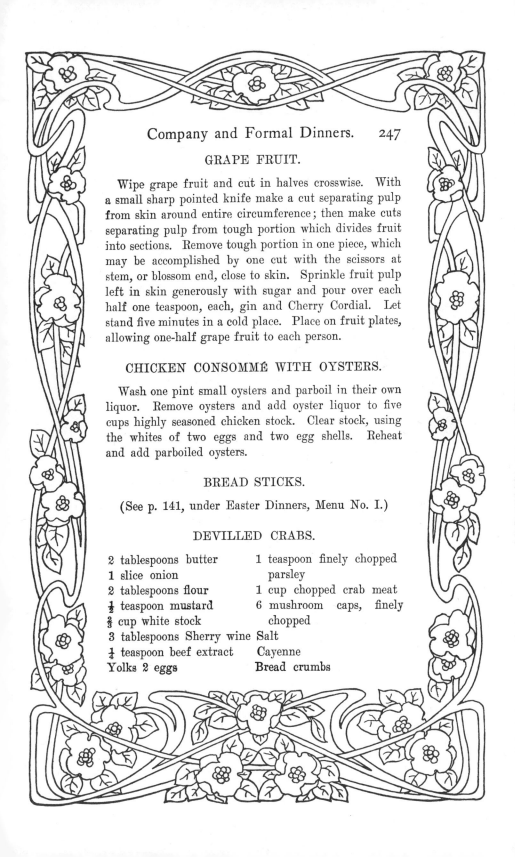

GRAPE FRUIT.

Wipe grape fruit and cut in halves crosswise. With a small sharp pointed knife make a cut separating pulp from skin around entire circumference; then make cuts separating pulp from tough portion which divides fruit into sections. Remove tough portion in one piece, which may be accomplished by one cut with the scissors at stem, or blossom end, close to skin. Sprinkle fruit pulp left in skin generously with sugar and pour over each half one teaspoon, each, gin and Cherry Cordial. Let stand five minutes in a cold place. Place on fruit plates, allowing one-half grape fruit to each person.

CHICKEN CONSOMMÉ WITH OYSTERS.

Wash one pint small oysters and parboil in their own liquor. Remove oysters and add oyster liquor to five cups highly seasoned chicken stock. Clear stock, using the whites of two eggs and two egg shells. Reheat and add parboiled oysters.

BREAD STICKS.

(See p. 141, under Easter Dinners, Menu No. I.)

DEVILLED CRABS.

2 tablespoons butter	1 teaspoon finely chopped
1 slice onion	parsley
2 tablespoons flour	1 cup chopped crab meat
½ teaspoon mustard	6 mushroom caps, finely
⅔ cup white stock	chopped
3 tablespoons Sherry wine	Salt
¼ teaspoon beef extract	Cayenne
Yolks 2 eggs	Bread crumbs

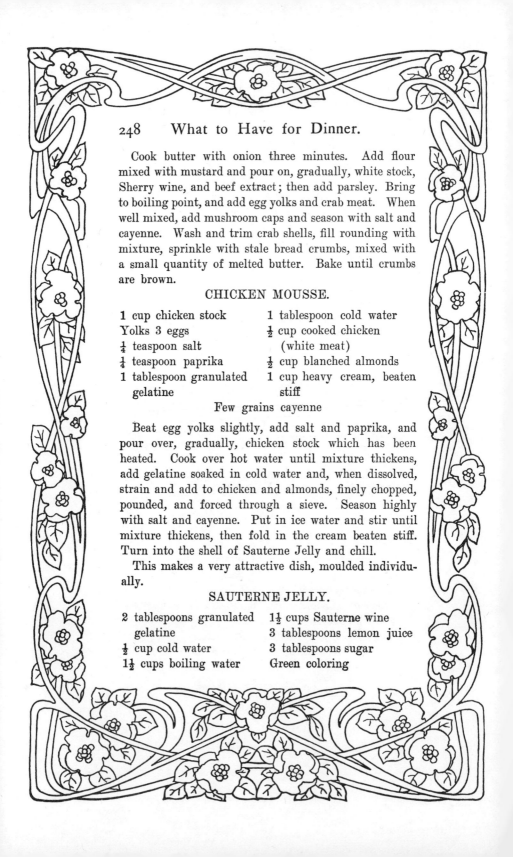

Cook butter with onion three minutes. Add flour mixed with mustard and pour on, gradually, white stock, Sherry wine, and beef extract; then add parsley. Bring to boiling point, and add egg yolks and crab meat. When well mixed, add mushroom caps and season with salt and cayenne. Wash and trim crab shells, fill rounding with mixture, sprinkle with stale bread crumbs, mixed with a small quantity of melted butter. Bake until crumbs are brown.

CHICKEN MOUSSE.

1 cup chicken stock	1 tablespoon cold water
Yolks 3 eggs	½ cup cooked chicken
¼ teaspoon salt	(white meat)
¼ teaspoon paprika	½ cup blanched almonds
1 tablespoon granulated gelatine	1 cup heavy cream, beaten stiff

Few grains cayenne

Beat egg yolks slightly, add salt and paprika, and pour over, gradually, chicken stock which has been heated. Cook over hot water until mixture thickens, add gelatine soaked in cold water and, when dissolved, strain and add to chicken and almonds, finely chopped, pounded, and forced through a sieve. Season highly with salt and cayenne. Put in ice water and stir until mixture thickens, then fold in the cream beaten stiff. Turn into the shell of Sauterne Jelly and chill.

This makes a very attractive dish, moulded individually.

SAUTERNE JELLY.

2 tablespoons granulated gelatine	1½ cups Sauterne wine
½ cup cold water	3 tablespoons lemon juice
1½ cups boiling water	3 tablespoons sugar
	Green coloring

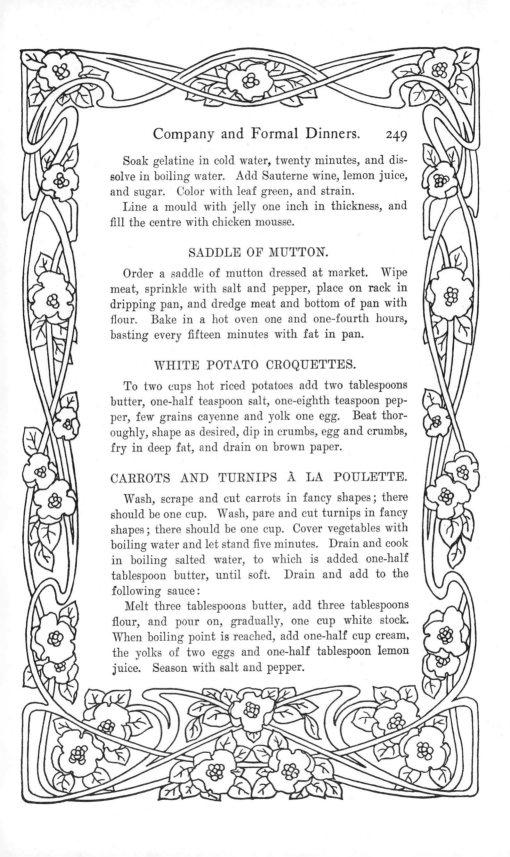

Soak gelatine in cold water, twenty minutes, and dissolve in boiling water. Add Sauterne wine, lemon juice, and sugar. Color with leaf green, and strain.

Line a mould with jelly one inch in thickness, and fill the centre with chicken mousse.

SADDLE OF MUTTON.

Order a saddle of mutton dressed at market. Wipe meat, sprinkle with salt and pepper, place on rack in dripping pan, and dredge meat and bottom of pan with flour. Bake in a hot oven one and one-fourth hours, basting every fifteen minutes with fat in pan.

WHITE POTATO CROQUETTES.

To two cups hot riced potatoes add two tablespoons butter, one-half teaspoon salt, one-eighth teaspoon pepper, few grains cayenne and yolk one egg. Beat thoroughly, shape as desired, dip in crumbs, egg and crumbs, fry in deep fat, and drain on brown paper.

CARROTS AND TURNIPS À LA POULETTE.

Wash, scrape and cut carrots in fancy shapes; there should be one cup. Wash, pare and cut turnips in fancy shapes; there should be one cup. Cover vegetables with boiling water and let stand five minutes. Drain and cook in boiling salted water, to which is added one-half tablespoon butter, until soft. Drain and add to the following sauce:

Melt three tablespoons butter, add three tablespoons flour, and pour on, gradually, one cup white stock. When boiling point is reached, add one-half cup cream, the yolks of two eggs and one-half tablespoon lemon juice. Season with salt and pepper.

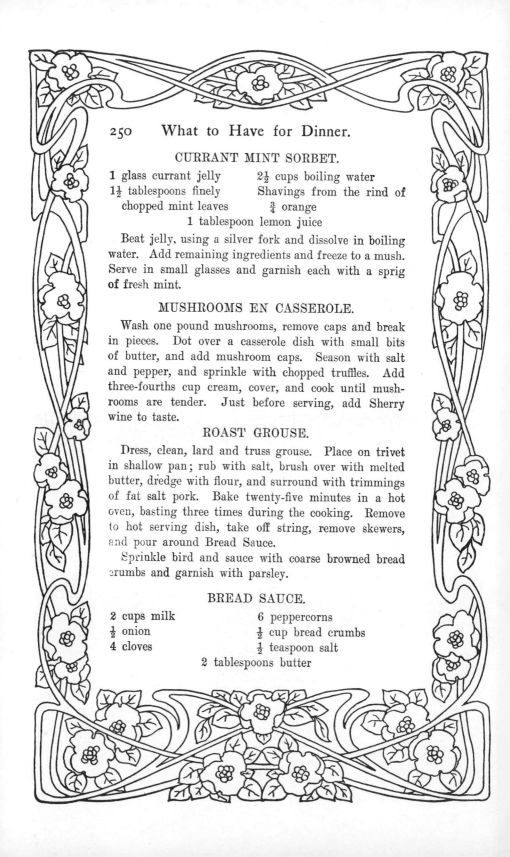

CURRANT MINT SORBET.

1 glass currant jelly
1½ tablespoons finely chopped mint leaves
1 tablespoon lemon juice
2½ cups boiling water
Shavings from the rind of ¾ orange

Beat jelly, using a silver fork and dissolve in boiling water. Add remaining ingredients and freeze to a mush. Serve in small glasses and garnish each with a sprig of fresh mint.

MUSHROOMS EN CASSEROLE.

Wash one pound mushrooms, remove caps and break in pieces. Dot over a casserole dish with small bits of butter, and add mushroom caps. Season with salt and pepper, and sprinkle with chopped truffles. Add three-fourths cup cream, cover, and cook until mushrooms are tender. Just before serving, add Sherry wine to taste.

ROAST GROUSE.

Dress, clean, lard and truss grouse. Place on trivet in shallow pan; rub with salt, brush over with melted butter, dredge with flour, and surround with trimmings of fat salt pork. Bake twenty-five minutes in a hot oven, basting three times during the cooking. Remove to hot serving dish, take off string, remove skewers, and pour around Bread Sauce.

Sprinkle bird and sauce with coarse browned bread crumbs and garnish with parsley.

BREAD SAUCE.

2 cups milk
½ onion
4 cloves
6 peppercorns
½ cup bread crumbs
½ teaspoon salt
2 tablespoons butter

Scald milk with onions, cloves and peppercorns, strain, add bread crumbs and cook in double boiler twenty minutes. Add salt and butter.

WATERCRESS SALAD.

Wash, remove roots, drain and chill two bunches watercress. Arrange in salad bowl, and pour over two tablespoons vinegar mixed with one-half teaspoon salt and a few grains paprika.

WILLARD SOUFFLÉ.

1½ tablespoons butter	3 tablespoons powdered sugar
2 tablespoons flour	
½ cup milk	Whites 3 eggs
Yolks 2 eggs	Fresh strawberries

Melt butter, add flour, and when well blended, pour on, gradually, while stirring constantly, milk. Beat yolks of eggs until thick and lemon colored and add, gradually, while beating constantly, powdered sugar. Combine mixtures, cool slightly, and cut and fold in whites of eggs beaten until stiff and dry. Cover bottom of individual cases with strawberries cut in halves and sprinkle with sugar. Put in mixture to fill cases three-fourths full, and bake in a slow oven until firm and delicately browned.

Serve with each soufflé a slice of Strawberry Ice Cream.

STRAWBERRY ICE CREAM.

(See p. 183, under Company Dinners, Menu No. II.)

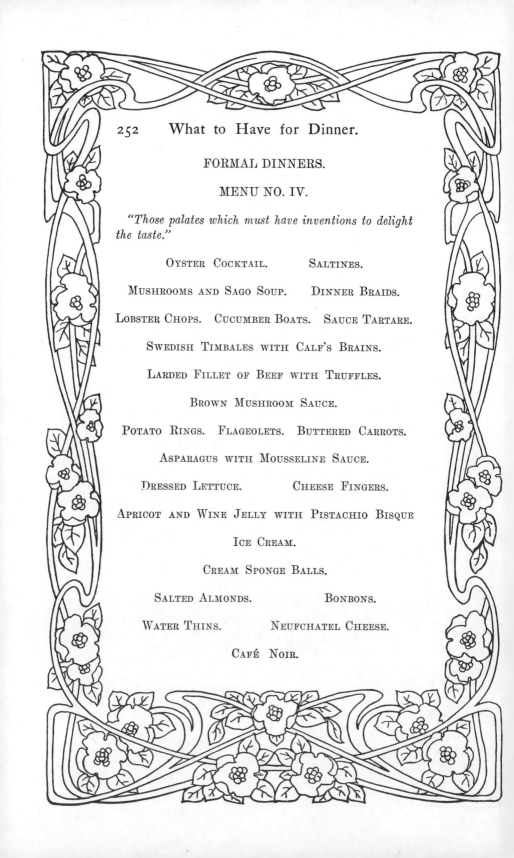

FORMAL DINNERS.

MENU NO. IV.

"Those palates which must have inventions to delight the taste."

OYSTER COCKTAIL.   SALTINES.

MUSHROOMS AND SAGO SOUP.   DINNER BRAIDS.

LOBSTER CHOPS. CUCUMBER BOATS. SAUCE TARTARE.

SWEDISH TIMBALES WITH CALF'S BRAINS.

LARDED FILLET OF BEEF WITH TRUFFLES.

BROWN MUSHROOM SAUCE.

POTATO RINGS. FLAGEOLETS. BUTTERED CARROTS.

ASPARAGUS WITH MOUSSELINE SAUCE.

DRESSED LETTUCE.   CHEESE FINGERS.

APRICOT AND WINE JELLY WITH PISTACHIO BISQUE

ICE CREAM.

CREAM SPONGE BALLS.

SALTED ALMONDS.   BONBONS.

WATER THINS.   NEUFCHATEL CHEESE.

CAFÉ NOIR.

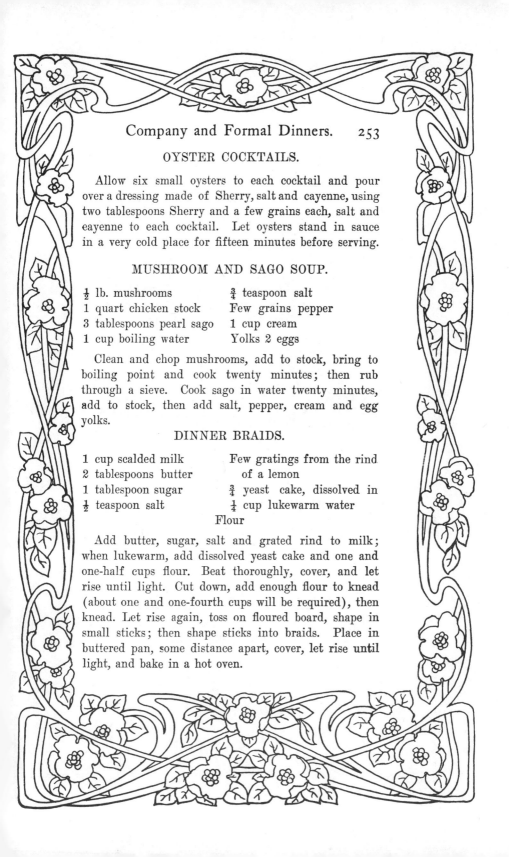

OYSTER COCKTAILS.

Allow six small oysters to each cocktail and pour over a dressing made of Sherry, salt and cayenne, using two tablespoons Sherry and a few grains each, salt and eayenne to each cocktail. Let oysters stand in sauce in a very cold place for fifteen minutes before serving.

MUSHROOM AND SAGO SOUP.

$\frac{1}{2}$ lb. mushrooms	$\frac{3}{4}$ teaspoon salt
1 quart chicken stock	Few grains pepper
3 tablespoons pearl sago	1 cup cream
1 cup boiling water	Yolks 2 eggs

Clean and chop mushrooms, add to stock, bring to boiling point and cook twenty minutes; then rub through a sieve. Cook sago in water twenty minutes, add to stock, then add salt, pepper, cream and egg yolks.

DINNER BRAIDS.

1 cup scalded milk	Few gratings from the rind
2 tablespoons butter	of a lemon
1 tablespoon sugar	$\frac{3}{4}$ yeast cake, dissolved in
$\frac{1}{2}$ teaspoon salt	$\frac{1}{4}$ cup lukewarm water
	Flour

Add butter, sugar, salt and grated rind to milk; when lukewarm, add dissolved yeast cake and one and one-half cups flour. Beat thoroughly, cover, and let rise until light. Cut down, add enough flour to knead (about one and one-fourth cups will be required), then knead. Let rise again, toss on floured board, shape in small sticks; then shape sticks into braids. Place in buttered pan, some distance apart, cover, let rise until light, and bake in a hot oven.

LOBSTER CHOPS.

2 cups chopped lobster meat	2 teaspoons lemon juice
¾ teaspoon salt	Yolk 1 egg
Few grains cayenne	1 teaspoon parsley, chopped finely

1 cup Thick White Sauce

Mix ingredients in order given and add white sauce. Spread on a plate to cool; then shape in form of chops. Dip in crumbs, egg and crumbs, fry in deep fat, and drain on brown paper. Insert a small claw in small end of each chop and arrange around a mound of parsley or watercress.

THICK WHITE SAUCE.

Melt three tablespoons butter, add one-third cup flour, and pour on, gradually, while stirring constantly, one cup milk or one-half cup each, milk and white stock. Bring to boiling point, and season with one-fourth teaspoon salt and one-eighth teaspoon pepper.

CUCUMBER BOATS, SAUCE TARTARE.

Select three long, regular shaped cucumbers, cut a thin slice from both the stem and blossom end of each, and cut in halves crosswise. Remove pulp, and seeds, if possible, in sufficiently large pieces to cut in cubes for another salad. Cut sections so as to make boat shape. Arrange each boat on a single lettuce leaf, and fill with

SAUCE TARTARE.

(See p. 17, under Family Dinners, Menu No. IV.)

SWEDISH TIMBALES.

⅓ cup cornstarch	⅓ cup beer or
⅓ cup flour	Same quantity liquid, using
⅓ teaspoon salt	equal parts milk and wa-
Yolks 2 eggs	ter

1 tablespoon olive oil

Mix dry ingredients, add liquid gradually, and beaten yolks of eggs; then add olive oil. Shape, using a hot timbale iron, fry in deep fat until crisp and brown; take from iron and drain on brown paper.

CREAMED CALF'S BRAINS.

Soak calf's brains in cold salted water one hour. Remove blood vessels and cook in boiling, salted, acidulated water, twenty minutes. Drain and plunge into cold water to harden. When cold, cut in three-fourths inch cubes and add to the following sauce:

Melt three tablespoons butter, add one slice onion and cook until yellow; then add three tablespoons flour, and pour on, gradually, one-half cup calf's head stock and one-half cup milk. Bring to boiling point, remove onion, and add one-fourth cup cream, yolks of two eggs and one tablespoon lemon juice. Season with salt and cayenne. Do not allow sauce to reach the boiling point after the cream and egg yolks have been added.

LARDED FILLET OF BEEF WITH TRUFFLES.

Wipe, remove fat, veins and any tendinous portions from a fillet of beef. Lard upper side with grain of meat, and between lardoons insert small pieces of truffle, using a sharp pointed knife to make cuts. Use one truffle for the fillet. Place meat on rack in small

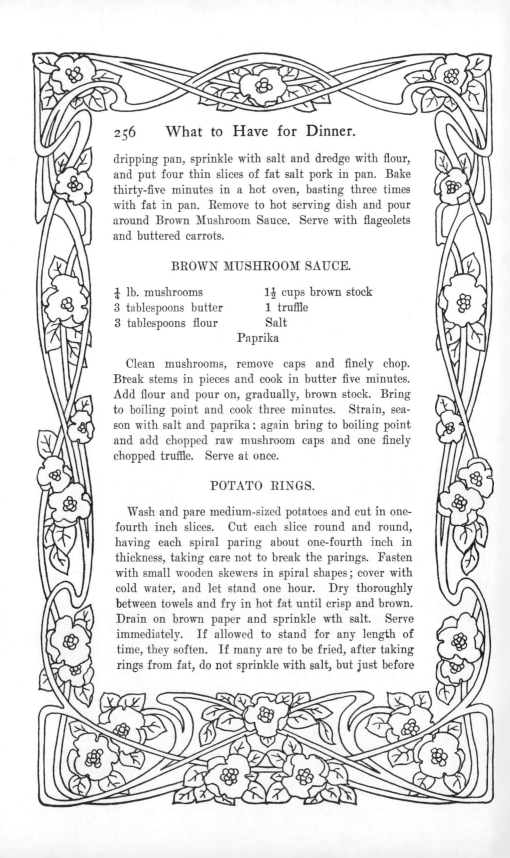

dripping pan, sprinkle with salt and dredge with flour, and put four thin slices of fat salt pork in pan. Bake thirty-five minutes in a hot oven, basting three times with fat in pan. Remove to hot serving dish and pour around Brown Mushroom Sauce. Serve with flageolets and buttered carrots.

BROWN MUSHROOM SAUCE.

$\frac{1}{4}$ lb. mushrooms	$1\frac{1}{2}$ cups brown stock
3 tablespoons butter	1 truffle
3 tablespoons flour	Salt
	Paprika

Clean mushrooms, remove caps and finely chop. Break stems in pieces and cook in butter five minutes. Add flour and pour on, gradually, brown stock. Bring to boiling point and cook three minutes. Strain, season with salt and paprika; again bring to boiling point and add chopped raw mushroom caps and one finely chopped truffle. Serve at once.

POTATO RINGS.

Wash and pare medium-sized potatoes and cut in one-fourth inch slices. Cut each slice round and round, having each spiral paring about one-fourth inch in thickness, taking care not to break the parings. Fasten with small wooden skewers in spiral shapes; cover with cold water, and let stand one hour. Dry thoroughly between towels and fry in hot fat until crisp and brown. Drain on brown paper and sprinkle wth salt. Serve immediately. If allowed to stand for any length of time, they soften. If many are to be fried, after taking rings from fat, do not sprinkle with salt, but just before

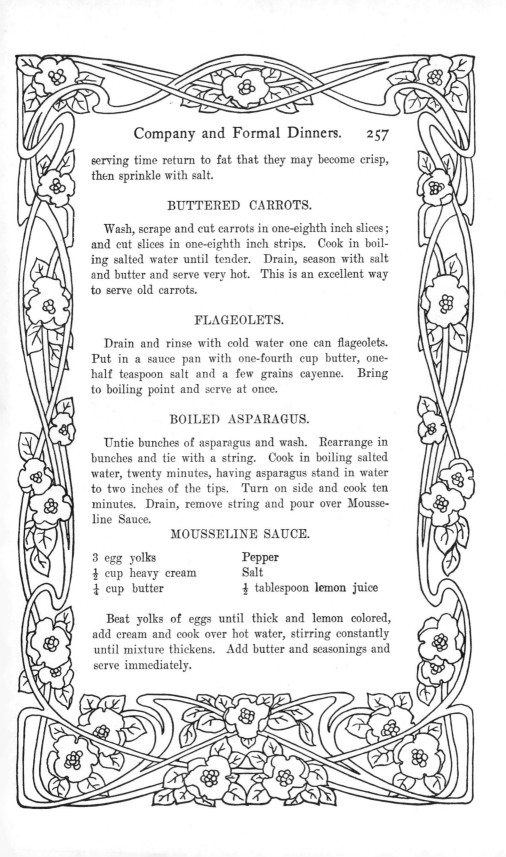

serving time return to fat that they may become crisp, then sprinkle with salt.

BUTTERED CARROTS.

Wash, scrape and cut carrots in one-eighth inch slices; and cut slices in one-eighth inch strips. Cook in boiling salted water until tender. Drain, season with salt and butter and serve very hot. This is an excellent way to serve old carrots.

FLAGEOLETS.

Drain and rinse with cold water one can flageolets. Put in a sauce pan with one-fourth cup butter, one-half teaspoon salt and a few grains cayenne. Bring to boiling point and serve at once.

BOILED ASPARAGUS.

Untie bunches of asparagus and wash. Rearrange in bunches and tie with a string. Cook in boiling salted water, twenty minutes, having asparagus stand in water to two inches of the tips. Turn on side and cook ten minutes. Drain, remove string and pour over Mousseline Sauce.

MOUSSELINE SAUCE.

3 egg yolks	Pepper
½ cup heavy cream	Salt
¼ cup butter	½ tablespoon lemon juice

Beat yolks of eggs until thick and lemon colored, add cream and cook over hot water, stirring constantly until mixture thickens. Add butter and seasonings and serve immediately.

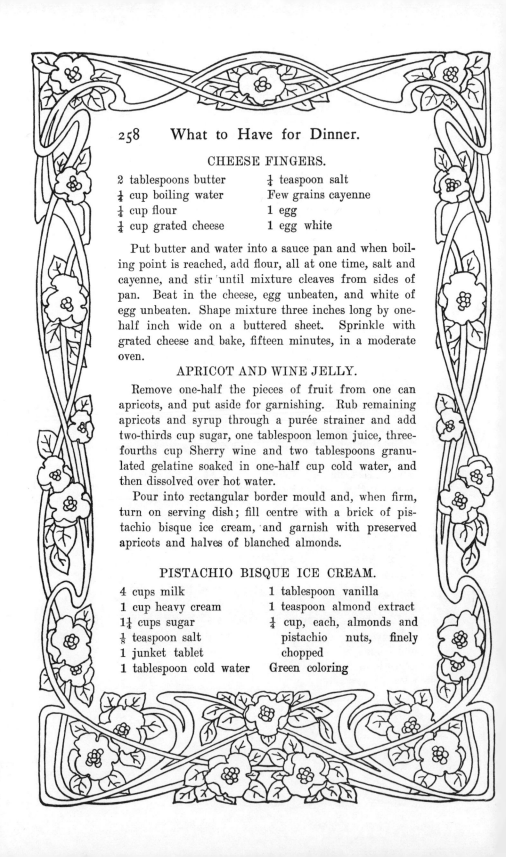

CHEESE FINGERS.

2 tablespoons butter	¼ teaspoon salt
¼ cup boiling water	Few grains cayenne
¼ cup flour	1 egg
¼ cup grated cheese	1 egg white

Put butter and water into a sauce pan and when boiling point is reached, add flour, all at one time, salt and cayenne, and stir until mixture cleaves from sides of pan. Beat in the cheese, egg unbeaten, and white of egg unbeaten. Shape mixture three inches long by one-half inch wide on a buttered sheet. Sprinkle with grated cheese and bake, fifteen minutes, in a moderate oven.

APRICOT AND WINE JELLY.

Remove one-half the pieces of fruit from one can apricots, and put aside for garnishing. Rub remaining apricots and syrup through a purée strainer and add two-thirds cup sugar, one tablespoon lemon juice, three-fourths cup Sherry wine and two tablespoons granulated gelatine soaked in one-half cup cold water, and then dissolved over hot water.

Pour into rectangular border mould and, when firm, turn on serving dish; fill centre with a brick of pistachio bisque ice cream, and garnish with preserved apricots and halves of blanched almonds.

PISTACHIO BISQUE ICE CREAM.

4 cups milk	1 tablespoon vanilla
1 cup heavy cream	1 teaspoon almond extract
1¼ cups sugar	¼ cup, each, almonds and
⅛ teaspoon salt	pistachio nuts, finely
1 junket tablet	chopped
1 tablespoon cold water	Green coloring

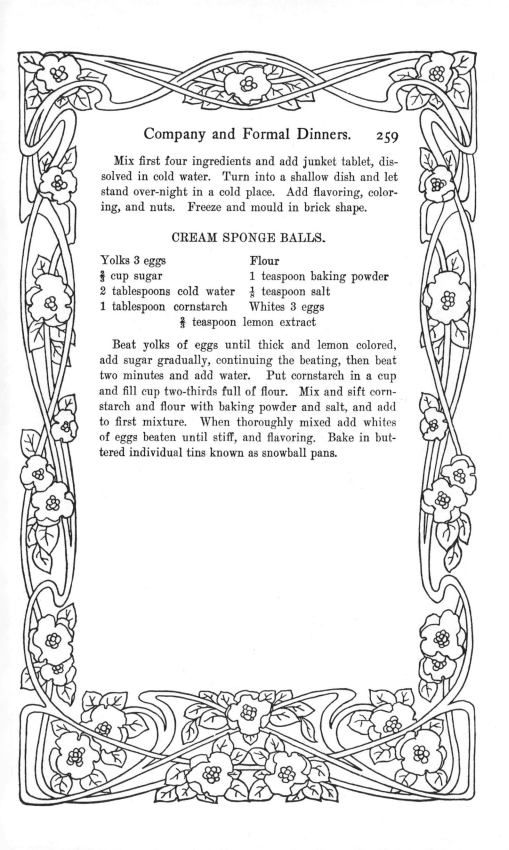

Mix first four ingredients and add junket tablet, dissolved in cold water.   Turn into a shallow dish and let stand over-night in a cold place.   Add flavoring, coloring, and nuts.   Freeze and mould in brick shape.

CREAM SPONGE BALLS.

Yolks 3 eggs	Flour
⅔ cup sugar	1 teaspoon baking powder
2 tablespoons cold water	⅛ teaspoon salt
1 tablespoon cornstarch	Whites 3 eggs
	⅔ teaspoon lemon extract

Beat yolks of eggs until thick and lemon colored, add sugar gradually, continuing the beating, then beat two minutes and add water.   Put cornstarch in a cup and fill cup two-thirds full of flour.   Mix and sift cornstarch and flour with baking powder and salt, and add to first mixture.   When thoroughly mixed add whites of eggs beaten until stiff, and flavoring.   Bake in buttered individual tins known as snowball pans.

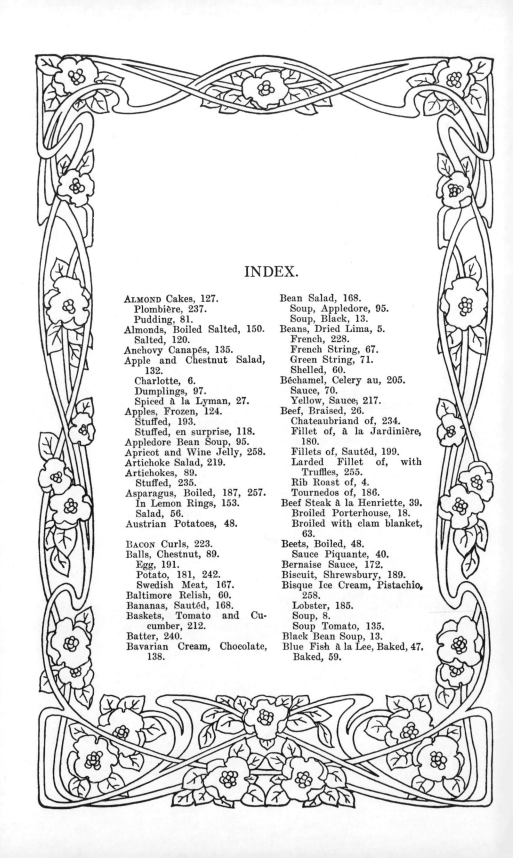

INDEX.

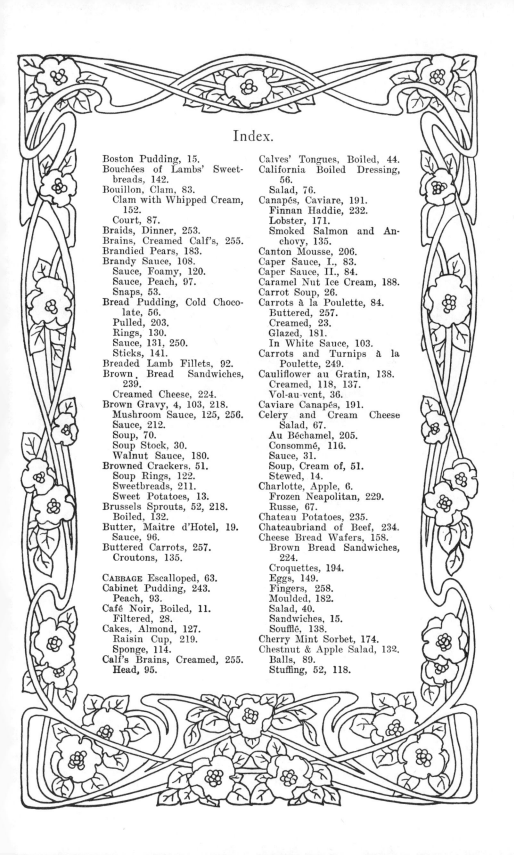

Index.

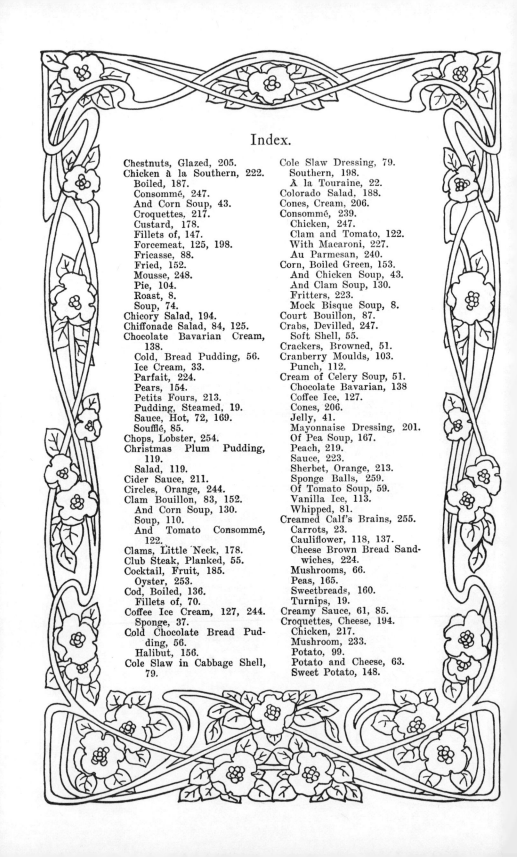

Index.

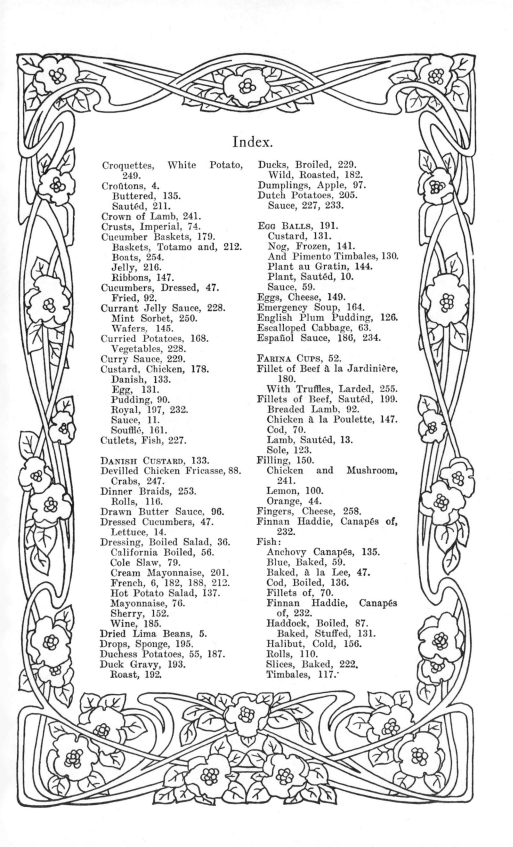

Index.

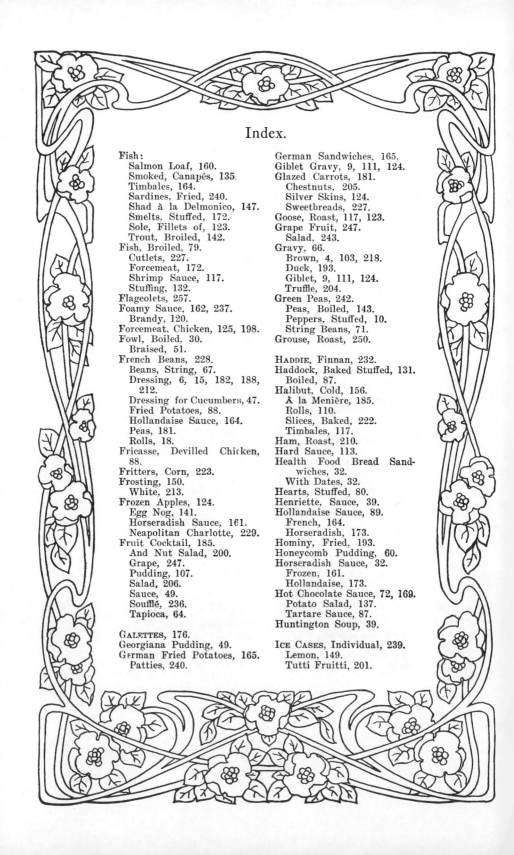

Index.

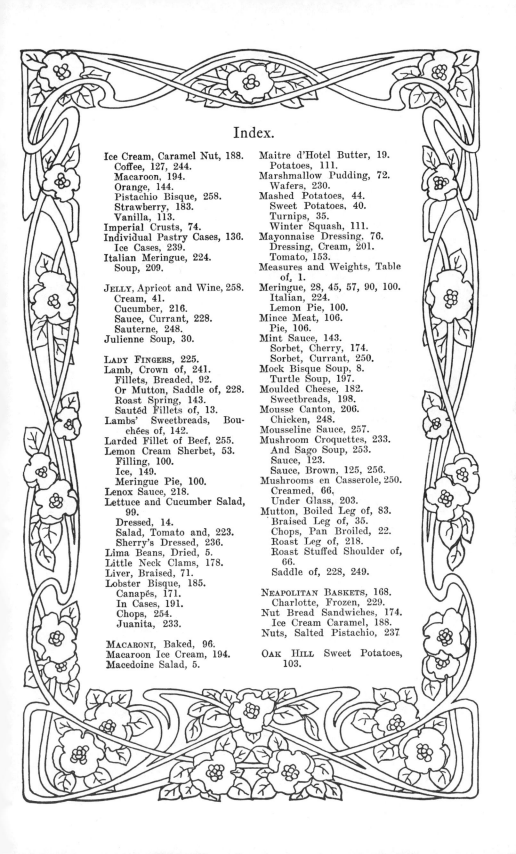

Index.

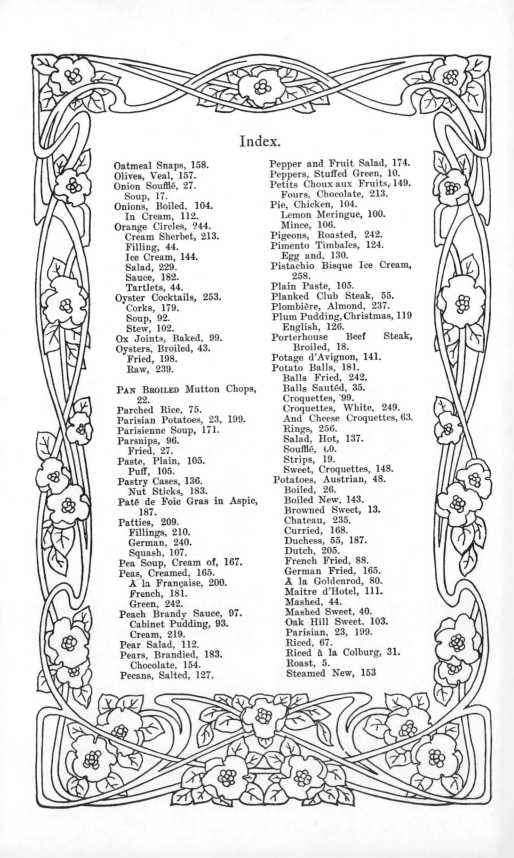

Index.

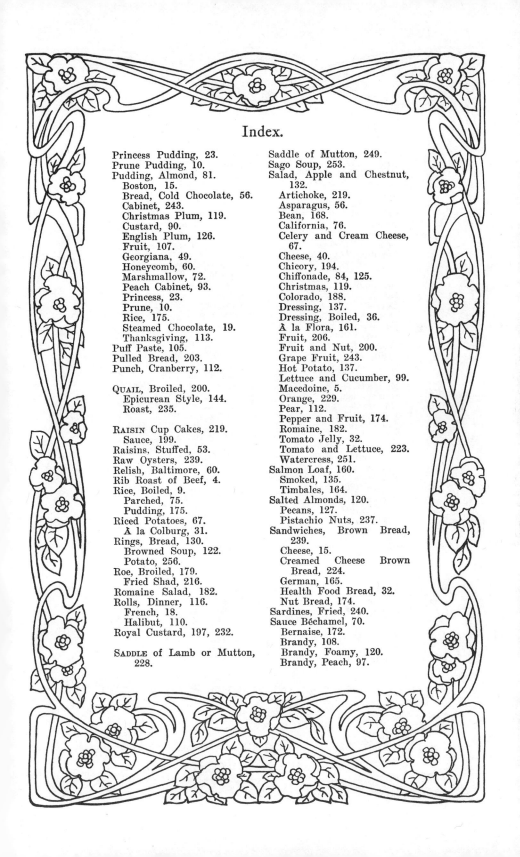

Index.

Index.

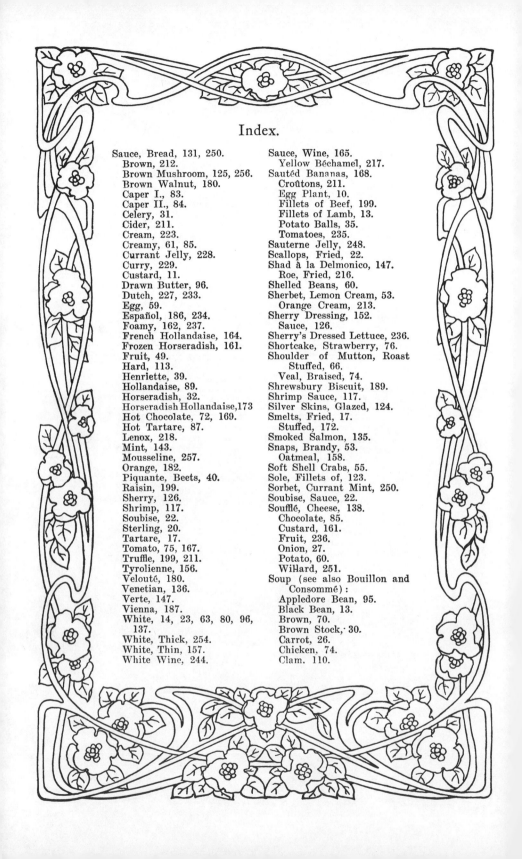

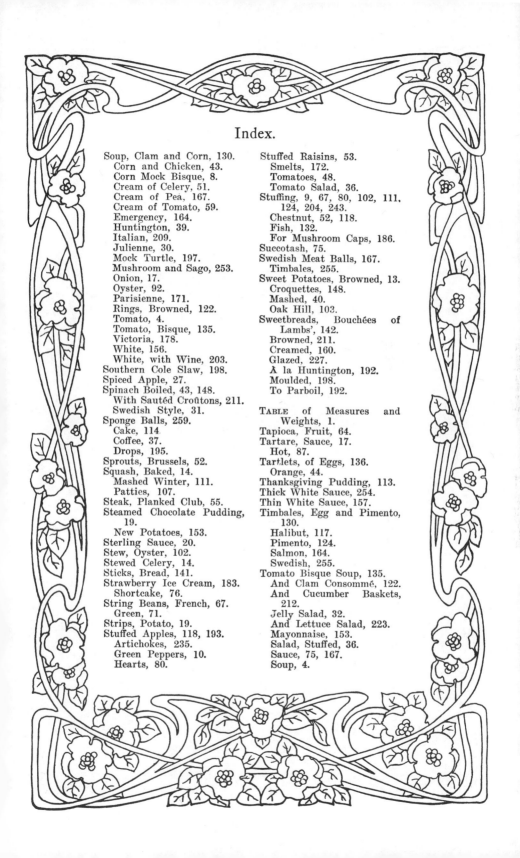

Index.

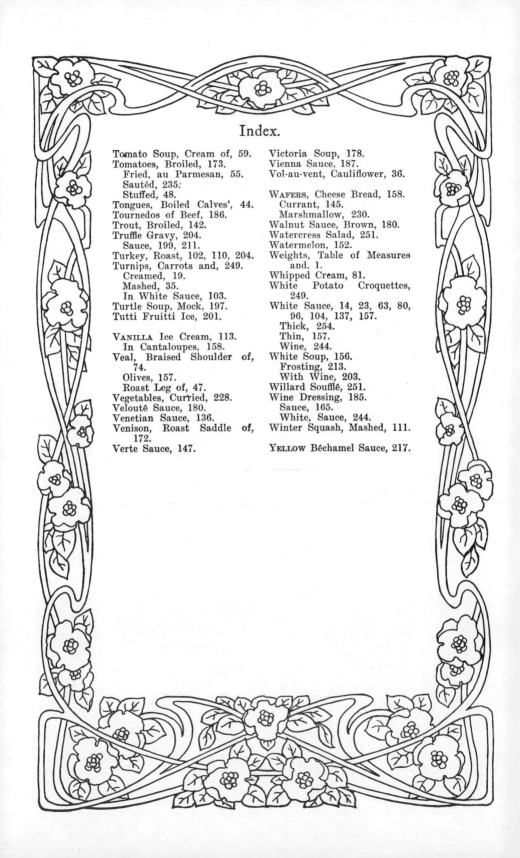

Index.

Notes

Notes

Notes

Notes

Notes

Notes

Notes

Notes

Notes

Notes

Notes

Notes